AER
DOGS

AER DOGS

TOM LYONS

IRELANDIA PRESS

This edition published 2025 by Irelandia Press,
Dublin, Ireland

Irelandia Press
6-7 Barrow Street
Dublin 4
D04 H3F8
Ireland

www.irelandiapress.ie

© Tom Lyons, 2025

The right of Tom Lyons to be identified as the Author of this work has been asserted in accordance with the Copyright, Designs and Patents Act 1988.

All rights reserved. No part of this book may be reprinted or reproduced or utilised in any form or by any electronic, mechanical or other means, now known or hereafter invented, including photocopying and recording, or in any information storage or retrieval system, without the permission in writing from the Publishers.

ISBN: 9781917105002

Design & Typesetting by Fiachra McCarthy
Printed by Sprintbooks

*To all the Aer Dogs, thank you for sharing
your stories. And to Lynne, Robyn, and Martha,
thank you for your love and letting me do it.
Tom*

CONTENTS

Foreword x
Cast of Characters xii
Aer Dogs xv
Preface xvi
Chapter 1: Almost Famous 1
Chapter 2: A Wall Street Wolf 14
Chapter 3: The Protector - Anthony 23
Chapter 4: Leaving Ryanair 27
Chapter 5: Moving away from metal 33
Chapter 6: A Rare Dog 39
Chapter 7: An Amicable break-up 44
Chapter 8: Nearly 6 in dog years 48
Chapter 9: Crocodiles carry no passports 60
Chapter 10: Tony the real Tiger 69
Chapter 11: Dirty tricks in Oz 84
Chapter 12: A Tiger Roars 90
Chapter 13: IPO and an exit 99
Chapter 14: Las Vegas and the dogs 107
Chapter 15: The original Aer Dogs 123

Chapter 16: The Goode Years 126
Chapter 17: Viva Mexico 131
Chapter 18: The Max Factor 138
Chapter 19: India to Turkey 143
Chapter 20: The Medellín Cartel 149
Chapter 21: Mo'exits 154
Chapter 22: A Kidnap Attempt 160
Chapter 23: The end (and start) of an era 165
Chapter 24: Shaw bites the dust 170
Chapter 25: Mexico not loved in NYC 174
Chapter 26: A new airline for Latin America? 182
Chapter 27: Tensions Rising 190
Chapter 28: The night of the long (Mexican) knives ...197
Chapter 29: A wildcat and Guatemalan chickens 203
Chapter 30: The Mexican Wave 208
Chapter 31: A changing of the dogs 216
Chapter 32: Shaw returns to Viva 220
Chapter 33: 'Make them fear losing' 225
Chapter 34: The Wings Club 231
Chapter 35: The Paris Air Show 239
Chapter 36: Good Karma 245
Chapter 37: Back as top dog 251
Chapter 38: Don't cry for me Argentina 260
Chapter 39: A lion looking at a zebra 263
Chapter 40: The Cartesian Equation 269
Chapter 41: Who you gonna call? 273
Chapter 42: Pandemic 276
Chapter 43: Project Air - Restructuring Team 283
Chapter 44: At war with GECAS 289
Chapter 45: El Dog 298

Chapter 46: Gurdian of Avianca 304
Chapter 47: The bad boy of Brazilian finance 308
Chapter 48: A merger and a marriage 320
Chapter 49: A baton passes...326
Chapter 50: Viva Colombia, viva Irelandia 330
Chapter 51: Sunset in Miami..335
Chapter 52: 20/20 Hindsight..338

FOREWORD

For someone whose career has been all about innovation and breaking the mould, Declan Ryan has always taken a surprisingly intense interest in history. That's something he shares with two of his father's protégés, Denis O'Brien and Michael O'Leary, who both have a deep and profound interest in the subject. But Declan Ryan has also taken that fascination a step further as an initiator of the historical writing process.

I remember first meeting Declan Ryan in 2008. He had invited me into the Irelandia offices to discuss writing a biography of his father Tony Ryan—the founder of GPA and Ryanair. Frankly, I was skeptical about the project, so I set out my stall. That it had to be a proper biography. That a hagiography would be a waste of his time and mine. I would want access to Tony's papers and his contacts; and I would need it explicitly understood that I was independent and would tell the story however I saw it. "Fair play to you," Declan said. "The last thing Tony would have wanted was someone blowing smoke up his backside. And I don't want that either.

FOREWORD

So yeah, just write the book." He stuck to his word, not only giving me access to the papers at Lyons Demesne, but having them properly catalogued for future generations by a UCD archivist, and then not interfering in the writing process. Did he agree with everything I wrote? No. But he also understood that his father's achievements were best served by being written about critically by a professional historian.

Now in *Aer Dogs*—the story of Irelandia and the airline startups that followed after Ryanair—Declan Ryan has repeated the trick. By giving full access to the distinguished Irish business journalist, Tom Lyons, he has allowed the story of Irelandia to be told in all its rich complexity. That licence to roam lets Tom bring out not just the drama, but also the subtleties of a story where time and again the difference between success and failure turns on the finest of margins. Nowhere is that more the case than with Viva, the low cost carrier Irelandia started in Colombia and likely to be its most successful investment return since Ryanair went public in 1997. To say that these "Aer Dogs" were dancing on a volcano during those Viva years, which included the pandemic, would be an understatement. The story is one of such turbulence and intricacy that it requires a Tom Lyons to tell it properly. In doing so, he demonstrates that the baton has been passed, not just from me to him as a chronicler of this extraordinary Irish entrepreneurial venture going back half a century, but also from Tony Ryan to Declan Ryan and his Aer Dogs as figures who have helped make Dublin the centre of excellence in global aviation that it is today.

Richard Aldous, April 2024

CAST OF CHARACTERS

Roberto Alcántara - *chairman of Group IAMSA. Mexican entrepreneur*
Richard Aldous - *professor of history, biographer of Tony Ryan*
Felix Antelo - *CEO of Viva*
Jason Bewley - *CFO of Viva*
Barry Biffle - *former CEO of Viva, CEO Frontier Airlines*
Alan Bird - *former CFO of VivaAerobus, advisor to Irelandia Aviation*
Ruairi Blaney - *Associate Irelandia Aviation, fleet manager in Viva*
David Bonderman - *co-founder of TPG, former chair of Ryanair, investor in Indigo Partners*
Richard Branson - *British entrepreneur, founder of the Virgin Group*
Anthony Carragher - *former CFO of Irelandia*
Charlie Clifton - *early Ryanair employee, airline advisor*
Louise Coen - *finance manager in Irelandia*
Miguel Cortés - *CEO of Grupo Bolivar, key backer of Viva*
Tony Davis - *former chief executive of Tiger Airways, former partner in Irelandia*
Paula Doherty - *former CFO of Irelandia*
Kong Dong - *former chairman of the Chinese National Aircraft Corporation*

CAST OF CHARACTERS

Germán Efromovich - *Bolivian entrepreneur, former controlling shareholder in Avianca*
Tony Fernandes - *cofounder AirAsia, Malaysian entrepreneur*
Bill Franke - *Airline investor, co-founder of Indigo Partners*
Maury Gallagher - *Airline investor, chief executive and chairman of Allegiant Air.*
Aoife Gallen - *head of finance in Irelandia*
Monica Gil Coca - *chief executive of Viva Foundation*
Joe Gill - *Aviation analyst*
John Goode - *senior partner in Irelandia, head of aviation*
José Gurdian - *co-founder of a private equity firm Caoba Capital*
Juan Luis Bosch Gutiérrez and Juan José Gutiérrez - *Guatemalan entrepreneurs whose family owns Latin American food conglomerate CMI*
Gorur Ramaswamy Iyengar Gopinath - *founder of Air Deccan*
Fred Jacobsen - *cofounder Viva, former chief executive of Viva*
Ellen James - *Dec's PA in Irelandia*
Alan Joyce - *former CEO of Jetstar Airways (Today chief executive of Qantas)*
Roberto Kriete - *El Salvadorean aviation investor, chair of Avianca*
Natalia Laverde - *Irelandia consultant based in Medellín*
Michael Lynch - *partner at Irelandia*
Maurice Mason - *Airline investor and director, former consultant to Irelandia*
Steven Maxwell - *managing partner of Irelandia*
Conor McCarthy - *former Ryanair executive, co-founder of AirAsia (Today executive chairman of Emerald Airlines)*
Howard Millar - *director of Viva, former deputy chief executive of Ryanair*
James Muldowney - *former co-head Irelandia Aviation*
Tom Mullins - *managing director Raymond James*
Brian Mulvihill - *director of Irelandia, co-founder of TippAero*

Adrian Neuhauser - *former investment banker, chief executive of Avianca*
Colin O'Brien - *partner KPMG*
Michael O'Leary - *chief executive of Ryanair, former PA to Tony Ryan*
Juan Emilio Posada - *cofounder of Viva, former CEO of Viva*
Cathal Ryan - *former Ryanair director, the eldest son of Tony Ryan*
Danielle Ryan - *entrepreneur, daughter of Cathal Ryan*
Declan Ryan - *executive chairman and founder of Irelandia, middle son of Tony Ryan*
Shane Ryan - *investor, youngest son of Tony Ryan*
Tony Ryan - *founder of GPA, founder of Ryanair*
Ali Sabanci - *Turkish businessman, founder of Pegasus Airlines*
William Shaw - *cofounder of Viva, former CEO of Viva*
Rupert Stebbings - *English stockbroker based in Colombia, director of Viva, author of* The Viva Effect
Chew Choon Seng - *former CEO of SIA*
Kieran Wallace - *head of restructuring KPMG*
Paul White - *partner in A&L Goodbody, legal advisor to Irelandia*
Peter Yu - *managing partner, Cartesian Capital*
Juan Carlos Zuazua - *CEO of VivaAerobus*

AER DOGS

I never thought we would write a book about the team at Irelandia Aviation. It simply isn't our style but sometimes you need to change your mindset. Quite simply, this story needed to be told. This story is about an extraordinary group of people, most of them young and Irish. They are world beaters but are not widely recognised. To the rockstars at Irelandia, many thanks - you are brilliant and extremely resilient. I really regard it as a privilege to be a part of this incredible story. This privilege is also having the brightest and best people around me. I'm beyond proud.

Dec Ryan

PREFACE

The weak died along the way

I glance out the window of Viva's new A320neo aeroplane before take-off from Bogotá, the capital of Colombia. It is January 2022, and our destination is Cartagena, a beautiful historic city on its Caribbean coast. From the window seat, you can see a sparkling yellow wingtip. A middle-aged woman tugs at my sleeve. She is asking in Spanish how her seatbelt works.

As I show her, it is obvious that this is her first time ever on a plane. This is not unusual for Viva. Since its first flight on 25 May 2012, the low fares airline has made flying accessible to millions of Colombians who could never afford to fly before. Afterwards, I messaged the owner of the airline, the aviation entrepreneur Declan Ryan, to tell him this story. "That makes my day," Declan Ryan replies.

It is January 2022, and I had met Ryan for coffee a few days earlier in the Click Clack hotel in Medellín on a visit to Colombia. Ryan is the chief executive of Irelandia, a tiny, yet world-beating, company headquartered in Dublin. He had deployed aeroplanes in Colombia worth cumulatively billions of dollars over the previous decade and he employs 1,000 people there, but nobody recognises him. Ryan has none of the trappings of the successful gringo businessman: no expensive watch, no branded clothing, no security entourage. He arrived for coffee in shorts and a t-shirt.

Ryan's hair is a little long, and he has a broad smile. He is a pioneer in low fares travel but retains a low profile. Irelandia has IPO-ed three airlines (Ryanair, Tiger Airlines, Allegiant) on three continents, and also built an airline in Mexico (VivaAerobus) that it later sold out of at a profit.

And then there is Viva, the airline that is perhaps closest to Ryan's heart – maybe even more than his first love Ryanair. From a standing start in 2012, Viva had become the second largest airline in Colombia, a country of forty million people. Since Viva began, more than thirty-one million people have flown in its airlines in either Colombia or Peru.

While its larger regional rivals Avianca and LATAM filed for bankruptcy during the pandemic, Viva didn't.

When we met in Medellín, Viva had survived the pandemic, and as pent-up demand for travel in Colombia surged, the airline was rebounding. Ryan was in the middle of a deal that could see him merge Viva with its rival Avianca, the world's second oldest airline. The plan, which was subject to regulatory approval, was to create a new Latin American regional airline champion, one in which he would be a shareholder and a director.

I had travelled to Colombia in anticipation of this deal closing imminently, but as frequently happens with complex deals, it was taking longer than expected. Ryan was restricted in what he could say. He spoke in code, promising to fill me in more as soon as he was able.

Over breakfast that morning, our conversation moved from the early days of Ryanair to the battle to keep an airline afloat during a pandemic. We detoured to Ryan's passion for Colombia, a country he believes in, even though it came close at times to breaking him, and the history of his firm Irelandia.

After I met Ryan, I travelled on. On the plane I flicked through a book called *Shoe Dog*. Recommended by Ryan, it told the life story of Philip Knight, the founder of Nike. There is a line in it on the first page where Knight is thinking about a lesson that he learned from the best teacher he ever had.

It reads: "The cowards never started," he'd tell me. "And the weak died along the way – that leaves us."

The Pandemic

Howard Millar leaned across the table in a restaurant in Lima, Peru. The 59-year-old former deputy chief executive of Ryanair had seen it all in the four decades he'd spent working in low fares airlines. Now he wanted to say something to John Goode, the 36-year-old head of aviation with Irelandia. It was 9 March 2020, the night before a board meeting of Viva where Millar was a non-executive director. Goode had mentioned a new virus that was emerging in China and appeared to be rapidly spreading around the world. He had been working for Irelandia for only a few months in 2009 when swine flu shut down flying in Mexico where he was employed by one of its airlines, VivaAerobus.

He knew Irelandia had come through that shutdown in Mexico, and, although it was before his time, he was aware of how it had previously navigated its way through the SARS virus in Asia. Irelandia had lost millions from both viruses, but it hadn't been existential. Goode figured Viva was facing a similar torrid period of months.

Millar, however, had a different view, raising a dark eyebrow, he said: "John, there is something I've got to tell you," Millar said. "Ryanair is seeing bookings fall off a cliff because of this virus. It is preparing for a very tough time. Nobody knows what is going to happen."

Ryanair had €4.5 billion in cash on its balance sheet. Yet, it was worried.

Viva, based between Colombia and Peru, had not felt even a tremble in its bookings. There were reports about the virus, but they were on the inside pages of the newspapers. At Viva's board meeting the next day, its management reported that trading was ahead of target. Steven Maxwell, the 32-year-old CFO of Irelandia, told the meeting that the airline's strategic committee preparing for an IPO felt this was the type of performance it needed to float. Viva was led by its charismatic tall Argentinian chief executive Felix Antelo and its new American chief financial officer Jason Bewley. Antelo was providing leadership, and Bewley had tightened up all its financial reporting lines, so Maxwell was pleased that Viva was turning a corner. Antelo was previously chief executive of LATAM Airlines Peru, so he knew the challenges facing Viva.

Bewley was a former president of Silver Airways, Florida's oldest commercial carrier. He had taken over from Stephen

Rapp, an aviation veteran who Ryan had moved to run Viva in Peru. Bewley had previously worked for AirTran Airways, helping its flotation on the New York Stock Exchange in 2001, before Southwest Airlines bought the business in 2010 for $1.4 billion. It was only Bewley's second board meeting, and the agenda, prepared only days earlier, was all about growth. Already it seemed horribly dated.

On the agenda were plans to launch new routes to Puerto Rico in June 2020, closing a big new bank debt line, and an update on Viva's pipeline of new planes worth billions of dollars that were rolling out of Airbus' manufacturing facility in Toulouse.

At the board table Millar was adamant Viva should do nothing new. "Put the brakes on," he warned. "Guys, this is a tsunami coming and we'd better get ready for it. Hold onto cash at all costs." Some of the board pushed back, noting they had survived previous health crises with other airlines. "I'm just telling you what I'm seeing," Millar said. "The pace of the explosion of Covid cases is way beyond anybody's expectations."

That night the board of Viva, along with some senior executives and their partners, dined together. There were no masks, and no temperature checks. It was just twenty people enjoying a meal. Nobody thought it would be over eighteen months until they met again in person. That was Tuesday.

By Sunday 15 March, Argentina was preparing to close its borders the following day. Peru was next, just twenty-four hours later. Argentina was Antelo's home country. He couldn't believe it and felt Colombia would never overreact and shut things down. The next day it did, closing its borders

PREFACE

from Tuesday 17 March until 30 May. It also announced that it had already identified fifty-four cases of Covid-19. It already had its first death.

Declan Ryan was in New York as the pandemic gripped the Americas and Europe. He'd flown there after Viva's board meeting in Lima on business, arriving in time for St Patrick's Day. It was a city he loved since first passing through it in his twenties to work for an airline called American West where he did everything from cleaning the aisles to being a flight attendant.

The founders of American West, Ed Beauvais and Mike Conway, had been pioneers of low fares airlines, creating the United States' eighth biggest airline. However, in the 1990s they went broke losing $1.2 billion and putting thousands of people out of their jobs. "It was something I would think about time and again in my own business career – the human cost when things go wrong," Ryan said.

As he packed his bag and left the deserted streets of a city of eight million people, Ryan couldn't help but wonder if this was one of those times. The World Health Organisation had upgraded Covid-19 to a pandemic. Hospitals and mortuaries were filling. "I never thought I would see anything like it in all my days in my industry," Ryan said. He dashed back to his home in Medellín, Colombia, arriving just as its borders closed. He flew down using Avianca, the biggest airline in Colombia. The airline was his arch-rival, but it was the last flight available.

He arrived to panic. His CFO, Bewley, had only just moved into an apartment in Medellín, but now he was leaving to be with his partner in Fort Lauderdale. Nobody knew when they could come back. Viva was days from closing a new $50 million debt deal with an American investment bank to fund it growth. The bank pulled the plug after months of negotiation. Nobody was lending to the aviation sector. Viva had raised $50 million in new equity the previous year, but Ryan knew this was not enough. He had 1,000 people on the payroll and more than twenty planes on the ground. Another thirty were due. Ryan had to figure out what to do. John Goode and the youngest member of his team, 28-year old Ruairi Blaney, stayed with him.

Over the next two years sixty-eight airlines around the world would go bust. Irelandia was determined Viva would not be one of them, but the odds were stacked against it. If Viva went bust Ryan risked losing most of his fortune. The world's media would undoubtedly have drawn the comparison between his failure, and that of his father Tony Ryan when his revolutionary aviation leasing business GPA went bankrupt almost thirty years before. Ryan wasn't afraid about his reputation, but he did fear everyone in Viva was going to lose their jobs. All the sacrifices Irelandia had made to create Viva would have been for nothing. Everything was on the line.

CHAPTER 1: ALMOST FAMOUS

More than twenty years ago, Declan Ryan started to keep a journal. It was a private diary that started in 2002 and tracked what was going on in his life and how he felt about it at the time. Every year, he wrote down his mistakes. Ryan was an avid reader, as well as a journaler. He despised Amazon, and always wanted real books, not electronic ones. He loved independent bookshops and had even funded a community bookshop called Books@One near his holiday home in Louisburgh, Co Mayo. After aeroplanes, books were his great passion.

Tony Ryan loved reading and writing too. He had wanted to record his story but despite several conversations with a publisher had never gotten it down. On his deathbed Tony Ryan spoke to his son Declan about telling his story with a special focus on ensuring what he described as "some of the wankers" in his life getting a special mention.

After his father died Declan Ryan asked the historian Richard Aldous to fulfil his father's wish by writing a biography of him called *Tony Ryan: Ireland's Aviator*.

It was a best-seller that told the story of a disruptor who was first an aviation leasing pioneer who created and then lost an empire called Guinness Peat Aviation (GPA), before he recovered it all as the founder of low fares airline Ryanair.

GPA made Ireland a capital of aviation finance, and many of the world's biggest leasing firms are led by its alumni. Ryanair changed how Europeans travelled, opening up countries to each other by offering fares that were lower than any seen before.

Ryan gave Aldous access to his father's papers and didn't interfere with his conclusions — good or bad — about an extraordinary Irishman. The book came out in 2013 when Irish business was at a low point as it recovered from a severe financial crash. Ryan wrote a short preface that concluded: "I think regularly what Tony would have done in the current crisis. What I know for certain is that it wouldn't be standing still or lamenting our mistakes. That determination never to give up is the real lesson of this story."

I knew Declan Ryan a little from over the years in journalism, but he'd always done his best to stay out of the media. I interviewed him once in December 2008 in the Morrison Hotel in Dublin when I was working at *The Sunday Times*. Our interview lasted less than thirty minutes and had no restrictions other than he declined to pose for a photograph.

Afterwards the paper's London picture desk had insisted on scouring the archives for a picture: "Get a fucking picture of junior Ryan, there has to be one." Only a grainy shot from a decade earlier could be found. It was scanned from an old Ryanair annual report and unusable, so the story was illustrated with a picture of a plane instead. It was a grey

CHAPTER 1: ALMOST FAMOUS

winter morning when we met, and Ryan was wearing a dark green baseball cap, and open-necked shirt. He spoke about founding airlines all over the world with his team in Irelandia. Most of the airlines received little or no coverage back home. It was hard to keep up as we moved from continent to continent.

I asked Ryan why so few people outside aviation circles knew anything about him, other than who his father was "My style is low profile. I have always been like that. I have four kids and I want them to be good guys. Because you are a [Denis] O'Brien, a [Tony] O'Reilly or a [Bill] Gates that's irrelevant. You just need to get on with your life," he replied.

Ryan said his endgame when backing airlines was always the stock market as that was where the money was. "We will float anything," he said. "If you are ordering big capital expenditure items [like aeroplanes] you need to be publicly quoted."

He added: "We are traders. The family owned 100 per cent of Ryanair in 1996 and we own a small per cent now and that is probably worth a load more than it was in 1996."

Over the next twelve years, I bumped into Ryan maybe three or four times. We shared a pint once in a pub on Baggot Street with his niece Danielle after a chance encounter. The bar was packed but nobody recognised him. Ryan is a good conversationalist, but he gives little away.

Then in March 2021, Declan Ryan texted unexpectedly after *The Currency,* an online publisher I co-founded, published an article about AerCap buying GECAS for $25 billion to create the world's biggest airline lessor. "Buenos Días from Medellín," Ryan messaged. "Confidentially the AerCap takeover feels like a full circle for GPA. Many people have texted me about that point. It's a real pity Tony isn't around!"

AerCap was led by a former GPA alumni, Aengus Kelly, and part of it could be traced back to AerFi, a company salvaged from the wreckage of GPA after it collapsed in 1992 after GPA failed to float on the stock market. GECAS had bought the parts of GPA that didn't go into AerFi, so it too had firm Irish roots.

After making that initial contract, Ryan told me a little about how business had gone for him as he tried to run airlines in Latin America in a pandemic.

In May 2021, he contacted me again unexpectedly. We went for a walk down Dún Laoghaire pier in south Dublin. It was in between Covid-19 waves, so Ryan had worn a mask on the train out.

We discussed Irelandia, and all the challenges it had faced. Maybe there was a book in it. I asked about the book about his father, and Declan Ryan mentioned he had also turned his journals into a short book.

Only fifty copies had ever been printed in 2018. It was called *Almost Famous*, a term a girl had once used to describe him in a pub in Louisburgh, Co. Mayo.

The book was for his family, and written after his father died. Ryan gave me a copy of *Almost Famous* a few days later.

On its first page it says: "Life is so precious and we are all so fragile. The best lesson I've learned is that we all screw up."

The book you are now reading draws upon *Almost Famous*, but it is a different book.

It is about airlines, people, crises and never giving up. *Almost Famous* does, however, look at the early days of Ryanair, the airline that inspired Irelandia to do what it did next. The following is an extract from *Almost Famous*:

CHAPTER 1: ALMOST FAMOUS

It was typical Tony. 'Get your arse home, we got the Dublin-Luton licence.' He put Ryanair in the names of his three boys: Cathal, Shane and yours truly. We got 30 per cent each; Christy Ryan [a friend of Tony who had helped set up the airline] had a 10 per cent share.

On 8 July 1985 we ran our first flight from Waterford to Gatwick on a thirteen seater turbo prop. On 4 December 1985 the Irish government announced we had the licence to fly from Dublin to Luton. A return ticket was priced at IR£99. The first flight took off on 26 May, 1986. An Irish low-cost airline was born.

Looking back, I realise this was the turning point, maybe the *turning point, in my life. I could have told Tony, 'Forget it, I'm not your errand boy. I'm going to Wall Street.' But honestly I thought it was a great opportunity. Tony was a domineering guy, a control freak in many ways, so it would have taken a lot of balls to have stayed put. But I hardly even thought about not coming home.*

I knew from working in American West Airlines that Ryanair was going to be a slog. The last people ever to make money out of a new airline in those days were the owners. It was the leasing companies like GPA and all the suppliers who had first call on profits. But I liked that Tony wanted me involved. He was upfront that he was setting up the airline to get me and Cathal back to Ireland. Cathal was a pilot in Sri Lanka at the time. In its own way it was the most affectionate thing he'd ever done.

When I got to Ryanair it was total chaos. My official title was company secretary — the guy who signs the contracts and approves the cheques — but I soon realised it was just a title and I needed to be involved in everything and anything. It's my first rule of business: you have to be prepared to do any task yourself.

I was still only twenty-two, but I was one of the few at Ryanair who had any recent hands-on experience of working in an airline. We couldn't attract good people from Aer Lingus, because we couldn't compete on the perks, the pensions or even the potential.

Tony put Eugene O'Neill in charge in the early days. It seemed nuts to me what he did with the money, spending like there was no tomorrow.

For me those early days were a nightmare, as month after month it looked as if the whole thing would go under. Cash was our oxygen and we were running out of it virtually every day. Most Saturdays I'd trudge down to Kilboy (his father's home in Tipperary) to give Tony an update. At that time he was making $20 million a year from GPA, so I was saying to him, why are you throwing money away? He had that look in his eye, like the guy in the casino who keeps betting against the house. Ultimately he was right of course, but at the time it felt like pure madness, driven by his personal pride.

Those early days took a massive toll on me. Whenever Tony phoned me, it was always about business. There was never any chat about life or family. Because Ryanair had no business strategy, every decision was

CHAPTER 1: ALMOST FAMOUS

a drama. Everything became about survival. Not just for Ryanair, but for me too.

I had pains in my chest. My diet was terrible and I put on weight. I drank too much. Eventually I went to see a heart specialist in the Mater hospital. He was blunt. 'If you keep this up,' he told me, 'you won't get to thirty.' I was working crazy hours, worrying about the airline day and night, terrified about the massive losses and that we had no business model.

I could literally see Tony's wealth haemorrhaging money. There were too many people working for the company who thought they had hit the jackpot. I remember at one engineers meeting to discuss a new auxiliary power unit for one of the BAC 1-11s that was going to cost thirty thousand quid, one of the engineers piped up, 'Dec can take it out of his confirmation money.' I could have levelled him, but it was an attitude. Money was no object if the Ryans were paying.

Had Ryanair gone bankrupt, I don't know what would have happened to me health-wise. But I couldn't face slinking away in defeat. Deep down, I didn't want to disappoint Tony and my family.

I didn't have the maturity to realise that Ryanair failing would not have been the end of the world. The time when Eugene was fired was probably the worst of those early days.

I had written Eugene a private note about the losses and my concerns about running out of cash. He assumed Tony had written it for me, so he circulated it to the *whole board, trying to show that his position was being undermined. In fact Tony knew nothing about it. Later at a meeting in his suite at the Westbury Hotel Tony bollocked me because I hadn't even shown it to him. The board held a meeting about the issues raised in the memo and hauled Eugene over the coals, telling him that I was right. That was the beginning of the end for him. My intention was never to get him fired.*

Afterwards, Tony said to me, 'Right, you run with it.' I told him I felt that I would never be the right person for the job of CEO, but he said I was the only one who could do it. So I did it for a year while he looked for a new CEO. In those twelve months I had one focus: to stop us haemorrhaging money. Breaking even would be a bonus.

That year we carried around 700,000 passengers. Those were impressive numbers for a startup challenging a state-run airline like Aer Lingus. But we still lost IR£7 million. Every passenger flown cost us a tenner a head. It was utterly deflating when Michael O'Leary, Tony's accountant and rottweiler, did a stark financial assessment one Saturday morning in Tipperary. We were busting our arses for literally nothing.

When PJ McGoldrick came in as CEO, he took one look and told Tony to invest more money or close it down. He took over from me when I was still in my twenties and I was relieved that someone else was taking the strain. That year Conor was born and I got married to Kate, so it was the start of a much happier time in my life.

CHAPTER 1: ALMOST FAMOUS

I worked well with PJ, but his real rows were with Michael O'Leary. He was taking more interest in the business now. Sometimes I got caught in the crossfire of that relationship, and maybe I sided more with Michael than PJ. But I always felt PJ didn't get the credit he deserved for turning a massive deficit into a small profit. He gave Ryanair a bit of order and I learned that there was a more cool-headed way to do business than always riding Tony's rollercoaster.

It was different with another CEO, Conor Hayes. He was an accountant and I never warmed to him. Michael and I removed ourselves and let Conor get on with it. He did an alright job, cutting everything he could see. That was good for our low-cost model, although it was also the point when I started to worry that our cheap and cheerful airline was becoming cheap and nasty. Later Conor moaned that he didn't get enough plaudits for his part in the Ryanair success story — that it was all about Michael and Tony. I suppose he has a point that history hasn't been kind to the CEOs before Michael, myself included.

If you're the founder's son you are always going to be a bit tarnished. 'What does Tony's boy know?' That kind of stuff never annoyed me. The bitching side was like water off a duck's back. That was the rugby hooker in me. In some ways it was quiet arrogance, but not because I thought I was brilliant at business. It's because I know who I am and what I do. If I could have been a soccer player, I would not have been Ronaldo or Messi. I was Denis Irwin.

Solid, quiet, never misses a game. Sir Alex Ferguson said Irwin was the first man on the team sheet every week. No-one messed with Denis. Keane, Beckham, Cantona and whoever else was around would get all the plaudits, but he didn't care. He was just glad to be playing for Manchester United. That's how I saw myself. Professional. Dogged. Get the job done.

These were good skills to have when Tony's world collapsed in 1992. I didn't have anything to do with GPA, but when the share floatation tanked, the company suddenly had a massive impact on my life. The business was going down like the Titanic.

It was hard to watch Tony at this time as he lost his life's work. Our job was to ringfence any assets that didn't belong to him. Michael [O'Leary] was great in helping with that task. From the moment the GPA IPO failed, my total focus became Irelandia — the holding company for the family's assets. The banks came after us to claw back Tony's $35 million personal debt. That was not fun, even if it was character-building. The banks tried to make us say that Ryanair, which we owned, was really Tony's business. The irony is that we had offered it as security against the original loan from Merrill Lynch, but they had said it wasn't worth anything.

It was a tough time. Tony had gone into a depression and was very fragile. There was guilt about all the people who lost their jobs in GPA and the staff who had taken out loans to buy shares in the IPO. I remember at one stage trying to raise some money in London on Good Friday by selling a BAC-11 aircraft to a Swedish airline. We needed a profit of a million on it, so I dug in, having overheard the Swedes saying they wanted to catch a flight home to Stockholm for the Easter holidays. After I got the deal done, I caught a packed train to Luton to get the last Ryanair flight to Dublin. I hadn't eaten all day and the food trolley only had stewed tea and a dodgy egg sandwich. I hate egg sandwiches and I hate tea, but I had them both, sitting on the floor of the train, and thinking to myself, 'How is this the reward for clearing a million-quid profit?'

In the end, I got through the whole GPA situation by being like a Jack Russell who will just not back down. As the banks got closer and closer, circling like sharks, ultimately they could not get past one single fact. Ryanair was owned by Tony's sons, not by Tony himself. We just about managed to get Tony off the hook after GPA. He ended up paying about ten cents on the dollar on a massive debt. Not bad, all things considered. But with everything else gone, Ryanair suddenly became very important to everyone.

Tony Ryan was now forced to negotiate hard against Merrill Lynch to avoid being bankrupted. It was a stunning reversal in fortune for the self-made entrepreneur who had turned GPA into Ireland's biggest private business with revenues in

1991 of $2 billion, and profits of $280 million. GPA needed access to the stock market where it had hoped to raise $850 million in fresh equity, allowing it to borrow $3 billion more to finance its huge advance order book of aeroplanes. Once the IPO failed in March 1992, its bankers lost confidence in GPA, and it went into a downward tailspin as it ran out of cash. Nearly 40 per cent of its 317 employees lost their jobs, and their shares were wiped out in value. Tony Ryan had expected his shares to be worth $200 million post the float, and he had borrowed $35 million from Merrill Lynch on the strength of this value. Now his shares were nothing, and the investment bank moved hard to secure its position. Declan Ryan and Michael O'Leary backed Tony Ryan all the way as he fought the bank. In the summer of 1993 Merrill Lynch said it would accept $14 million to pay off Tony Ryan's loan of $35 million. Typically, Ryan refused, and made a counteroffer of just $5 million saying this was all he could afford. Months of painful negotiations took place before the bank was beaten down to accepting this offer. At the last minute Tony Ryan said he was $500,000 short, and offered $4.5 million. Merrill Lynch was coming towards its financial year end and eager to close the matter out, so it accepted this sum with the proviso it was paid by 5 April 1994. To raise the money to pay off his debts Tony Ryan bought five Boeing planes for $20 million. Ryanair then bought these planes from him for $24 million to expand its fleet. Ryanair was then owned entirely by Ryan's sons through a trust so it could bail out Tony Ryan if it wished. O'Leary was supportive of the move. The Ryan sons were happy to help their father, as they knew the only reason Ryanair still existed was because

CHAPTER 1: ALMOST FAMOUS

he had saved it by putting tens of millions into it over the previous decade to keep it going.

Six days after paying off Merrill Lynch, Tony Ryan resigned from GECAS, a subsidiary of General Electric, which had seized control of most of GPA. Ryan had been forced by financial necessity to work for GECAS, but he was now free to leave. Ryan had been one of Ireland's wealthiest people as a builder of a global business. Now he was 58, and out of a job. His health suffered and he was advised to go on holiday.

Tony Ryan went to Spain and went on very long walks on the beach daily, as he tried to deal with what had happened. "Some asked me later how much I had lost. I said: '$300m and 20lbs,'" he told the *Irish Times* in a 1995 interview. It was a typically hard-nosed comment made three years later, but at the time Tony Ryan was distraught by GPA's failure.

Declan Ryan was only 31, and far more interested in Ryanair than he had ever been in GPA, which he saw as his father's passion. Long-term, GPA would become the bedrock of a multi-billion-dollar industry that would never have been headquartered in Ireland without it. But the short-term is less forgiving. The Ryans were out in the cold, with a lot to prove.

CHAPTER 2: A WALL STREET WOLF

By the early 1990s, Ryanair had racked up losses of £20 million. There had been offers to buy the airline, but Tony Ryan kept turning them down. Ryanair had decided to adopt Herb Kelleher's Southwest Airlines low-fares model which Declan Ryan was familiar with from working in America. Another £20 million went into Ryanair to try and turn it around, and it had begun to do so. In 1994 Michael O'Leary became chief executive. Ryanair was by then no longer a basket case and beginning to show green shoots, but O'Leary drove the airline to another level with a relentless focus on costs. This was a critical time in Ryanair's history, as Declan Ryan recalls in *Almost Famous*:

> Tony, Michael and I now ran the show between us. I don't think it's claiming much to say that I was probably the nicest of the three of us. Frankly it wasn't hard to be nicer than Tony or Michael. They were ferocious. Mick had a chip on his shoulder that made him desperate to succeed. He had an incredible hunger.

CHAPTER 2: A WALL STREET WOLF

Tony recognised that in him and just kept feeding the beast.

My relationship with Mick was more complicated. Sometimes he was wary around me, wondering if he could trust me. I was Tony's son. I had known him on and off since Clongowes. His brother Eddie was in my class. Michael was quiet at school and certainly not the character he later became in business. Clongowes was a rugby school and Michael played golf, so there wasn't much of a connection. He also had that thing of having been a couple of years ahead of me at school. Sometimes he would call me 'the lad.' It was half affectionate, half wind-up.

When the two of us were together with Tony, there was a lot of testosterone in the room. I was still the Jack Russell, biting everyone's legs. But there was also a hierarchy that I didn't mind. At the regular Saturday morning meetings, I felt part of the team, but I knew I was always No 3 in the pecking order. I spoke my mind, but I never tried to get one over on Michael in those meetings. For the most part I saw my job as smoothing things out between him and Tony, keeping two brilliant characters from killing each other.

Some of the rows were spectacular, but when it came to outsiders we always stuck together, even if sometimes one or other of us wanted to tear our hair out. When Aer Lingus came in with an offer to buy Ryanair for IR£26 million, Tony said 'No, we won't take less than 29.' Michael and I just looked at him as if he'd gone completely mad. However hard we pressed him, he just would not back down so the negotiations collapsed. It was days like this I felt like just walking away.

That failed Aer Lingus deal was one of our many attempts during the early 90s to get the bigger airlines to buy Ryanair. Talks never got anywhere with the UK airlines honestly because I think they thought we were straight out of the bog. Bob Ayling at BA always had that smug air about him. I didn't care much for Bob, but at least he was professional. Richard Branson on the other hand I just found very strange. In the mid-90s he was trying to crack the low-cost model with Virgin Express and thought we might be a way to do it. I met him in London a couple of times, at his house in Holland Park, and on a barge that he kept on the River Thames. He seemed to me to be a bizarre mix of the too informal and super-paranoid. I recall that he would write everything down. He was taking minutes, but seemed pretty determined not to miss anything out. If I said, 'How are you Richard?' I felt he would write it down on his notepad.

This was the era of BA's 'dirty tricks' campaign against Branson. He didn't fool us though. When he stepped outside, Mick and I looked at each other and said, 'We're not doing this.' We made our excuses and left. Soon afterwards Tony sent the Virgin boss a letter instructing him on the meaning of the word 'bollix.' I don't think there was much disagreement between any of us that Branson was one of those.

Part of our success in those days was a 'You'll never beat the Irish' attitude. In return, the Brits often

CHAPTER 2: A WALL STREET WOLF

looked on us as gobshites coming in to turn them over. Sometimes, they could have a sense of humour about it. At one meeting with Mercury Communications, a British telecommunications company, I was chatting to the CEO's assistant who asked me, 'Do you come to the mainland much?' Deadpan, I replied, 'No, I haven't been to Germany for years.' The CEO came in just as I said it and roared with laughter, telling her she deserved the retort. For the most part though, the attitude of the PA was the one we ran across in the UK. I would watch people's eyes and I can see them thinking, 'It's just the bloody Irish.' Even The Financial Times *never tired of taking potshots at us. The irony is that today UK business schools run classes on the Ryanair model. Irish aviation is used as a global template for businesses across the world, because it was done on the basis of cost. So while the Brits never took us seriously, we were leading a revolution in air travel.*

The only good thing that came out of talks with Branson was that it did help us find a new partner on the other side of the Atlantic. In 1995, Branson wanted a 51 per cent stake in Ryanair. Negotiations were led by David Bonderman. A founding partner of TPG and a legend on Wall Street, Bonderman is like a wolf. The minute you talk about a deal, it's like feeding time for him. He's a deal junkie, but the difference between him and the people we were talking to in London was that he was respectful of what we'd done. He admired the company, liked the low-cost model and wanted to work with us, not against us. He understood how good the Paddies were, recognised what Mick was doing as CEO, and knew we were on the crest of a wave with the low-cost model.

David Bonderman's name resonated on Wall Street. Bonderman was born in Los Angeles and was a graduate of Harvard Law School. He had also spent two years studying Islamic law in the Middle East. He'd planned to be an academic but after a year teaching decided to work for the US attorney general Ramsey Clarke instead. Clarke was a champion of civil rights under Democrat presidents John F Kennedy and Lyndon B Johnson, and Bonderman found his legal work in this area inspiring.

When Republican Richard Nixon was elected in 1968, Bonderman could see it was time to move on. He became a corporate lawyer and started to work for Bob Bass, a billionaire whose family had made its first fortune in the oil industry. For ten years Bonderman worked for the Bass family along with Jim Coulter, an MBA graduate from Stanford University. In 1992 Bonderman started to crunch the numbers of Continental Airlines. It was the fifth biggest airline in the United States but had gone bankrupt twice.

"Everybody was down on the (airline) industry in general, and in particular the case of Continental. Nobody bothered to look at the facts," Bonderman recalled in a 2020 interview with a tech company called the Unit Network. Bonderman could see that Continental had made $900 million two years earlier and then lost it all again because of bad management

CHAPTER 2: A WALL STREET WOLF

decisions and the economic cycle moving against it. He tried to convince the Bass family to back him in acquiring Continental — nobody else was interested in buying it at the time. The family refused as they felt it was too risky and high profile, so Bonderman and Coulter left to co-found the Texas Pacific Group (TPG). They assembled a consortium and bought out Continental, and then turned it around by putting in proper management and convincing its trade unions to support a restructuring.

To rescue the airline, TPG let 4,000 of Continental's 40,000 employees go but ultimately ended up with 52,000 people as the business recovered. "We made ten times our money in three years on a $100 million investment more or less so that kind of put us on the map," Bonderman would later recall. TPG's first deal established TPG and it started to look for other deals around the world. It backed Richard Branson when he bought the MGM cinema chain in Britain in 1994. When Branson started to look at Ryanair, it made sense for him to ask Bonderman to help out. The American had a different personality to the brash Englishman. He was astute, pragmatic and had a sharp sense of humour that endeared him to the Ryans, unlike Branson. In Ireland, Bonderman's arrival as an investor in Ryanair was spun as a sign of weakness. "There was a lot in the newspapers saying that TPG were a vulture fund and that Ryanair must be in trouble, and they're coming in to rescue Ryanair. Not at all," Anthony Carragher, later a partner in Irelandia, recalled. "Ryanair was doing fantastically well, and TPG were jumping on that train, and helping to get it over the IPO hump."

To bring in David Bonderman's TPG as a new investor, the Ryans had to work out how many shares to sell and how much to leave for Michael O'Leary and themselves.

Tony Ryan sent in Declan Ryan as a "battering ram" to negotiate with O'Leary as he knew his son would fight his family's corner hard. O'Leary was happy for Tony Ryan and Declan Ryan to get shares, but he objected to Declan Ryan's brothers getting too many.

A row broke out. "I don't know how Michael and I didn't swing at each other. I was not offended that he wanted a reward for the work that he'd done," Declan Ryan said.

"But I was offended that he wanted me to sell my brothers down the river. None of us knew what Ryanair would be worth when we started out.

"Yes, it was like I had walked up twenty flights of stairs carrying the suitcases while the two other lads had taken the executive lift to the top floor. But there was always enough success to go around."

Eventually a deal was reached, with O'Leary getting 18 per cent, TPG 20 per cent, and the rest staying with the Ryans. Bonderman joined the board of Ryanair, but from early on the amount of swearing surprised him.

"Bonderman asked us about the different uses of the word bollocks," Ryan recalled. "He said he'd heard us use it six times in a different way, so he did a glossary right there from 'your man's a bollox' to 'dogs bollox.' He couldn't believe how a dog's balls could be the best thing!"

The arrival of TPG was a precursor to Ryanair floating, but as it prepared to do so its banks objected to Tony Ryan being chair due to his history with GPA.

Declan Ryan was told to break the news to his father. "Over my dead body," Tony Ryan said. Declan Ryan responded:

CHAPTER 2: A WALL STREET WOLF

"That's right because you're already a dead man walking."

Declan Ryan felt he had no choice but to be blunt, and O'Leary agreed with him. Tony Ryan accepted the decision, and blamed his banks as opposed to his son or O'Leary.

Relations between Tony Ryan and O'Leary worsened as time went on, however, for other reasons. "It wasn't master and apprentice anymore," Declan Ryan said. "Tony could have dealt better with letting go, but Mick could have shown a bit more respect. He didn't need to wind Tony up in every meeting and should have acknowledged who had been the visionary here.

"Mick was a brilliant CEO, without doubt the best I've seen to this day. But Tony was the entrepreneur, the pathfinder, the funder. Mick had wanted to close the airline down. So had I. Without Tony, there would have been no Ryanair."

David Bonderman became chair instead of Tony Ryan. His main task was to lead Ryanair's 1997 IPO. To Declan Ryan's surprise Bonderman said he would be hiking in the Himalayas at the time.

"When I heard he was going for a holiday in the Himalayas I lost it because of GPA and so on," Declan Ryan said. "Our guy in Morgan Stanley (an adviser on the Ryanair float) said, 'Dec would you calm down, he glows in the dark', I said, 'I don't care where he fucking glows, I want him in New York for the IPO.'"

"So, I rang David and I said, 'You have to be fucking there, this is our company dah, dah, dah.' He says, 'You know what Declan, I don't need to be there but for you I will bring a satellite phone', and he said, 'By the way it's going to weigh 10 pounds.'"

Ryan sent a note to Bonderman afterwards to make peace. "I said, 'Sorry I lost it. But it's really important to us, maybe the 10 pounds will help you lose a bit of weight!', and he comes back, 'Fuck no, the Sherpa will carry that for me.' It was typical of David's good-natured, deadpan humour," Ryan said.

"The guys in New York were right. Bonderman does glow in the dark, and if he puts his name behind a company, it's a bit like Warren Buffet. The IPO itself of Ryanair was fantastic. I was on the steering committee. I was eating, drinking and sleeping it."

Ryanair floated on 29 May 1997, and Declan Ryan flew back from New York to Dublin on the day it listed. He had a drink with Michael O'Leary in Davy Stockbrokers, and then went with him to the Coachman's Inn near the airport to meet Ryanair's team. "It was amazing craic. Everyone was there with all the Ryanair staff, the baggage handlers who'd been given shares and were making a few grand out of it. That was moving to witness," Declan Ryan recalled.

"One guy came over to me, laughing, all excited. But then he turned serious and said, 'Let me buy you a pint, you don't realise what you've done for me and my family.' That sounds like I'm giving myself a big pat on the back. But an airline that had started out with a single turboprop had put real money into this guy's pocket and he wanted to say thank you. It was one of the best moments of my business life."

CHAPTER 3: THE PROTECTOR — ANTHONY

The year before Ryanair floated in May 1997, Anthony Carragher went for a job interview with Tony Ryan in his office at 9 Merrion Square, Dublin 2. A brass plate on the door said Irelandia, but he knew nothing about what went on inside the finely restored property other than it had something to do with Tony Ryan. The name Irelandia could be traced to 1980, when it was the name Tony Ryan hoped to use for a new airline based in Ireland that would transform "the least developed aviation nation in Europe." This airline differed from what became Ryanair as it was to be based in Shannon and offer both short and long-haul flights to New York, Boston and London. "The keystones of Irelandia's operations will be low overheads, efficient operations and forceful marketing ... Irelandia will respond to the deregulation philosophy currently implicit in American aviation policy and now gaining ground in Europe," Tony Ryan explained in a draft position paper.

Ryan had started to lobby the government to support his vision for an Irelandia airline, but Aer Lingus had gotten wind of it and objected. Ultimately, Irelandia never became an airline, but in it could be seen the seeds of what became Ryanair. Irelandia instead became the investment vehicle for the Ryan family, but it didn't do that much in 1996 as the Ryan family were yet to make their float windfall.

Carragher was 25 years old, and a freshly-minted accountant who grew up in Kilmore West, a neighbourhood between Santry, Beaumont and Artane on the northside of Dublin. His father came from Co. Louth and was a welder, while his mother, a housekeeper, came from Monaghan. Carragher worked part-time with his father, but he wanted to study accountancy as it was a way of getting a qualification while earning money. He joined a mid-sized practice called Horwath Bastow Charleton where he became a corporate finance manager. His office overlooked the Grand Canal, and Carragher was advising an emerging new breed of Irish businessperson keen to utilise an eclectic array of state-promoted tax-based schemes to invest in everything from car parks to hotels, and from boats to aircraft to films. He also witnessed the other side of business working as a senior manager in its receivership department and winding down a number of Dublin coal yards.

Carragher had learned a lot, but he was ready to move on. A recruiter suggested he meet one of Ireland's wealthiest businessmen, Michael Smurfit, the chief executive of an international packaging giant. Smurfit offered him a job working on the finances of the K Club, a luxury golf resort his firm owned in Co. Kildare. The same recruiter said he should also talk to Tony Ryan in his office on Merrion Square. When he rang the doorbell, a 31-year-old opened the door. It was Declan Ryan. Carragher had been warned to expect a grilling, but instead he found the younger Ryan quick-witted and self-deprecating, and he decided to go with the Ryans when they offered him a job.

Day to day it was a tiny team, just Declan Ryan, Carragher and Margaret Kinane, who worked mainly on its property deals. The first thing Carragher had to do was to unravel the CDS Trust, which stood for the names of Tony Ryan's sons — Cathal, Declan and Shane. The trust's assets were Ryanair shares, and Carragher needed to restructure it to allow Ryanair to float on the market and sell these shares.

The Ryan family had already made some money from selling shares in Ryanair to David Bonderman's Texas Pacific Group prior to its float, but this was a different league. Ryanair floated with a market capitalisation of IR£300 million. The Ryans made tens of millions of pounds, and they held onto a stake worth over IR£100 million. The family wanted Irelandia to manage the Ryan wealth and ensure they didn't come close to losing it all again. "We had more money than we knew what to do with," Ryan said. "So we needed to work out how to control it, and not let it control or change us."

Declan Ryan was in charge of Irelandia, but it would hold regular board meetings attended by Tony Ryan and Cathal Ryan, and, when he was old enough, Shane Ryan. Anthony Carragher's task was to work with Declan Ryan on investing the Ryan family's fortune. He was the family's financial protector and gatekeeper. Everything was done privately. "I wouldn't have spoken about Ryan family business to anybody in my life — not a brother, not a sister, not my wife," Carragher said. "It was one of our core values: absolute confidentiality."

Ryan could afford to move from Sandymount to a large house in Killiney in south County Dublin. He was married, and Jack, Declan Ryan's third son, was born in 1996. He had two sons already, Conor (b. 1989) and Eoin (b. 1991) and a daughter Ana would arrive in 1999. Living in Killiney he discovered his next-door neighbour was Bono, the lead singer with U2. Bono didn't know who he was but would refer to him as 'neighbour' when they bumped into each other.

One day Bono bumped into Ryan and said: "Neighbour, can I have a word? I just wanted to let you know that Salman Rushdie is staying with me." Rushdie was living under a fatwa at the time after the publication of his book *The Satanic Verses* in 1988. Ryan couldn't help but slag Bono. "I thought I'd bought one of the most secure houses in Ireland. Now it turns out there's a guy living next door with a fatwa on his head. WTF?'" Bono didn't cop Ryan was joking, and got annoyed. "I don't know whether he was expecting me to say 'Wow!' or whether he genuinely thought he was being neighbourly," Ryan recalled. "But he didn't expect me to be making jokes about little red lasers on our heads from the Iranian special forces!"

CHAPTER 4: LEAVING RYANAIR

Aviation analyst Joe Gill first met Declan Ryan shortly after he had stepped down from the board of Ryanair in 2003. Gill had recently returned to Dublin from London to work for Ireland's second biggest stockbroker, Goodbody. He recalls meeting Ryan at an aviation conference in New York organised by investment bankers Raymond James. The investment bank had helped Ryanair float a few years earlier and one of its partners, Tom Mullins, was close to Ryan.

"Declan was talking about the idea of investing in low-cost airlines in growth markets as against developed markets like Europe," Gill recalled. "I knew he was Tony's son so I was trying to work him out. I knew Ryanair was a success but I didn't know if he was the real deal. Will he be able to pull off what he is talking about or is he a spoiled kid?

"I think a lot of people back then didn't know whether he was real or not. Dec had to doubly prove himself because he was Tony Ryan's son. He was coming out from under his father's huge legacy and shadow, as well as Michael O'Leary's shadow too."

Ryan had barely any profile. His name carried weight — both good and bad — in the airline industry.

Gill came away from New York liking Ryan but knowing little about him.

Declan Ryan had been a director of Ryanair from 1985 and was chief executive from 1989 to 1990. He grew up lower middle class and didn't always have money. Few knew him outside the close-knit airline business.

Ryan had been thinking of leaving Ryanair since it floated on the stock market, but he only did so on 23 June 2003. Thirteen days earlier, he and Michael O'Leary had both sold four million shares in Ryanair, making €24 million each. The two men had grown up together. They'd tried to convince Tony Ryan to cut his losses by closing Ryanair, and then helped him turn it around. Now both were wealthy in cash terms for the first time. Ryan's resignation was barely marked. Mary Finan, a spokesperson for the family, said: "He's been on the board for 18 years. He felt it was time to do other things."

Ryan felt it was a release to leave Ryanair. "There were very strong people on the board. It was Michael, Tony (Ryan) and (David) Bonderman. I was kind of in the championship versus the lads who were in the premiership," he laughed.

O'Leary was ahead of Declan Ryan in school at Clongowes Wood College in Kildare, and felt he was the senior as a result. O'Leary was quiet in school, but that was changing.

"Myself, Michael and Tony were like the Marx Brothers. We met together every Saturday morning for four or five years in the Ryanair/GPA days," Ryan said. For years O'Leary would pull in his car near Kilboy House and wait

CHAPTER 4: LEAVING RYANAIR

for Declan Ryan to arrive, rather than risk being roasted by Tony Ryan alone.

"We used to say we were the cannon fodder for Tony and his Monday morning meetings at GPA. I was the boy of the holy trinity. The guys were not dismissive, it was just that I was two years younger than Michael and I was Tony's son," according to Ryan.

"Tony and Mick would love kicking the shit out of each other. They were like the young bull versus the old bull and I was in between them. It wore on me a bit.

"I have huge respect for Mick but it gets a bit tiring, and it was getting boring as it was getting bigger." Ryanair was now a listed business. It wasn't a start-up anymore.

When O'Leary took over as chief executive in 1994, he drove it hard and didn't always treat customers and staff well. This caused a rift between him and the Ryan family.

"When we set up Ryanair, the model that I always had in my mind was American West — a low-cost carrier that was friendly. It was about making what was a luxury product available to everyone," Ryan said. "At Ryanair we stopped smiling and started barking."

In 1998 Declan Ryan had sent a memo to O'Leary telling him he was "disappointed but not surprised" that a strategy document the Ryanair chief had prepared "did not cover the areas of customer service." O'Leary didn't listen to him, or similar protestations from Tony Ryan. "In hindsight Mick came to realise Tony was right and changed Ryanair's policies years after Tony's death," Ryan said. "But back then we were the Millwall of the airline world, 'No-one likes us, we don't care.'"

On 24 January 2002, Ryanair placed an order for 100 Boeing 737-800 aircraft with an option for fifty more, in a deal worth $9.1 billion. Declan Ryan had driven this deal hard in the wake of 9/11 as Ryanair played Boeing off against Airbus to get the best deal. When British Airways chose Airbus, Ryanair knew it had the whip hand. "It became a slam-dunk that we were going to go with Boeing. They need us badly," Ryan said. "At one stage during a board meeting Mick turned around and said, 'I'm even starting to feel sorry for Boeing.' We just couldn't believe the price they were offering."

Ryan felt elated after the Boeing deal, even more than when Ryanair floated. "I started thinking then it would be a good time to go," he said.

Tony Ryan didn't want his son to leave. "Tony was annoyed with me," Ryan recalled. "He wanted Ryanair to be one of those great family businesses."

"Mick (O'Leary) was very nice about it. He rang me up and said 'Who's going to be there for me?' I said, 'Mick, I'm always here for you, it doesn't matter if I'm on the board or not you know.'"

What Declan Ryan planned to do next wasn't clear. He had a hunch that the business principles of Ryanair could be exported to new airlines around the world, but he was looking at lots of non-aviation ventures too.

Howard Millar remembers hearing Declan Ryan was resigning. He'd just been made deputy chief executive of

CHAPTER 4: LEAVING RYANAIR

Ryanair along with Michael Cawley reporting into Michael O'Leary. "I was surprised because Ryanair was so much in Declan's DNA. He'd helped get it up and running. To walk away from your child when it was grown up and listed in Dublin, London and on the Nasdaq, just after we had signed the order with Boeing and were ready to grow, I was taken aback." Millar joined Ryanair in April 1992 when he was hired by O'Leary's predecessor Conor Hayes so he'd worked closely with Declan Ryan. From Santry, north Dublin, after graduating with a business degree in Trinity College Dublin in 1982, Millar worked in leasing for Renault Ireland. In 1988 he went to Saudi Arabia to work for Masstock, an Irish agri-food group, founded by the McGuckian family which had a big joint venture there with a local partner. Hayes had previously been CFO of Masstock so he asked Millar to join Ryanair. Millar initially wasn't interested as Ryanair was seen as likely to go bust, but his wife encouraged him to take the job as she missed Ireland. Hayes interviewed him around Christmas 1991. "Conor said, 'Look, Ryanair is a mess, but you might get six months out of it, a year max, but sure you will be home then and can see about other jobs,'" Millar recalled. Millar joined as finance director and was promoted to CFO in the run-up to Ryanair's IPO. "I would have a lot of communication with Declan at that time," Millar recalled. "Declan was on the board and heavily involved in the process. The IPO was the opportunity for the Ryan family to recover from the disaster that was GPA. Ryanair was the last piece of silver in the cupboard, so it had to work for them." When Ryan stepped down Millar was surprised but he could see the logic. "Tony was a very forceful character,

Bonderman was very forceful, and Michael [laughing] was not exactly shy and retiring! The board meetings could be interesting. Frank and open exchange of views is normally the phrase but that is the Ryanair style … I could understand Declan's decision."

CHAPTER 5: MOVING AWAY FROM METAL

Eleven days after the Twin Towers terrorist attack in New York in 2001, Tony Ryan and Anthony Carragher went to Prague. The two men had heard that investors in the US were desperately trying to dump properties in Central Europe in order to bring money back home as the world's biggest economy was reeling. AIG, the world's largest insurer, was facing $800 million in claims in relation to the Twin Towers alone. It was involved in a joint venture with another firm, Lincoln, to develop office blocks in Prague to house a new headquarters for PWC as well as a hotel and medical centre. Irelandia offered to buy out its position. Over the next three years Irelandia invested in property in Poland and the Czech Republic. Yes, it was involved in aviation. But it was also looking at diversifying its position.

In 2004, Ryan and Carragher attended a meeting with estate agents Jones Lang in Prague when they heard there were more Irish people down the hallway looking at deals. It was Seán Quinn, then Ireland's richest man, who was going on a buying spree worth hundreds of millions from

Central Europe to Russia. "I turned around to Anthony and said it is time to look somewhere else," Ryan said. "Seán Quinn was throwing money at stuff and we knew we couldn't compete."

Irelandia felt the property market was overheating. "I thought the prices being offered were ridiculous," Carragher recalled. "They were offering the same prices as in Germany. There was a sense of madness." By this stage Irelandia had a portfolio worth hundreds of millions of euro but it decided to sell it all. Cathal Ryan argued against it as he loved the Czech Republic and Poland; Declan Ryan said it was time to sell. "Declan was always a trader," Carragher said. "He did not need to own things forever. He has a mind that loves new things, new people. He was ready for the next thing and we were being offered crazy money so he wanted to sell." Carragher agreed. "We didn't see the entire market crashing but we got out."

Irelandia also had property assets in Brussels, Paris and Barcelona. It sold those also. It had more than doubled its initial investment in property.

The Ryan family was determined that Irelandia would invest widely, making it bullet proof against any single investment going bad.

"The Ryans used the term 'peeling the onion' about Ryanair," Anthony Carragher said. "The onion will keep growing and we'll keep peeling a layer off it but what's left behind will actually be bigger no matter how much you peel off because it was such a fast-growing airline."

Tony Ryan loved hearing about what Irelandia was investing in, and was never afraid of giving his views. But he had just

CHAPTER 5: MOVING AWAY FROM METAL

bought the Lyons Estate in Co. Kildare for £3 million, and restoring it became his great love. "There was no logic to some of the spend," Carragher laughed. "There was never a time, it was not over budget." Tony Ryan restored Lyons to a level described by restoration expert Hugh Montgomery-Massingberd as "the largest, most ambitious and exhaustive programme of restoration ever undertaken in a private capacity in the history of the Irish state".

After restoring the house, Ryan moved on to redeveloping the nearby village of Lyons, which had been burnt by English soldiers in 1641, establishing a restaurant, series of boutique shops and eventually guesthouses on the site.

"Tony found these old Italian murals behind the rotting wallpaper and he shipped in these guys from Rome that had experience of restoring this stuff," Carragher recalled. "He loved the challenge of it and once he started restoration works we saw less of Tony in Merrion Square."

Irelandia had significant funds from Ryanair, and the question became what to do with it. "Tony was our biggest fan and nobody revelled in our success more than he did," Declan Ryan said. "We invested in all kinds of businesses and Anthony was central to the success that we enjoyed."

Back home, Irelandia looked at buying consumer brands including crisp maker Tayto, and Tipperary Water – but it couldn't find the right deal. In 1998 it bought a stake in glass maker Tipperary Crystal, so it had some experience with consumer brands.

Irelandia invested in overseas private equity funds, bought bonds, and took stakes in technology companies. Irelandia sold out of bonds at a forty-five-year high and did well from most of its managed investments.

In April 2001, it teamed up with Tom Barrack's Colony Capital to buy the Château Lascombes vineyard in the Margeaux region of France near Bordeaux for $67 million.

The 117-hectare Château was steeped in history, tracing its name to Chevalier Antoine de Lacombes, who owned it in the seventeenth century. Brewers Bass Charrington then bought the vineyard in 1971 from a French wine merchant, and the quality of its wines slipped after that. Dominique Befve, a former technical director from Château Lafite Rothschild and Château l'Evangile, along with renowned oenologist Michel Roland, were hired by lead investor Colony to turn things around.

A survey of the soil in the vineyard concluded that twelve of its hectares were clay-limestone and clay-gravel, making them more suitable to Merlot than to Cabernet Sauvignon. Befve restructured the vineyard to better match its soil to grape variety and increased the density of vines.

The vineyards' cellars were modernised to add more flavour, and new systems were installed to cool its grapes, increasing tannins, colour and aroma. "Properly managed, the wine business is a very good business," Tony Ryan said in a 2003 interview in the *Sunday Independent*. "Any new investors coming into a business look at what is needed and make the necessary changes in procedures and management."

All told, €35 million was put into the estate, allowing it to make 500,000 bottles annually, making it the highest producer of any Margaux estate. A decade later, the vineyard was bought by French health insurance company MACSF for €200 million, including about €50 million in stock. Irelandia made a significant profit from its part of the sale.

Around the time of Château Lascombes, the Ryans also invested with others in a new €25 million fund called Growcorp led by Professor Michael Donnelly. Donnelly was an electronics engineer who had left Ireland to join Narco Scientific, where he developed new ways to save premature babies.

"From a personal perspective, I had difficulties myself when I was born. And from that respect, I was always interested in the area," he told me in a 2004 interview in the *Irish Independent*.

Donnelly then worked with the US Department of Defence on ways to protect soldiers from biological weapons. In the late 1990s he returned to Ireland and started talking to Irelandia. Donnelly convinced Irelandia to fund the acquisition of the original drug delivery business created by Don Panoz, the founder of drugs company Elan, as well as to take stakes in various start-ups spun out of Dublin City University. Irelandia bought the old Elan business for €3 million after the Irish midlands-based pharma company had invested €100 million in it over more than a decade.

Growcorp rebranded the old Elan business as Merrion Biopharma and it started working on new ways of giving drugs orally using a patented delayed release technology.

In December 2007, Merrion Biopharma floated on the Irish Stock Exchange. It licensed its technology to other firms and after surging in value, was eventually taken private.

"I thought buying Elan's assets was a great opportunity, but Growcorp is a great example of when we didn't get it right," Ryan said. "It didn't reach its potential."

Irelandia took risks but was prudent. "Each investment was an island," Carragher said. "Any leverage or debt was limited recourse to that asset alone so no one domino would ever be able to take it all down. No personal guarantees, no cross-collateralisation. If a deal died, it died alone. That was the strategy."

CHAPTER 6: A RARE DOG

The original task of Irelandia was to ensure that the Ryan family's wealth wasn't exposed entirely to the aviation sector. But even still it couldn't help but be drawn to it. Irelandia had made two early investments in aviation leasing after GPA. Tony Ryan had some residual shares in AerFi, an aviation leasing company led by GPA alumnus Patrick Blaney. Aerfi's assets included part of the old GPA. Later Tony Ryan put more money in, and in 2000 this business was sold to AirFinance, the aircraft-leasing division of the Daimler Chrysler Group, for $750 million.

Tony Ryan had made almost $50 million from the sale. The Ryans also backed two former GPA alumni, Domhnal Slattery and John Morrissey, who had set up a new aircraft-leasing company called International Aviation Management Group (IAMG) in 1998.

Morrissey said IAMG considered Tony Ryan as a "sumitomo" in investing terms, a reference to the Japanese phrase meaning royal family. It was a complex deal in which to invest. Irelandia needed someone to guide them on the tricky nuances of private equity investing. James Osborne, a director of Ryanair and long-term adviser to Tony Ryan, recommended they use a then 33-year-old lawyer called Paul White, who worked for A&L Goodbody. Declan, along with Anthony Carragher and White, were dealing with the Cayman Islands, where the business was based, as well as in Dublin, where the deal was negotiated, and San Francisco, where the IAMG lawyers were based. Carragher and White got on together.

"It was my first deal with Irelandia," White recalled. "We were in the trenches, and there was a fair bit of testosterone flying around given the big characters involved."

Julian Yarr, later a managing partner of A&L, had just joined the Dublin firm as a recently qualified lawyer from Belfast, and he too was thrown into the deal to assist Irelandia. "We were working around the clock in three time zones for weeks as we tried to close the deal. It felt a bit like being in a tumble dryer," White said.

As the relationship developed, Slattery and Tony Ryan inevitably clashed. "There was a lot of respect there but it was also like two bulls bucking heads," Morrissey recalled. IAMG ended up buying out the Ryans for what they put in.

Slattery would go on to nearly go bust in the financial crash when he set up a private equity firm called Claret Capital, only to make an incredible comeback by co-founding Avolon in 2010, one of the world's biggest aviation leasing companies. Irelandia could have done without making the IAMG investment, but it did bring White into its world. He would be its trusted legal adviser over the coming decades. "Irelandia always fearlessly backed itself and its team, and it was never boring. Working with them has often been a swashbuckling experience," White reflected. Around the same time White started working with Irelandia, so too did another influential figure: Maurice Mason. Declan Ryan and Mason's paths had already crossed.

The first time they met was in the rugby dressing room in Wanderers, one of Ireland's oldest rugby clubs "Maurice comes over to me," Ryan recalled. "And as you know I was born with a cleft palate. Maurice comes over to me and says how did you break your nose? I looked up at him like a Jack Russell about to bite.

"Another guy called Rusty O'Callaghan, an officer in the army who was from Cashel in Tipperary, says: 'I don't know if he broke his nose Mo but I know how yours is going to get broken!' That is Mo, he always says it how he sees it!"

Mason was from near Killiney in south County Dublin, the son of a doctor and a teacher. He was a boarder in Castleknock College, who had studied law in Trinity College Dublin, before dropping out to do engineering. Mason was fascinated by the mechanics of a Rolls-Royce aircraft engine, but he never thought he would work in aviation. Instead, he went to London to work for Procter & Gamble, where he developed a lemon-scented version of Fairy Liquid. He missed home, and he spotted an advertisement for a job with GPA in the back pages of the *Sunday Tribune*, a newspaper Tony Ryan had previously owned in the 1980s with the journalist Vincent Browne.

Mason sent in his CV, and was rejected, only to get a phone call asking him for an interview. He was rejected again, only to get another call asking him for a second interview with

Colm Barrington, chief operating officer of GPA. Barrington was a keen sailor, and he knew Mason from a sailing club in Bray. "For whatever reason ... and Colm always takes the credit, I was given a chance," Mason said. Early on, Mason was in GPA's London office walking along a narrow corridor towards Brian McLaughlin, a lawyer in GPA. Tony Ryan was a smaller man, so Mason didn't see him behind McLaughlin until they almost collided with each other. "Tony greeted me by saying 'Hello overhead,'" Mason recalled. "It certainly marked my card." Mason knew nothing about GPA or aviation leasing. He was sent to Shannon and ended up working on leasing contracts only because there was a spare seat. Colm Barrington and Patrick Blaney were setting up GPA Capital, a new division in the business, and they took him under their wing.

"I wasn't afraid of numbers so they found me useful," Mason said.

Blaney was trying to find non-traditional sources of capital to invest in aeroplanes, a practice which is common today but then nascent. Mason was helping out, and he met his future wife Mairead, who worked in public relations for GPA at the time. The pace in GPA was frenetic. "You wouldn't hesitate to get on a plane and go anywhere," Mason said.

When GPA failed to IPO, confidence in the business dried it up and it failed. Tony Ryan was sidelined by his bankers, and GPA was broken in two. GE Capital bought half, with the rest left to Blaney to sift through. Mason helped Blaney with this, but then GE Capital asked him to move to Stamford, Connecticut to work for it. Mason didn't want to go, so he asked Karl Essig, an aviation financier who'd advised GPA,

CHAPTER 6: A RARE DOG

for a job in Morgan Stanley. "I basically said you guys have a hole in Europe, and I think I could fill it," Mason said. For the next four years Mason worked in the aviation capital markets. "I learned, and learned and learned," he said.

By 2002 and in his mid-30s, Mason was a managing director in Morgan Stanley. He was getting rich, but he missed home. His wife Mairead was still friends with Tony Ryan. Tony Ryan suggested to Mason that he should meet Declan Ryan, who was by then thinking about founding new airlines. Back then, to succeed airlines needed to IPO, so Tony Ryan figured Mason's experience in London would be useful. Mason started working for Irelandia as an unpaid consultant, but he could invest alongside it if the right deals could be found.

Declan Ryan had enjoyed investing in property, life science, technology and wine. But he didn't love those sectors. "For all the strain and cost to my health of the early days of Ryanair, it was running the airline as a start-up that had given me the greatest buzz I'd enjoyed in business," Ryan said. "I learnt a lot of lessons about how to make the low-cost model work. Now I wanted to replicate the success story in other parts of the world."

CHAPTER 7: AN AMICABLE BREAK-UP

Declan Ryan had run Irelandia for the best part of a decade from the early 1990s. He was responsible for the family money and had made several hundred million for the Ryan family. Nearly everything he did was below the radar, but Declan knew it would be impossible to start founding new low-fares airlines and not attract attention. He also knew the level of risk required would be much higher, as airlines, especially fledgling ones, often go bankrupt. As he thought about founding a platform to develop new low-cost carriers, he decided to pull the plug on managing his family money.

Also, it was putting a strain on relations between him and his father and siblings. "I remember one year Cathal (Ryan) said 'That's great Dec,' when we reported a 22 per cent increase in profit," Declan Ryan recalled. "And then he said, 'Is there any chance we could get it up to 25 per cent?'" The remark was tongue in cheek, but only partly. "The lads had started to see me as the family's business guy, not their brother, when to be honest Sunday lunch with them and my pop was more important to me," Ryan said.

CHAPTER 7: AN AMICABLE BREAK-UP

"Tony begged me to keep doing it, but I told him I had some plans of my own. He could invest in them. They all could. But I wanted to distance myself from their business activity."

It wasn't just this strain that caused Ryan to divide out Irelandia; it was also the case that interests had diverged between him and his family.

Tony, Cathal and increasingly Shane Ryan had all fallen in love with the equine industry. Between them they had set up 'Four Farms', representing the family's bloodstock interests. As this business scaled, it was taking up a significant amount of Irelandia's time to manage.

Cathal Ryan and Tony Ryan owned studs in Kildare, while Tony Ryan owned Castleton Lyons in Kentucky, and Sefton Lodge in Newmarket, England too. Combined, these were assets worth in the hundreds of millions. In Castleton, Tony Ryan had even built a life-size replica of the tower of the Rock of Cashel to remind him of his home in Tipperary.

"Bloodstock was becoming a big, big thing," Carragher said. "But Dec wasn't interested." A final factor was that when Irelandia was founded, Shane Ryan was a boy, so his family had made investment decisions for him. He was now a man, and understandably wanted to do his own thing.

"Was there friction? There probably was by the end," Carragher said. "But for a family who invested in so many businesses with high stakes, they were remarkably close and friendly."

Irelandia divided its money between the three brothers and their father. Shane Ryan set up Maroon Capital, while Cathal Ryan set up Portico as their personal investment vehicles. Irelandia stayed with Declan Ryan. Ryan decided to turn

Irelandia into three divisions: an aviation division to build and invest in low-cost carriers, a more low-risk investment division, and finally the One Foundation.

Ryan's idea for the One Foundation was to set up Ireland's first venture philanthropy fund with a lifespan of ten years. It would ultimately invest in dozens of start-up charities as an investor in Social Entrepreneurs Ireland, and it put growth capital into established nonprofits to help them scale. It also backed campaigns such as children's rights and Ireland's marriage equality referendum.

To help Irelandia do all this, Irelandia hired Paula Doherty, a young graduate from KPMG. Doherty was born in Galway but she had lived in Scotland before settling in Donegal. She had wanted to be a veterinarian surgeon but didn't get the examination results and so went to study business in a technical college in Derry. She got a part-time job in Galliagh to the north-west of Derry, where families driven out of the Bogside and Creggan in the 1970s had moved. It was a Republican area that policed itself. Her job was in The Baltimore bar, and Doherty remembers her customers as decent. Yet, it could also be dangerous. "One night a massive fight broke out and we had to barricade the doors," she said. "You couldn't ring the RUC as they wouldn't come to that area in the middle of the night." The bouncers in the bar made a phone call, and then the noise stopped. "The biggest, burliest guys you've ever seen walked in," she said. "I didn't know who they were, but the men outside did and they scarpered."

Doherty did well in college, and managed to get into the University of Ulster, and then get a work placement in Washington with a US law firm. She graduated with a first

CHAPTER 7: AN AMICABLE BREAK-UP

class honours degree in business and got hired by KPMG. Doherty ended up auditing Irelandia, under KPMG partner Colin O'Brien. She recalls being struck by the hundreds of companies within Irelandia, which employed less than ten people directly. After four years in KPMG she left to travel, before O'Brien rang her to ask if she would work for Irelandia. Anthony Carragher offered her a job in 2004 as financial controller. "I came in at the tail-end of the split in Irelandia," Doherty said. Her job was to trace every euro in the business to ensure it was split up among the Ryans correctly. "It was mammoth, but it gave me a brilliant picture of the whole thing," Doherty said. Doherty met Tony Ryan a handful of times in his home in the Lyons Estate as part of her work. "I did find him quite scary, I'm not going to lie," Doherty said. "But as long as you answered his questions, he respected you and would move on." Doherty fell in love with Kildare – which is famed as the home of horses in Ireland – on her drives down there. "I used to drive around going, I would love to live here," she recalled. Doherty would become part of the tiny engine room that drove Irelandia.

CHAPTER 8: NEARLY 6 IN DOG YEARS

On 7 September 2003, Declan Ryan turned forty. He had reorganised Irelandia into its three divisions. The One Foundation was up and running and managed on a day-to-day basis by co-founder Deirdre Mortell. It would become a big part of his life over the following decade. In 2011, I saw Ryan speak about his vision for the One Foundation at the European Venture Philanthropy Association (EVPA) in Turin. "We don't buy into a business without working out how to exit, and it should be the same with social enterprises. If we could see more business principles [in social enterprises], more business people would invest," Ryan said. "Philanthropy shouldn't be about donors feeling good, but about results – social impact."

One's focus was on Ireland and Vietnam. Carragher said he first heard about Ryan's plans in 2002. "He just came into the office one day and said: 'We're doing this,'" Carragher said. "It was classic Declan." The founders of One felt areas like young people's mental health, LGBT support and refugees were underdeveloped in Ireland, and they wanted to help address this.

CHAPTER 8: NEARLY 6 IN DOG YEARS

Over the next decade the One Foundation gave away €85 million. Its name was inspired by "One", a song written by Ryan's old neighbour Bono.

The scale of Ryan's giving was a significant portion of his wealth and being able to give to it is key to understanding his motivations for what was to come.

Irelandia had now sold its fine office overlooking Merrion Square in the heart of Georgian Dublin and moved to a new rented headquarters on Mayor Street in the International Financial Services Centre, just north of the river Liffey.

Anthony Carragher recalls Declan Ryan coming into the office one morning to tell him about his plans to bring Ryanair's DNA to the world.

"Declan said, 'what do you think?'" Carragher recalled. "I said, 'we're well positioned everywhere so we can take the risk'. When Declan said let's do low-fares airlines ... I remember thinking well that makes sense as Declan knows how to do this."

Irelandia decided not to invest in Europe as it didn't want to compete with Ryanair. There was a risk to the Ryan name if one of its investments failed, but Carragher said Ryan wasn't worried about that: "Declan's brave, and he had Tony's support, so we were going to do it."

The first deal Irelandia looked at was introduced to them by Ryan's friend, Conor McCarthy.

Conor McCarthy started his aviation career as a sixteen-year-old apprentice in Aer Lingus in 1978 working in a hangar in Dublin Airport. By twenty-eight he was chief executive of Aer

Lingus Commuter, the national carrier's regional division that flew between Dublin, Galway, Sligo, Cork and Shannon. But at the time Aer Lingus was on the cusp of bankruptcy after the Gulf War began in August 1990, so experienced executives didn't want to go near it. Things worsened following the failure of GPA, as Aer Lingus had hoped to make a fortune from its shares as an early backer of Tony Ryan. "It was totally irresponsible and reckless of Aer Lingus to put me in charge when I was so young," McCarthy admits. He rose to the challenge, and when in 1993 businessman Bernie Cahill was tasked with restructuring Aer Lingus he gave McCarthy more responsibility as head of group strategy and special projects. McCarthy's first task was to fix its transatlantic business, which was heavily loss-making. By 1995, McCarthy had turned around the airline's Atlantic routes. He was then asked to convert Aer Lingus Commuter into Aer Lingus Express, a low-cost carrier to challenge Ryanair. "It was only then I really understood the philosophical challenges of trying to create a low-cost business within a full-service business. Within about six or nine months I realised I'd been given an impossible job because of the fiefdoms that existed in a 60-something-year-old business," McCarthy reflected.

According to McCarthy, Declan Ryan led him to the life changing decision to join Ryanair. "Declan watched what was happening in other airlines, more than Michael (O'Leary), who had his head down focused solely on Ryanair," McCarthy said. Ryan suggested to O'Leary he contact McCarthy to offer him a job.

Michael O'Leary rang McCarthy in his office. The conversation went as follows.

CHAPTER 8: NEARLY 6 IN DOG YEARS

> O'Leary: "Hi, is that Conor?"
> McCarthy: "Yeah."
> O'Leary: "Michael O'Leary here, I want to offer you a job."
> McCarthy: "Alright, I have one of them."
> O'Leary: "No, I'm talking about a job that gets you out of bed in the morning,"
> McCarthy: "I have one of them as well."
> O'Leary: "Do you want to meet up?"
> McCarthy: "Actually, I do want to meet up, yeah, I haven't met you before."

O'Leary, then aged thirty-five, arranged to meet the year younger McCarthy. "We had a very interesting dinner where we were jousting about brand versus price, value proposition versus cheap fares, profitability and so on," McCarthy told Ian Kehoe in a 2020 interview in *The Currency*.

"We were modelling what we thought was Ryanair's profitability and he was saying, 'You've got to be kidding'. He said, 'I'm embarrassed how much money we're making; I'm hiding the money in maintenance reserves, anywhere I can. If the word gets out how much money we're making on these old machines,' he said, 'I'll be toast'."

In November 1996, McCarthy joined Ryanair as director of group operations. Not long after he suggested he should hire another rising star in Aer Lingus, Alan Joyce, who he knew from working together on Aer Lingus Express.

"Alan is smart, self-effacing, not at all arrogant. He is open and friendly," McCarthy said. "Michael met Alan shortly after I joined Ryanair and it just didn't work. Alan then moved to Australia and the rest is history."

Joyce will feature again later in our story, as a competitor of Irelandia as chief executive of the Jetstar Group and later Qantas in Australia.

After joining Ryanair, McCarthy got to know Declan Ryan.

"Declan was very much his own man," McCarthy reflected. "He's different to Tony, he has a bit of his father and his mother. He's a good businessman with a huge heart. Tony wouldn't necessarily have displayed that as much as Declan would."

McCarthy added: "When I joined Ryanair, it was like swapping industries. "We had the aircraft in common but the approach to business was very refreshing. It was 'If we're making money here then we're interested. If we're not making money, we're not interested.'

"There was absolutely no romance. It was all about cost. The customer was always going to favour the incumbent so our only salvation was costs. There was a hard-charging atmosphere but there was no ambiguity. It was very clear what we had to do, whereas in Aer Lingus you'd be trading off different decisions and compromises."

In December 2000 Conor McCarthy decided to leave Ryanair; the reasons were not dissimilar to those that motivated Ryan three years later. "By thirty-six, I was able to clear my relatively small mortgage. It was unbelievable," McCarthy recalled.

McCarthy was ambitious, and he could see he might be waiting many years to get the chance, if ever, to lead Ryanair.

"Michael wasn't going anywhere," McCarthy said. "He used to always tell us, 'I'm going farming next year, it's up to you guys to figure out who's going to run this place', but

CHAPTER 8: NEARLY 6 IN DOG YEARS

I figured out very quickly he loves that job, and he does it very well so he was going nowhere."

"Unless you're willing to fight with Michael it's very hard to survive in there," McCarthy said. "You have to get into the cage and when you do you come out bloodied and bruised. It's a tough environment where the bar was raised incessantly.

"I'd kind of stopped enjoying it to be honest. When you stop enjoying something it doesn't take very long for you to move on, so I moved on."

After McCarthy left, Tony Ryan asked him to work full-time with Irelandia, but McCarthy turned him down. "I felt I'm just after leaving one megalomaniac, I'm not joining another," McCarthy laughed. "Don't get me wrong. I enjoyed working with Tony. He had a fantastic sense of humour, a real dry sense of humour. He was very intelligent, and had a big vision."

McCarthy did take a one-day-a-week job with Irelandia managing Tony Ryan's private jet and helicopter, which were owned by a company called Starair. "Tony wanted to offset the cost of these toys because they're quite expensive by renting them out to other people," McCarthy recalled.

The Celtic Tiger was now underway. The economy was booming. There was plenty of demand. McCarthy would visit Tony Ryan occasionally to discuss business on the Lyons Estate. "I remember I said to him once, ''Jesus, this is some gaff Tony, how many are living here?' He didn't even answer the question, just raised one finger."

McCarthy's main focus remained setting up a low-fares advisory consultancy called PlaneConsult. He picked up consultancy work in Europe with Ray Webster, the chief executive of Easyjet, and he did some work with Aer Rianta, Ireland's then state-owned airport agency.

But then McCarthy was asked to meet a Malaysian entrepreneur called Tony Fernandes by John Higgins, an Irish airline executive who worked with GE Capital Aviation Services (GECAS). Fernandes got the idea to go into the airline business after watching an interview with Stelios Haji-Ioannou, the founder of Easyjet, in a London pub in 2001.

He created a business plan to fly domestic routes in Malaysia and fly long-haul 767s to Europe into low-cost airline hubs where travellers could connect to Easyjet or Ryanair. Fernandes' background was in the music industry, and he knew nothing about airlines. In his autobiography, *'Flying High: My story from AirAsia to QPR'*, Fernandes recalled meeting McCarthy in a coffee shop at Stansted Airport, where the Irishman told him his concept was "crazy", as no European low-fares airline would bother to work with him. Fernandes said McCarthy told him to, "set up a domestic airline, single-class, single-aircraft type, fill it, stack it high, sell it cheap and sell it through the internet directly to the consumer. You'll never look back."

McCarthy said he had never been to Malaysia but he became interested when Fernandes told him that the population of Malaysia was more than twenty-four million and that the market was dominated by flag carrier Malaysia Airlines. Fernandes said he wanted to buy a loss-making airline with two planes called AirAsia, and McCarthy said he would help him.

"What we wanted to do was an absolute clone of Ryanair," McCarthy said. He helped Fernandes take over AirAsia by convincing the airline's $20 million debt holders to take $10

CHAPTER 8: NEARLY 6 IN DOG YEARS

million upfront, with a repayment plan for the rest.

Conor McCarthy was now working hard as a consultant to Fernandes, and he also had a 7.5 per cent stake in AirAsia. He could see Tony Fernandes' abilities even if he was an aviation rookie. He could also see the scale of the opportunity for AirAsia. He was commuting to Malaysia once a month, leaving his four children, all of whom were below the age of six, and his wife behind. McCarthy had raised some money from friends and family in Ireland to put into the fledgling airline, but he knew it needed more.

Tony Ryan asked McCarthy how things were going. "We might be interested in that," Ryan told him.

Tony Ryan said he'd like to meet Fernandes in Malaysia, so, ahead of the trip, McCarthy helped broker a potential term sheet between Irelandia and AirAsia.

"Tony was an eternal negotiator," McCarthy said. "We had an agreed valuation, and an agreed sort of investment structure. He was going to put money in, in a similar way to what Bonderman did in Ryanair. He was going to put in a small amount of real hard equity, and then a loan which had a coupon. He was buying a significant share of the business."

At that stage, AirAsia was valued at $20 million, and Ryan's investment would give him a large minority stake. "Tony would have not far under half of the business," McCarthy recalled. Ryan also wanted significant control. Ryan flew to meet Fernandes in Malaysia with two others, a former GPA executive and an executive who worked for investment vehicle Newbridge Capital, TPG's Asian affiliate. "The idea was they were going to look at the airline and some of its operations in the old Kuala Lumpur Subang International

Airport," McCarthy said. McCarthy didn't accompany Tony Ryan on the trip as he was busy, but he waited to hear back what happened. The first call was from an unhappy Tony Fernandes. "I got one call from Tony Fernandes saying, 'Hey this guy is just after shitting all over us here as soon as he got off the plane. He's not talking about giving us $10 million, he's talking about giving us $2 million. He's putting in a loan but the interest rate on the loan is huge and he's also talking about controlling everything, he's talking about nominating the CEO, nominating the CFO, you know all this stuff.' I said yeah, that's his style, he'll negotiate, he says, yeah but he also said that look, we're not committing to this, don't tell us anything you don't want to tell us because we're thinking we might start our own airline in this region and that was like dropping the bomb, the minute that was said."

After he came home, Tony Ryan asked McCarthy to meet him at his office on the Lyons Estate. "Tony said I understand that you're after telling the boys to forget about doing a deal with me," McCarthy recalled. McCarthy denied doing that, saying that he had brokered Ryan's term sheet with Fernandes and his team. "The lads thought that they were talking to you about you going ahead with that deal but the minute you got off the plane, you started to negotiate with them," McCarthy said. "It's a different style down there, they don't work that way and the second thing, which really put the mockers on it is that somebody said we might start our own airline, so don't go telling me stuff you don't want to."

"Tony (Ryan) said, 'I didn't say that', and I said, 'Well somebody said it', and he said, 'Well I certainly didn't say it' and I said, 'Okay but unfortunately whoever said it dropped

CHAPTER 8: NEARLY 6 IN DOG YEARS

a bomb and the boys said, well forget that then because we're not giving someone else information to help them on their way.'" The deal was revived: "The deal wasn't killed or anything. There was a bit of to and fro and then Declan got involved," he said.

Declan Ryan considered McCarthy a "rockstar" so any deal he recommended had to be looked at. He was enthusiastic about Asia as a region, but not certain of AirAsia. "Tony was a very likeable Malaysian guy but all I could think of was Richard Branson," Declan Ryan recalled. "There's many people who try to be the local Richard Branson. But selling records is easier than selling airline seats."

Declan Ryan didn't like the deal. "The guys in AirAsia just wanted our name," he said. "We're not passive investors, we are active investors. So it wasn't a fit."

Anthony Carrager recalled: "If there's failing in Declan, and he doesn't have that many of them, he will form an opinion based on character early on. He is often right, but he can get it wrong."

"Declan takes a view on different people, but he was never somebody who knocked other people. We've left good deals behind, often for that very reason, Declan just couldn't be arsed doing business with that guy or girl."

Maurice Mason asked around about Fernandes, and he was vouched for by his old friends in Morgan Stanley. "I could see the potential," Mason said. "Conor McCarthy was involved which was a great plus, but I was dubious too as it felt a bit Branson-ish. Branson is about brand rather than operational substance, so we turned Tony down."

"I just didn't think it would work – I was wrong," Ryan

said. AirAsia would go on to become a multi-billion-dollar airline, and a formidable competitor to Irelandia. McCarthy was disappointed Irelandia didn't invest, but it wasn't the only one to discount AirAsia. The year after Irelandia turned down the AirAsia investment, McCarthy met David Bonderman at an airline conference in Dublin, and he too admitted he'd turned Tony Fernandes down.

Irelandia didn't know at the time that Fernandes would go on to become successful. AirAsia did, however, get Irelandia thinking about Asia. Declan Ryan had lived in Thailand for three years when his father leased planes to Air Siam for Aer Lingus.

Ryan had adopted a daughter called Ana from Vietnam in 1999, while Cathal Ryan had a daughter called Danielle Ryan, whose mother Tess de Kretser is from Sri Lanka. Declan Ryan knew the market, and he felt it was ripe for disruption.

"The lowest-hanging fruit at that time was South East Asia because it didn't have a plethora of low-cost carriers," Carragher said. Demographics, rule of law, inefficient local carriers and a growing middle class were all signals a low-cost carrier might work. Ryan started to spend months in Asia figuring out where to begin. He got wind that Macau, China's version of Las Vegas, might be looking for a new low-fares airline to bring gamblers and tourists to the island on the Pearl River delta.

It had a modern airport, but it was only running at half capacity. The opportunity was to serve the island, and potentially create a hub into mainland China.

"We saw Macau as like Luton Airport was for Ryanair and London," Ryan explained. Irelandia started talking

CHAPTER 8: NEARLY 6 IN DOG YEARS

to Dragonair, a subsidiary of Cathay Pacific, but then it encountered Kong Dong, chairman of the Chinese National Aircraft Corporation, which owns Air China.

"He was called Mr Dong, which I'm sorry to say meant the Irish team found it hard to say with a straight face," Ryan laughed. Nonetheless, Ryan took Dong seriously, as he was a powerful figure in China.

Irelandia tried to convince Dong to sign a letter of intent to make it Air China's exclusive partner. Over a dinner of many hours, Ryan tried to win Dong over via translators.

Eventually Dong leaned over to Ryan and said in perfect English: "That is never going to happen. China is for the Chinese."

"I appreciated his honesty, but in the end he'd been true to his name," Ryan said. The deal was dead, but in pursuing it another opportunity had arisen.

CHAPTER 9: CROCODILES CARRY NO PASSPORTS

Tiger Airways was launched in late 2003 in a television studio in the business district of Singapore. Tony Ryan and Bill Franke appeared awkwardly on the screen together. Tony Ryan was an airline legend with the success of Ryanair known worldwide. Less well known was Bill Franke, an American and former chairman of America West, who had recently founded Phoenix-based air transport private equity firm Indigo Partners. Now the two men had teamed up to launch a new low-fares airline for Asia called Tiger Airways.

Both Ryan and Franke were alpha males, so they didn't get on. Just before going on air, Franke ordered Tony Ryan not to mention any plans to IPO the airline in the future. Almost the first thing Tony Ryan said when the cameras turned on was to say he hoped to bring Tiger Airways to the stock market.

Watching on in the wings of the studio, Declan Ryan couldn't help but laugh. It was December 2003, and afterwards Ryan and Franke briefed the newspapers. It was a packed room as Tiger was a serious proposition that was also backed by both Singapore Airlines (SIA), the flagship carrier of Singapore,

CHAPTER 9: CROCODILES CARRY NO PASSPORTS

and Temasek, its sovereign wealth fund. Inside the Millenia Singapore, a series of five landmark buildings, the tallest of which at forty-one storeys tall was designed by Dublin-born architect Kevin Roche, Tony Ryan was in full flow. "I am confident that the new airline will deliver the benefits that low-cost carriers can bring in terms of tourism and job creation, not only in Singapore but also to the other countries it serves," Tony Ryan told the press. "Asia is a vast market with lots of small businesses."

Declan Ryan was pleased to see his father ably deal with any questions fired at him. "It wasn't just a nice gesture," he explained. "Tony still carried a lot of weight as the guy who started Ryanair, which by this stage was well on its way to being Europe's most successful airline. He hadn't lost any of his old appetite for the game." Asia was a new frontier for low-fares airlines, and the decision by SIA to back Tiger Airways was partly a defensive move to protect itself against encroachment.

Tiger was being launched based on Ryanair principles. However, due to regulatory barriers with other neighbouring countries, it was forced to fly medium-haul rather than short-haul. An unprecedented number of airline start-ups were trying to break into the market at the time. Analysts were already predicting that not all would survive. A group of former SIA executives planned to launch a new airline called Valuair, while Indonesia had two new fledgling carriers called Lion Air and Air Paradise.

Malaysia meanwhile had the fast-growing AirAsia, which was looking at setting up a joint-venture carrier in Thailand with Prime Minister Thaksin Shinawatra's Shin Corp.

In Thailand, a new airline called Orient Thai was being planned, and Richard Branson had also expressed an interest in setting up a new low-fares airline with the country's biggest airline Thai Airways. "The trick for these operators will be to see who will be the last man standing," said Christopher Gee, a strategist at JP Morgan & Chase, told Reuters. "Tiger Airways has four shareholders who are very deep-pocketed and they have more access to capital than any other operator out there." *The Wall Street Journal* was sceptical about whether all the new low fares airlines would survive, writing a long feature with the headline: 'Lions and Tigers in Air? Oh, my! Airlines in Asia pick "cat" fight.'

Charlie Clifton, Ryanair's fifth employee and interim chief executive of Tiger, was confident, however. "The population base within our radius is 500 million people who haven't been exposed to low-cost travel at all. I think there's more than enough to go around," he said at the time. Not everyone agreed. "Right from the word go, the market conditions it faces will be very different from its regional competitors like AirAsia, which have a significant domestic market," Vincent Ng, aviation analyst at S&P Asian Equity Research said. "It will be an international carrier right from the start. That being the case, it is hard to see Tiger Airways duplicating AirAsia's success in the last two years."

Irelandia had invested a year in trying, unsuccessfully, to break into China, before it came across the opportunity

CHAPTER 9: CROCODILES CARRY NO PASSPORTS

to found a new airline in Asia. Declan Ryan was in Hong Kong when he picked up in the aviation industry that SIA, a state-owned legacy airline, was looking at building a low-cost carrier. He emailed SIA's chief executive Chew Choon Seng straight away asking for a meeting. Known simply as CS, the Singaporean executive was bright and eager to defend Singapore Airlines from the encroachment of new low-fare airlines like AirAsia. "We clicked immediately," Ryan recalled. "They needed a partner to avoid problems with the unions, who wanted the same conditions as SIA staff. Now they could put up their hands and say, 'Listen, this Irish crowd is running the show, so there's nothing we can do,' so it worked for everyone."

Ryan added: "It was a golden era for SIA, which was doing really well. CS was a hero down there, but they needed to bring in some Irish bouncers to stop others coming into their market."

Choon Seng put his strategy succinctly. "The low-cost model requires completely different methods and procedures, marketing approaches and skills," he said. "It is hard to be both premium full service and low cost, no frills at the same time." Declan Ryan rang David Bonderman to see if he would like to co-invest with Irelandia in Tiger. "He loved the idea, and he brought in Indigo," Ryan recalled.

Indigo Partners was at that stage only a year old. Bonderman's TPG was an investor in Indigo, which had already looked at one deal in Australia which hadn't worked out. Led by Bill Franke, Indigo had a relentless focus on operational efficiency. But Franke could be blunt and confrontational when expressing himself. The Tiger investment structure was that SIA would hold 49 per cent of the airline, allowing the Singapore airline to truthfully say it did not own it.

However, Temasek, an investor in SIA as Singapore's sovereign wealth fund, had 11 per cent, so in effect the Singaporean side of the partnership had control. Irelandia took 16 per cent, while Indigo took the remainder. In total about $20 million was budgeted to be put up by the consortium to get Tiger up and going.

This was a tiny amount but reflected the experience and balance sheets of its backers. Aircraft makers, airports and suppliers knew there was no need to worry about Tiger when it came to funding.

Irelandia only needed to put in $1 million, but it brought its expertise to the table in ensuring the airline stuck to its low fares principles.

Despite the wealth of its investors, Tiger's strategy was to be tight with capital. "We were very parsimonious with it. You don't give airline guys too much money as they'll spend it," Ryan said.

Irelandia could seek risks with Tiger, but there were also powerful forces moving in its direction. Irelandia knew there weren't enough people in Singapore to support its ambitions, but it was prepared to bet that the region was going to deregulate, allowing a huge population to fly, often for the first time.

If this didn't happen fast enough, however, the downside risk was it could find itself stuck in a tiny market surrounded by huge ones to which it wasn't allowed to fly. Even with its strong partners, it was taking a big risk on geopolitics.

CHAPTER 9: CROCODILES CARRY NO PASSPORTS

The Tiger name was arrived at when Declan Ryan was kicking around names with his father Tony on the Lyons Demesne. Located on 600 acres, the estate was bought by Tony Ryan in 1996 in disrepair from the Faculty of Agriculture in UCD.

In his papers Ryan described Lyons when he bought it as "close to ruinous condition, yet it seemed to possess an indomitable spirit that challenged restoration or retreat. I chose the former."

Tony Ryan met Declan Ryan in Lyons Demesne, to discuss naming the new Asian airline. The name they had fixed on was Southeast, in homage to Southwest in the United States.

Neither Ryan was convinced, and over breakfast, as Declan Ryan's kids played around them they tried to come up with something better. "Out of nowhere Jack was having his breakfast and goes 'Why don't you call it Tiger?'" Declan Ryan recalled. Jack Ryan was just eight at the time, but he caused his father and grandfather to pause.

"Myself and Tony looked at each other and thought silently, 'Einstein!" Ryan remembered. Declan Ryan told his son he loved the name, but Tony Ryan took out a €20 note. "Tony says to Jack: 'You can have that if you give me three reasons why you would call it Tiger?'" Declan Ryan recalled. "Jack said: The beer, the golfer, and the animal: they're all great." Convinced, Tony Ryan handed over the money.

"Obviously that was his mother's genes, he didn't get it from us," Declan Ryan laughed.

Declan Ryan told his Singaporean partners about the

name, and they said Tiger was also a slang name for lap dancing clubs locally. Tony Ryan said: "That's a fourth good reason then but I'm glad Jack didn't know it!" Tiger later called one of its planes after Jack, but at the time there was little in it for him. Declan Ryan insisted he split his €20 with his siblings. "In the end Jack only got a fiver for his trouble," he said.

To get the new airline going, Declan Ryan was spending a lot of time in Singapore along with Anthony Carragher, Maurice Mason and Charlie Clifton. Clifton joined Ryanair in 1986, and he sold its first ticket to a passenger. He was energetic, and as director of ground operations with Ryanair from 1997 until 2002, had worked closely with both Tony and Declan Ryan as well as Michael O'Leary.

Clifton had negotiated many of the early airport deals for Ryanair, and he had helped build up its ancillary revenue. He made money when Ryanair floated, so he was working with Irelandia as a consultant. Irelandia wanted Tiger to be based in an airport in Johor, a Malaysian state about 300 kilometres south of the capital Kuala Lumpur. "We were trying to set things up like Ryanair. It was to be our low-cost Luton that wasn't too far from Singapore," Ryan recalled.

Chew Choon Seng said SIA would not support such a move and was adamant Tiger must be headquartered in Singapore. Ryan said it made economic sense, and CS was only rejecting it as a base because many Singaporeans look down on Malyasians.

"Declan this isn't true," CS said. "I'll give you $50 if you can give me an example of it." Two days later Ryan

CHAPTER 9: CROCODILES CARRY NO PASSPORTS

was reading a local newspaper in Singapore about how a crocodile had eaten a local farmer. The headline read: 'Malaysian crocodile eats Singaporean farmer.'

Ryan showed CS the paper and asked: "Since when do crocodiles carry passports?" CS gave him the $50 and said: "I get it. I get it."

He was not, however, prepared to budge on allowing Tiger to base itself outside of Singapore.

Charlie Clifton was Tiger's interim chief executive, but the plan was from the beginning to replace him with a local leader once the airline got close to launch. In March 2004 Clifton stepped aside to make way for Patrick Gan, a Singaporean with eighteen years of experience in pharmaceuticals.

Ryan wanted a female Singaporean from the waste industry to lead the airline, but the Singaporeans felt her background in the bins business would make it easy for their rivals to discredit Tiger.

They went with Gan instead, figuring Michael O'Leary hadn't an airline background either. There were cultural issues as Tiger's Singaporean investors adjusted to what it took to be a low-fares airline. "The first week an aircraft was grounded, leaving passengers delayed," Ryan said. "SIA said we need to get a replacement aircraft down there immediately, even if we have to lease another aeroplane. Charlie said no way. We're not making enough. We will do it after a week maybe, but they're going by bus, not luxury." Tiger's inaugural fares made an impact, with flights of only $1 from Singapore to Hat Yai, Bangkok and Phuket. Quickly its brand established itself, but there were also, it was becoming clear, differences between Tiger's chief executive and Irelandia and Indigo about what they believed was needed.

"Patrick was passionate about what we were trying to do," Mason said. "He was fifty and he wanted to be entrepreneurial. He was plausible but we realised he didn't have what it took. We needed somebody else."

"It is very hard to go into this industry and be a non-airline person. It is like Pfizer putting someone in charge of Disney. You just don't know if it will work," Declan Ryan said. "We tried to train Patrick up but either you get the low-cost thing, or you don't." Tiger needed a new chief executive.

CHAPTER 10: TONY THE REAL TIGER

Tony Davis tightened the Windsor knot in his tie. The Englishman was meeting Maurice Mason and Charlie Clifton in the office of recruitment firm Spencer Stewart overlooking London Bridge. He was determined not to be mistaken as another open-necked shirt-wearing low-fares airline boss.

Davis was thirty-nine but already an airline veteran. He joined British Airways at just nineteen in 1986, the year before the airline was privatised, starting as reservation agent and working his way up to pricing and marketing.

In 1992, BA bought a stake in USAir, allowing him to move to New York.

His next stop was Gulf Air in Bahrain before he was headhunted by British Midland, where he worked on alliances and public affairs.

Based in the East Midlands, British Midland, or BMI as it became, was already being squeezed by Ryanair and Easyjet. Then British Airways' low-fare airline, Go, announced plans to set up a base on its doorstep. "BMI can't decide whether to be full service or no frills, which is a recipe for commercial disaster," Barbara Cassani, the chief executive of Go said in 2002 as she announced plans to target its business.

"It was a declaration of war," Tony Davis recalled. "Or at least that's what my boss Sir Michael Bishop took it to be." Davis was instructed to found bmibaby, its own new low-fares airline subsidiary. His mission was to fight all three low-fares rivals. He was thirty-five, and as he stripped out costs in the new airline, it was like a "religious conversion".

"To sell tickets for £25 we needed a different cost base and a different structure," Davis recalled. Davis built bmibaby up into fifteen aircraft, and by 2004, the airline was making a profit of £3 million.

"Baby had the potential to get larger, but we were the subsidiary of another airline, so it was a defensive move rather than a big commitment to low fares. It was about stopping the other guy. We were making a profit but our parent company was making a loss," Davis said.

"I admired Michael Bishop, the owner of British Midland, enormously but it was fairly obvious there was never going to be an opportunity to have a share in Baby's success. But that said, I was financially comfortable, and I had my dream job running an airline."

Davis recalls that he had a good impression of Irelandia from his first meeting. "Maurice and Charlie were speaking the same language," Davis said. "We all just got each other."

Irelandia asked Davis to go to Singapore for further interviews. "Those interviews were more nerve-wracking," Davis said.

His SIA interview was tricky as it was still getting to grips with low fares, but Temasek went better. "After the interview

CHAPTER 10: TONY THE REAL TIGER

they sent me a Tigger, a stuffed Tiger teddy from Winnie the Pooh, so I thought I must have done okay," Davis laughed.

Davis had a good career in bmibaby but he wanted more. "The Tiger opportunity offered some ownership which was very attractive. I thought I could learn from the Ryans, Indigo and Singapore Airlines, so there was the possibility of it being a major stepping-stone," Davis said.

Despite being prepared to spend several years there, Singapore never felt like it would become a permanent home. He recalls going for dinner with the founder of modern Singapore, Lee Kuan Yeuw, and a small group of other expats, and each was asked where they planned to retire. Nobody said Singapore. "LKY kind of chastised us all for not saying Singapore," Davis recalled. "But he was right. You never felt like you were putting down permanent roots there."

Davis planned to start at Tiger in January 2005, but he was needed sooner. "The previous CEO, Patrick, didn't want to hang around so I got a call telling me to come out straight away as there is a risk Tiger's licence may not remain valid without you," Davis recalled.

Welcoming his arrival in November 2004, Franke described Davis as bringing "accomplished, battle-tested and focused leadership as we expand our reach in the increasingly competitive south-east Asian travel market."

His first board meeting was in early December 2004 in the curved-glass offices of Temasek on Orchard Road in an upmarket retail quarter in Singapore.

His own office was little more than a room at the time in Terminal 1 in Changi Airport. But it was enough, as Tiger had only two aircraft, with two more on the way.

At Davis's first board meeting Temasek announced it was investing in a rival low-fares airline called Jetstar Asia. "Temasek were the bedrock of the investment as a sovereign wealth fund and now they were telling us one of the directors was stepping down as they've formed a joint venture with Qantas to create Jetstar Asia – a direct competitor," Davis said.

Irelandia and Indigo were furious, but there was nothing they could do about it.

"We'd barely started, and Temasek were already hedging their bets," Davis said.

The second big surprise for Davis was how walled in Tiger was. "It wasn't until I got to Singapore that I realised Tiger was restricted from flying to Indonesia or Malaysia because of the bilateral aviation agreements," he said.

The population of Indonesia was over 220 million, while Malaysia had twenty-five million at the time. So, there were almost a quarter of a billion people living in countries on Tiger's doorstep, neither of which it could fly to.

This meant Tiger had to focus on Thailand and destinations to its north and Australia to the south. "The business model that worked for Ryanair was high frequency, short routes, but this wasn't even possible for Tiger as we were not allowed to fly to countries nearby," Davis said.

"So we had to create a new business model and effectively become a mid-range low-cost carrier and more importantly convince the Ryans and Indigo that it would make money." In Europe the average flight for Ryanair was about an hour, but Tiger's average flight was closer to two hours. Culturally, Singaporeans loved to travel and were prepared to fly four hours to Hong Kong just for a weekend break, so that was at least one plus.

CHAPTER 10: TONY THE REAL TIGER

Davis hit the ground running offering 10,000 one-way tickets to the resort island of Phuket and the town of Hat Yai in the south of Thailand for just $30. He also announced plans to add two new Airbus A320s to its fleet, doubling the size of Tiger.

Davis flew home to Europe for his first Christmas as chief executive, but on 26 December 2004, he got a phone call telling him that a tsunami had hit southern Thailand, killing 5,400 people. "Phuket airport was underwater, we were a new airline with a small team and I was trying to deal with a lot of issues from the other side of the world."

"It caused enormous disruption and we ended up doing a lot of empty flights into Phuket that were full on the way out as we helped repatriate people," he said.

Tiger decided to offer the baggage holds in its planes to the Red Cross and other charities to allow them to fly in badly needed equipment and suppliers.

Tiger played its part in assisting during the tragedy. But it was also an uncertain time as traveller demand to go to Thailand plummeted after the tsunami. Jet fuel prices meanwhile rose. In January, Davis told reporters: "We are reassessing our business model. Our goal for this year is to reach breakeven." Davis said Tiger was not thinking about an IPO in the near term.

"It's a bit premature to talk about a flotation – we have resources available from our shareholders," he said. "If the operation is successful then all options are open to raise additional capital." Davis also predicted that Tiger's competition would struggle. "Not all low-cost airlines will succeed. Of more than 50 LCCs in Europe only two are really successful. If history is repeated here in the Asia Pacific region, the majority of LCCs in Asia will fail," he said, adding that Tiger was already pushing to fly to Malaysia and that its market needed to be "liberalised".

As Davis settled in, he worked hard to find new routes for Tiger to fly to. Singapore's population was just four million, but there was an unmet need for affordable travel. "In some ways we had to start again with our business plan," Davis said. "The country is a relatively small island, so no domestic flying and it is not an open skies region like Europe, the challenges facing Tiger were different in many ways to the Ryanair model."

He added: "It was a chess game about getting access to different countries. It was felt by some that maybe Tiger was a vehicle for Singapore Airlines to get more capacity so some governments were wary of letting us in." Davis said Tiger was actually very independent in terms of its decision-making, but not everyone believed this. "A lot of countries and other airlines really didn't want us," he said. "We had to fight."

Tiger began to make an impact, pushing down fares in whatever markets it could.

"When we started flying to the Philippines for example," Davis said, "I remember getting a note from a priest thanking us for helping to reduce the divorce rate among Filipino expats as our fares were so low they could afford to go home and see their wives.

"I know Declan felt very strongly that Tiger was a force for liberating travel for people in Asia." When Tiger began flying to Ho Chi Minh city in Vietnam, Davis said he was surprised at how many Vietnamese wanted to visit Singapore, a relatively expensive place.

CHAPTER 10: TONY THE REAL TIGER

"I was at the airport when our first flight landed from Ho Chi Minh and I asked the young people on the plane why they were coming. They said they'd never had a McDonald's, or they wanted to buy Levi's. They had humble aspirations, but because our fares were so low they could now afford to fly," he said.

"We were going around Asia trying to find places where we could get a permit to land."

Davis pushed publicly for changes, telling *The Strait Times* in 2005: "Clearly, until we have a single open skies agreement in Asia, we are constantly having to make sure that not only is there an air services agreement, but also that we get chosen out of the five airlines to be given those rights."

Davis felt Tiger was allowing people to fly who hadn't before.

"If the model is done properly, you create markets where traditional airlines have said there isn't one and that's where Tiger has a significant advantage over our competitors," he told Dow Jones.

Tiger also looked at forming joint ventures with other Asian airlines as a way to get around restrictions, but it couldn't find the right one. Rivals, however, were consolidating, with Qantas subsidiary Jetstar taking over Valuair. Davis told *Reuter*s that this didn't concern him: "Combining two less-than-effective competitors usually doesn't make an effective one."

Tiger knew it needed a bigger footprint. "Just having a base in Singapore is not the strategy ... we need to expand our network beyond Singapore," Davis said.

Jetstar was a tough competitor in Asia and became more so as Tiger started to expand into Australia. It was led in Australia by a thirty-something Dubliner called Alan Joyce. He grew up in Tallaght in west Dublin, and was the first member of his family to go to university, studying first applied science before finishing a Master's in management science in Trinity College Dublin.

Joyce joined Aer Lingus, where he reported to Conor McCarthy. He'd learned about low-cost airlines when he'd worked with McCarthy on a plan to launch a low-cost carrier called Aer Lingus Express, essentially to challenge Ryanair.

In 1996 he moved to Australia to become head of network planning with Ansett Australia. Joyce impressed and Geoff Dixon, the boss of Qantas, poached him as a rising star. He was a formidable foe.

Tiger decided to fight him on home ground, and find new markets where competition was less.

"We had to evolve the LCC model away from the Ryanair model which had short routes and lots of turnarounds," Davis said. "We were looking for places we could fly to overnight and then back. We flew to India in the middle of night. We had flights going up to northern China. We went down to Perth in Australia, which was five hours away. The model was different than Europe because of the distance and regulation."

Declan Ryan said he was often asked if Ryanair was annoyed that he tried to emulate it with Tiger. "The simple answer is no," he said. "Don't forget David Bonderman, Ryanair's chairman, invested in Tiger. And to be honest Michael O'Leary thought I was nuts. He asked David O'Brien, an ex-army officer and the chief commercial officer of Ryanair, to look into it. David said it wouldn't work, which I suppose

CHAPTER 10: TONY THE REAL TIGER

from a strategic point of view, with all the risks involved, it probably shouldn't have done."

When Ryanair was founded, Ryan said the European Union was its great advantage due to its mantra of deregulation and open skies. This allowed Ryanair to compete on a level playing field. "Michael said that if you don't have a deregulated market in Asia, the low-cost model can't work. I had a different outlook," Ryan said. "Deregulation happens in the end, because ultimately ordinary passengers will push for it. Give people $50 fares and they will demand deregulation."

It was, however, pressurised for Tiger because of anti-competitive restrictions. To make money, Tiger had to be careful. "We had a really forensic focus on costs and efficiencies," Davis said. "We wanted to get the most out of every asset."

Tiger also focused on ancillary revenue. "We had the highest ancillary revenue of any airline in Asia because we were selling more things and charging for more things like hotels and car hire," Davis said. "Historically, in Singapore baggage was free, but we started to charge for it. We did this based on the promise of a really low fare of $10 or $20.

"One of the things Michael O'Leary said was to try and think more like a cinema. You want to make the admission as low as possible to get people through the doors but charge as much as you can for popcorn and Coke. We had very much the Ryanair mindset, trying to keep admission prices affordable, which is especially important when countries' disposable income is relatively low."

Tiger's average fare when it IPO'd was $50 but it was getting another $20 in revenue from ancillary activities, which was really adding to our bottom line.

Ryanair had been a late convert to the power of the internet to drive ticket sales, and encourage passengers to hire cars, book hotels and take out travel insurance. Declan Ryan pushed for a website in the late 1990s, but O'Leary dragged his heels. At the time he distrusted technology. "Michael O'Leary sent me a note to say the internet would never take off in the airline ticket sales sector," Ryan recalled. Does the note still exist? "He destroyed the evidence!" Ryan laughed.

Ryanair only launched its website with an online booking engine in 2000 as a result of this scepticism when it hired a 17-year-old student called John Beckett to create the site with a budget of just IR£20,000. Behind the scenes, Howard Millar, then Ryanair's CFO, grasped the importance of the internet. He ignored his boss's scepticism and put in the best available technology behind Ryanair's somewhat garish home page, making it capable of scaling to take millions of bookings.

Within the first year three-quarters of all bookings were being taken through the Ryanair site. O'Leary quickly embraced online booking, although it would be some years yet before the airline rebuilt its front page and developed a sophisticated app and so on.

From the start of Tiger, Irelandia and Davis pushed hard for investment in its website, and the ability to cross-sell other services to ticket buyers.

Tiger invested in its brand, calling the operating airlines Tiger Cubs, and the airline's call sign with air traffic control was Top Cat. The brand resonated in Asia, and the tail of its planes were marked with orange and black stripes. Tony Fernandes, the boss of AirAsia, was bemused. "It's an odd choice of name," he told the *Wall Street Journal*, noting that

CHAPTER 10: TONY THE REAL TIGER

the tiger is Malaysia's national emblem. Singapore's historic symbol was the lion, but this had been taken as the logo of Lion Air, an airline founded in Malaysia in 1999. When Tiger's name and logo was unveiled there was speculation locally this was Singapore sending a message to its neighbour, but the truth was this wasn't a consideration. The name was chosen by Tony Ryan's grandson, and the tiger took off as a symbol of a powerful animal associated in Asia with strength and good fortune.

Davis said his four shareholders meant he had a very strong board. "For a LCC it was maybe a bit more bureaucratic than some other LCCs but it meant that we behaved more like a listed company from the start. The transition when we decided to float wasn't that difficult," he said. "An IPO can be very disruptive for management as it can cause you to take your eye off the ball because of the amount of information and resources it requires. We deliberately split responsibilities from early on between day-to-day operations and the IPO so we were ready for it."

An airline IPO requires a growth story, and access to a steady stream of planes to fuel this. The next challenge for Tiger was to do a big airline order.

Airbus had won a series of big contracts in Asia with AirAsia and Jetstar. As a result, Boeing was eager to win a deal with Tiger. It was already supplying SilkAir, a regional airline owned by SIA, so it thought this might give them an edge. "There was a very competitive tender but in the end, Airbus offered the better deal," Davis said. "We leveraged the Irelandia name and all of our shareholders and got a really good deal." In June 2005, Airbus said it was planning to sell Tiger eight new

A320 planes capable of holding 180 people each. The planes were due in March 2006 and cost an estimated $500 million. It was the first time Tiger was buying its own planes, and it tripled the size of the airline. "Our shareholders are convinced that we have passed the first phase on the sustainability of the business model," Davis told *The Edge Singapore*.

As Tiger finished 2005 it had carried 500,000 passengers in its first full year, and Davis said he expected it would be another two years before it broke even. Tiger had plans to add another plane and hoped to carry three million passengers a year once this came on stream.

Davis was at the World Low-Cost Airlines summit in Amsterdam as Tiger celebrated its first birthday. "Our business model is very clear, to be the Ryanair of Asia," he told the summit. Tiger was doing well. It had been granted approval for new routes to Kolkata in India, and was preparing to move into a new specially designed low-fares terminal in Changi Airport to be called the Budget Terminal. In November 2005, Tiger announced plans to fly to Darwin from 19 December, thereby entering the Australian market, the home of Jetstar. The next month Standard & Poor's aviation specialist Shukor Yusof put out a note stating: "Tiger Airways is rumoured to be in talks with Malaysian authorities to set up a budget airline that will be controlled by Malaysian and Singaporean shareholders." Davis more or less confirmed the story, saying Tiger was "exploring collaboration with local parties to provide joint venture services", but these talks didn't work out.

Tiger was getting noticed, and there was pushback. At the start of 2006, Dow Jones quoted an official from the Philippines' Civil Aeronautics Board saying Tiger would be fined for selling tickets on a route to Manila's Clark International Airport without having received its renewed operating permit.

Davis said he was "confused" by the report as Tiger was acting within the rules. "It's a route that many parties would like to see us not succeed. Whenever that's the case, there are people who are trying to trip us up or cause us problems," he said.

Tiger sorted things out in the Philippines, but other markets kept their borders firmly closed. Indonesia had closed its main airports to low-fares airlines. As 2006 began Santoso Eddy Wibowo, director of air transport at the Indonesian Ministry of Transport, said: "'We are not reviewing our policies on foreign low-cost carriers with regard to the four major cities. However, there is no problem if they want to fly to our secondary destinations, subject to bilateral agreements." Davis told *The Strait Times* not being able to fly to either Indonesia or Malaysia was a "source of frustration", but there was nothing he could do about it other than keep pushing. Tiger was now flying to thirteen cities, and it had got a permit to fly to three Chinese cities from April 2007, so it was far from all bad news.

In February 2006, the Associated Press revealed that Tiger and Qantas were both in talks to buy a stake in Indonesian budget airline Adam Air. This would have allowed Tiger to break into Malaysia. "I met Tiger's Tony Davis at the Grand Hyatt in Singapore Friday morning and discussed cooperation between the airlines ranging from code-sharing to possibly Tiger taking a stake in Adam Air or vice versa," Adam Adhitya Suherman, the airline's president, said. "I've had similar discussions with Qantas earlier."

Tiger was now accelerating past the one million passenger mark in March 2006, and when it emerged that Orangestar Investment Holdings, the holding company of Jetstar Asia and Valuair, was short of capital it offered to take over its routes. Davis said Tiger had "strong cash flow and the vast majority of our shareholders' initial investment remains unutilised". Davis also complained that Qantas had broken the rules by investing in Valuair, allowing it to enter the Singaporean market. "Not only is this not good for consumers, it's also unfair for Qantas to use Jetstar to benefit from Singapore's pool of very scarce air traffic rights which should be exclusively reserved for Singaporean carriers," Davis said.

In July 2006, Davis announced a change in tack where Tiger would establish new operating airlines or "Tiger Cubs" in the south Asia region. He also hinted publicly at an IPO for the first time. "It will be a shareholders' decision. As the management, we have to set the groundwork now so that when the timing is right we can carry it out smoothly," he said. AirAsia listed in late 2004, and it had taken a similar route with bases in Thailand and Indonesia. In October 2006, Tiger announced its first overseas operations by partnering with South East Asian Airlines (SEAir) in the Philippines. SEAir was an eleven-year-old airline but Tiger was helping it step up its offering by leasing it two of its new Airbus jets.

Davis said Tiger's plan was to add another four or five bases to allow it to cover the region. Meanwhile it continued to focus on cracking the Australian market by adding a new route to Perth in early 2007. His rival Alan Joyce announced plans for Jetstar to offer low-cost flights long-haul, but Davis said he wasn't tempted to follow suit. "There is a limit, in

CHAPTER 10: TONY THE REAL TIGER

terms of the aircraft, in terms of the operating model that we have, where we can still operate that low-fare model and get the efficiencies from our business model," Davis said. "If we set up bases in other parts of Asia, we might be able to go to new markets out of those places." Despite many obstacles, Tiger was now aiming for the stock market.

CHAPTER 11: DIRTY TRICKS IN OZ

On the edge of the fourth annual Asia Pacific Low Cost Airline Congress in January 2007, Tony Davis sat down with *The Business Times* of Singapore. He had big news to share.

"We should be in a position (to list on the market) by the end of this year," Davis told the newspaper. "My job is to give shareholders flexibility in deciding when they want to go to the market."

AirAsia's float in 2004 had been a pathfinder and now the Malaysian airline was rumoured to be preparing a rights issue to fund the purchase of 100 more planes from Airbus. Besides an IPO, Davis also hinted that Tiger was close to forming a second partnership with another airline but he declined to say which one.

On 8 February, Tiger revealed even more ambition, as Davis announced plans to try and enter the Australian domestic route market and break the "cosy duopoly" between Qantas and Richard Branson's Virgin Blue. "Fares are too high in Australia. We see the opportunity to deliver consistently low fares on all

CHAPTER 11: DIRTY TRICKS IN OZ

our routes," Davis said. Davis had joined the board of Western Australia's Skywest Airlines leading to speculation that this would be the access point for Tiger but this was denied.

Australia's Deputy Prime Minister Mark Vaile said he welcomed the "increased competition", but warned it would need to satisfy Australia's stringent safety and security requirements which had prevented airlines in the past gaining a foothold. Davis told the Australian Associated Press that Tiger would shake up the market. "We're committed to bringing in a completely different level of pricing to Australia," he said. "We don't have the complexity of lounges, frequent flyer programmes, all those things cost money and ultimately the fares have to be higher to cover it."

On 9 February 2007, Tiger showed more of its hand. At a press conference in Australia, it said it hoped to be flying there by the end of the year if given the go-ahead by the Foreign Investment Review Board and the Civil Aviation Safety Authority. Tiger said it planned to put five 180-seat A320s into Australia where it hoped to carry two million passengers a year.

"We are looking at a comprehensive national network and we are committed to bringing the low fares that we offer to as many people in Australia as we can," Davis said at the time. "We see a clear and present need in the Australian market to break the high-fare cycle created by the duopoly [between Qantas and Virgin Blue] and we are the right people to do it."

Jetstar's Alan Joyce poured cold water on the plan. "They talk a good game but they don't implement a good act," he said. "We don't think Tiger will offer anything new." Tiger's plans attracted attention across Australia but *The Sydney Morning Herald* took a more geopolitical view.

It made Singapore Airlines deny that it was behind Tiger's plans to enter Australia some four years after it abandoned plans to launch a new domestic airline in Australia. "We addressed the issue of our future involvement in the domestic market back in 2003," a Singapore Airlines spokesman said. "Our position on that hasn't changed. Tiger has seen the opportunity."

Ian Thomas, a consultant with the Centre for Asia Pacific Aviation, said he wasn't convinced. "It's more Singapore Inc establishing an Australian [domestic presence] and using Tiger as the most appropriate vehicle," he claimed.

As Tiger was announcing its plans for Australia, there was an intense focus on ownership of airlines in Australia. In December 2006, a private-equity-backed consortium called Airline Partners Australia had made a $9 billion bid to take Qantas private. The group was made up of domestic and overseas backers, including David Bonderman's Texas Pacific Group and Macquarie Bank. The bid was structured to comply with Australian ownership rules which said Australian international airlines must be 51 per cent owned by Australians.

The bid would ultimately fail in May 2007 after it was blocked by shareholders.

There was certainly a perception in Australia that overseas airlines were coming and not everybody felt this was a good thing, even though Qantas was 40 per cent owned by overseas investors.

A few days after the announcement of its plans to launch in Australia, Tony Davis gave more detail about Tiger's plans in an interview with AFP, a news wire service. He said Tiger

CHAPTER 11: DIRTY TRICKS IN OZ

planned to become the Ryanair of Australia.

"Well, certainly the success of people like Ryanair in Europe has been that they could go into secondary airports, to go to regional airports and really create new markets and create new opportunities," he said. "It's about having a single aircraft type, it's about operating to regional airports and getting lower fees to use those airports, and it's about giving consumers the choice to purchase additional services if they require them. But at its core is a very efficient and very focused business model which allows very low unit costs, and those low unit costs mean sustained and consistent low fares."

He added: "We've been competing very aggressively in Singapore against Jetstar Asia, which Qantas brought into the Singapore market, and it's probably only right and proper that we reciprocate the favour by competing aggressively and effectively here in Australia."

The *Australian Financial Review* interviewed Davis at the same time, and it raised the issue of "sensitivity around foreign ownership". Davis, it noted, was an Englishman, who described Tiger as a "foreign" airline before correcting himself and saying it was "international". Davis was careful to say he believed Tiger would be creating a new market rather than taking from the existing duopoly. "I think definitely the European experience has been that we're not really interested in shifting market share; we're actually more interested in creating markets," he said. In Darwin, he said Tiger had increased the total number of people flying rather than stealing them from other carriers. "I think if you look at an air map of Australia it's concentrated around a few cities," he said.

"If you look at the Ryanair network in Europe, it's very comprehensive. It flies to major cities and very small regional cities and I think that's where there's a big opportunity for someone like Tiger."

He said Tiger had a much lower cost base than anyone in Australia and so would be a "trailblazer" both in terms of domestic prices and making international travel to Asia affordable. "Australian incumbent operators do not dispute that Tiger has the cheapest cost base, but they do claim that it is not a truly commercial enterprise and that it is being sent to Australia to upset Qantas's expansion of low-cost offshoot Jetstar," the *Australian Financial Review* said.

Davis said these fears were unfounded. "I could take some cheap shots that they probably had limited competition and very high fares whereas we've had extensive competition and offered very low fares," he said. "Our objective is to be a pan-Asian regional operator with an extensive route network that goes all the way from China through to Australia." Tiger, according to Davis, was not a Trojan horse for SIA. "We operate independently based around what's right for Tiger," he said at the time, adding that Tiger actually competed against SIA and its other subsidiary, Silk Air unlike Jetstar and its parent Qantas. "We don't coordinate with them in terms of our routes and our pricing."

In February 2007, Virgin Blue said it was looking at setting up its own low-cost subsidiary as it recognised its business was now costly. Virgin Blue chief executive Brett Godfrey denied this was in response to Tiger. "There has been a lot of rhetoric on what Tiger is going to do to the local industry but spare us – they are coming with five aeroplanes," he said.

CHAPTER 11: DIRTY TRICKS IN OZ

In March 2007, Australia's Foreign Investment Review Board gave Tiger the all-clear to set up Tiger Airways Australia. It still needed to obtain its Air Operators Certificate from the Civil Aviation Safety Authority in order to start domestic services in Australia later that year.

As Tiger tried to expand into Australia it faced a setback in the Philippines over unresolved regulatory issues after a presidential executive order had forced it to cut back services to Clark, north of Manila, from fourteen flights a week to nine. Qantas too was not taking Tiger's entry lying down, saying it would give its budget arm Jetstar thirteen more planes to compete against it. It said it would buy nine of these as new planes and redeploy four from its international fleet to the domestic market. Davis said Tiger wasn't intimidated.

"Unlike our competitors, we will not be forced into expensive and ill-conceived knee-jerk responses," Tiger CEO Tony Davis said in the statement. "We remain committed to becoming Australia's only true low-fare airline." Tiger had doubled passenger numbers from 800,000 to 1.5 million in its financial year ended 31 March 2007 but it was much more ambitious. In May 2007, it announced plans to set up a base in Melbourne, and said it hopes to create 1,000 jobs there. This was to be its beachhead, but its local rivals were lining up to take it down.

CHAPTER 12: A TIGER ROARS

In June 2007, Tiger Airways announced it had signed a fifty-aircraft deal with Airbus. By December the deal had been extended to add another twenty planes. This took its pipeline to seventy aircraft. Tiger was flying to twenty-five destinations in eight countries. The new planes were to help it expand, including building a domestic flying operation in Australia based out of Melbourne.

All in, Tiger had placed an order worth more than $2 billion. Boeing had fought hard to win the contract, with Davis turning up the heat a few months earlier by saying: "If we get a good proposal from Boeing we will certainly consider it. We need to continue growing so we need access to more aircraft." The Airbus offer, however, was too good to turn down.

"Tiger Airways has entered an exciting new phase of development, with continued strong growth of operations out of Singapore, the successful launch of services in Australia and a new start-up in Korea on the horizon," Davis said at the time.

"To IPO you have to have a reason to raise money and to be able to prove you're going to be profitable and grow." The deal with Airbus was intended to precede a float. "We needed to raise money to pay for all those planes we ordered," Davis said. Not everyone was convinced Tiger would ever make money. Alan Joyce told a gathering of journalists at the National Aviation Press Club in Sydney in June 2007 that he didn't think it would.

"Whilst Jetstar takes any new competitor seriously, one cannot help but think when Tiger's first year of pre-tax profit will come. Their operations have [lost] and continue to lose money – over $60 million Singapore dollars in two years – and at a greater rate than Jetstar Asia to our estimation in their last financial year ending in March," Joyce asserted.

Jetstar and Tiger were now in a price war domestically in Australia. The Australian Associated Press described it as "Flying Kangaroo and Tiger at war in the aviation jungle."

Tiger's fares were half what its competitors were prepared to offer before it entered Australia, but Jetstar knocked it for not being as low as had been speculated in the media.

"We're not too sure if we're playing with a Tiger or a cub," a spokesman said. Davis dismissed the jibes saying: "We're not going to get drawn into a public slanging match with our competitors by responding to some of the ridiculous rhetoric that they're pushing out. But what we will do is to continue to listen to our consumers and respond to their desire for lower airfares. That's what Tiger's about. It's not about gimmicks and short-term promotions: it's about sustainable and continuous low fares and that's what we're going to introduce to the Australian consumer." Jetstar decided to sell tickets at a loss in its drive to push Tiger out of Australia. It pledged in July 2007 to "double the difference" if its fares were undercut on any similar flight. Then it offered 10,000 $1 fares.

At a two-day Asia Pacific Aviation Summit Alan Joyce tried to turn up the heat on Tiger's Singaporean shareholders by calling for open skies in Asia during a panel discussion that included Davis.

"The only way that will happen is for liberalisation to happen, consolidation to happen and for governments to get out of airlines," Joyce said. "I'd like the 'big bang' approach because it would give us access into Asia and I think ourselves and Virgin would love to fly into Asia. Up in Singapore we can't fly from Singapore to Kuala Lumpur and I keep saying it's a very important market, very protected and yet we're not allowed to fly to that market.

"And yet, because Australia's very liberal, [Tiger Airways chief executive] Tony [Davis], if he wanted tomorrow, could fly to Sydney."

Davis said this comment was unfair as Tiger was blocked from flying into Kuala Lumpur too. "Time does enable change to occur and the big thing about Asia is... the market is six times bigger than the European Union," he said. "We have open skies with China, we have open skies between Singapore and Australia, so what we're doing is taking advantage of the liberalisation as it occurs."

Joyce also said that Tiger was controlled by the Singapore government and funded by its taxpayer. Davis responded by saying the Singaporean sovereign wealth fund was an investor in Tiger, but it was also an investor in Qantas subsidiary Jetstar Asia. He also noted that Qantas had recently appointed a former head of the Singapore mint to run its low-cost offshoot in Singapore. At one stage Davis accused Joyce of "cheap shots". After the panel ended, the pair were the only two

CHAPTER 12: A TIGER ROARS

not to shake hands. Davis told the *Singapore Business Daily* afterwards: "Everyone should just get on with running their businesses." Tiger was now seen as a certain IPO candidate. *The Wall Street Journal* said it was preparing to do so "in late 2008. The company's Irish investors have been pushing for an IPO for the middle of next year at the latest, but the company is busy setting up its Australian operations," it quoted an unnamed source as saying. "So if market conditions allow it, the IPO will probably be in late 2008." Tiger was now revealing abridged quarterly numbers in advance of its float that showed its year-to-date revenue numbers up 143 per cent. Bill Franke had stepped aside as chair, replaced by an independent chair Daniel Ee, chairman of Gas Supply, an importer of natural gas from Sumatra, and a former director of the Civil Aviation Authority in Singapore. Ee said Tiger was going to go to "greater heights", a comment that most considered a thinly veiled reference to the prospect of an IPO. There was now a four-way dogfight in Australia between Tiger, Virgin Blue, Jetstar and its parent Qantas itself.

Sir Rod Eddington, the former chief executive of Cathay Pacific, British Airways and Ansett, said he believed the market wasn't big enough to support all of them.

Speaking at a luncheon of the Australian British Chamber of Commerce on 30 October 2007, he said: "History shows that this market will support two-ish airlines. Now whether the past is a guide to the future, I don't know. Will this market support Tiger? It will be well run, Tony Davis who runs Tiger knows the business and it is well backed. Jetstar is looking to grow, Virgin Blue is looking to grow ... it is going to be a very competitive period and history suggests that not everyone stays the distance.

"What will be really interesting is if Tiger stepped up to twenty aeroplanes instead of five, then the game will really be afoot."

In late November 2007, Tiger Airways began flying in Australia. It had gone to the wire as it waited for last minute regulatory approval but had made it. Jetstar greeted its launch by offering fares for just five cents (including tax) from Brisbane to various locations in Queensland.

Tiger wasn't able to fly as much as it wanted. It said flights to Alice Springs had been delayed for three months after Qantas refused to supply ground handling. Davis said this showed a "contempt" by Qantas towards the people of Alice Springs, but its rival said it was under no obligation to help.

"It's been very telling that some of our competitors, one in particular, have been engaged in all sorts of antics," Davis complained in the *Australian Financial Review*. "When you see some of your competitors behaving like headless chickens, it's very telling. We have a long history of competing against Jetstar in Singapore. We are very comfortable ... that we offer a better product."

As Davis spoke, Tony Fernandes, the founder of AirAsia, predicted that Tiger would fail. Fernandes had just launched a spin-out airline called AirAsia X flying between the Gold Coast and Malaysia.

"There's a market for low-cost flights in Australia. Virgin and Jetstar have lost their way," Fernandes said. "[But] I think Tiger will be crucified by them because it does not have enough capacity. Tiger has so many issues in Singapore, it's surprising they tried to do something in Australia. I don't think they know what they are doing."

Davis said Fernandes's comments were "probably wishful

thinking. It's a misconception to say that Australia can sustain only two major airlines. It is not true in the modern era."

Davis said Tiger had twelve planes lined up to enter Australia and that it could go to seventy aircraft. "We will grow our business in Australia. The Ryan family are [16 per cent] investors in Tiger, and Ryanair is the most successful low-cost airline in the world. It carries more people internationally than any other airline," he said at the time.

"The shareholders of Tiger are not in the charity business, they are in the business of making money."

As the year 2007 ended Tiger told *Bloomberg* it would put twenty more Airbus A320s in to support bases in South Korea and expand into Australia, Malaysia and India.

"It's really a case now of adding density to the operation and filling some of the gaps," it said. The Centre for Asia Pacific Aviation estimated there was an "untapped" market of 300 million people who wanted to fly between South Korea, China and Japan alone. Everyone was now betting big, as the Asian market started to open up.

Tiger had helped crack open the market in Asia just as Ryanair did in Europe.

Tiger said it had an option for twenty A320s with a list price of $1.46 billion alongside thirty planes it had already ordered. This was a big jump for Tiger, which had 12 A320s active.

AirAsia meanwhile said it had ordered 175 A320s, while Lion Mentari, the biggest budget carrier in Indonesia, said it had signed for 122 Boeing 737-900ERs. Tiger added new routes to India, South Korea and Australia. It was even making headway back home where the Singaporean and Malaysian governments had agreed to end a three-decade-long near monopoly between its two flag carriers and its two capitals. "We would be very excited to develop our route network to Malaysia, especially east Malaysia," Davis told *Bloomberg*.

But then the 2008 financial crash came. Tiger had strong shareholders, so it wasn't in danger of going bust, but it knew the timing for a float was poor. In March 2008, Tiger's chief financial officer Peter Negline quit after just ten months. A former Hong Kong-based JP Morgan analyst, his departure was seen as a sign that Tiger might not be IPO'ing as the financial crisis began in earnest with the collapse of Bear Stearns in New York. Tiger restructured its routes, scrapping or scaling back some while expanding others. Tiger had to do it because of high fuel prices and capacity constraints in order to manage its yield. Alan Bird, a former colleague of Davis in BMI, had just left that airline. "When Tony heard that I'd fallen out and I was leaving BMI, he rang me," Bird said. By January 2008, Bird was in Singapore on a one-month contract. After Negline left, he was asked to become interim CFO, working on integrating financial reporting between Tiger's Singapore and Australia business. He hoped the role would become full-time. "I was working on what they call IPO readiness," Bird said. "We were putting together all the business plans and forecasts required ahead of the stock market."

However, not everybody wanted Tiger to get there. In April 2008, Tiger made a complaint to the Australian Competition and Consumer Commission about a "dirty tricks" campaign being run by its competitors.

CHAPTER 12: A TIGER ROARS

Davis described the activity as "despicable". "Obviously, (our) success is jeopardising the bonuses of executives at other airlines so they have been doing their best to disrupt our operation," he said. The public aspect of the complaint didn't name who Tiger believed was trying to nobble it, but it was obvious who it was. Qantas had approached Tiger's chief pilot, head of check and training, head of safety and head of fleet safety with job offers. All the approaches were made separately but within a six-week period, convincing Tiger it was a coordinated take out.

"All of them have been approached," a Tiger spokesperson said. "We all know there is a pilot shortage, but these guys have been offered positions not as general pilots. Had any one of these people left suddenly, our aircraft would have been grounded." Tiger was under attack because it was doing well. The airline said in April 2008 it had carried 2.25 million people, a 50 per cent increase on the year before. Davis was growing its fleet from 12 to 72 aircraft, and Tiger said it was setting up a new cadet pilot scheme as it would need 580 pilots in Australia in 2016. Tiger was the biggest international low-fare airline serving China, and it knew it had barely scratched that market. It told Airbus to speed up its order as Tiger said it was now looking for acquisitions to give it greater scale. Tiger said it planned to raise $225 million to finance its fleet expansion. Bird was interviewed for the role of full-time CFO, but he was turned down. "Tony told me later [that] the Singaporeans wanted a local CFO," Bird said. After not getting the job Bird returned home, but he was now connected to Irelandia.

Tiger's new CFO was called Chin Sak Hin. Hin was a close associate of Chew Choon Seng, who had held various senior positions in SIA.

In May 2008, Choon Seng revealed that Tiger had made its first profit of almost $10 million. "Tiger has performed better than its business plan," he said. Davis meanwhile emphasised that Tiger had "ended the financial year with very strong cash reserves".

The focus on cash came as oil prices continued to rise in the summer of 2008 above $120 a barrel. Goldman Sachs was predicting they could top $200 a barrel.

Virgin Blue and Qantas/Jetstar both announced they were closing unprofitable routes. Davis said Tiger would increase capacity as its rivals retreated.

"The price of fuel is the canary in the mine that has simply highlighted the lack of cost discipline of our competitors," he said. "We are keen to use our Australian-based aircraft and crews to mount international services to fill the gaps left by Qantas/Jetstar as soon as we can convince the Australian government to allow Tiger Airways Australia access to these routes."

Alan Joyce said the Australian government should not give in to this request from an airline "100 per cent foreign-owned".

He added: "We'd say to Tiger that if they're so keen on liberalisation of these bilateral rules that they should be talking to the Singaporean government first about relaxing their rules there before they dictate to the Australian government what it should do. Good housekeeping starts at home."

Tiger was still eager for an IPO but it had to wait two years until the financial crisis settled. Davis had become friends with Ryan during his difficult first years. He trusted him and could rely on him for advice when weaving through the complex politics of his board and region. Now they could both finally see a route towards the stock market.

CHAPTER 13: IPO AND AN EXIT

The 2010 roadshow lasted weeks, starting in Singapore and then moving on to Hong Kong, London, Boston and finally New York. Tiger was now five years old and had a compelling story. The Asian market had started to deregulate, and it had made ground in Australia. "By the time we got to New York our investment bank could say we're oversubscribed. The IPO will happen," Declan Ryan recalled. On 13 January 13, Tiger filed its prospectus with the Monetary Authority of Singapore. "We intend to use our net proceeds from the offering to fund the equity portion of our planned acquisition of Airbus A320 aircraft and the associated aircraft pre-delivery payments; to establish a potential new airline and/or operating bases; to repay all outstanding short-term loans which have been used to finance our aircraft pre-delivery payments; and for working capital," its prospectus said.

Tony Davis added: "We are now ready to embark on the next stage of growth, and believe that a listing will help fuel that growth." Tiger was flying to thirty-three airports in eleven countries and had seventeen A320s active and predicted 68 planes by December 2015. Citi, Morgan Stanley and Singaporean bank DBS were all lined up to advise. Tiger pitched itself at the maximum of its price range of 1.65 Singapore dollars (€0.83) per share. In Australia there remained sceptics. The *Australian Financial Review* noted: "Tiger makes as much in its prospectus of the lucrative Australian market as of the growth potential of the Asian one, but half-a-dozen Australian airlines have crashed and burned in the past 30 years trying to duplicate the profitability of Qantas by tackling it head on. Only Virgin Blue has survived."

In New York in the third week of January a dinner took place to mark Tiger knowing its IPO was oversubscribed with Tony Davis, the Irelandia team, its bankers from Singapore, and Bill Franke from Indigo. "We all went out to dinner in Manhattan and there was a feeling that was a combination of euphoria, relief and slight trepidation," Davis recalled. "The biggest thing for me was that we had gone to the investment community and people believed our story and were willing to back us."

"You know about 24 hours before if the book was filled and we'd sold it numerous times," Declan Ryan recalled, "it was a great success but we were exhausted. It's like doing a marathon. After you finish, you're tired and relieved."

Davis flew back the next day with SIA non-stop from New York to Singapore with four of his investment bankers. It was an eighteen-hour flight, but it ensured he was back in Singapore for its stock market debut.

It had been a frenetic but exhilarating few weeks. When the waiter asked for his room number at breakfast in Singapore,

CHAPTER 13: IPO AND AN EXIT

Davis couldn't remember it as he had stayed in so many hotels in the preceding period.

On Friday 22 January 2010, Tiger floated on the Singapore Stock Exchange, with its shares finishing up 5 per cent on its first day trading. "We are proud to be the first low-cost airline to list on the SGX-ST and would like to welcome all our new shareholders as we embark on our new journey as a listed company," Davis said. Tiger floated in the same week that Japan Airlines, one of Asia's oldest and biggest full-service airlines, declared bankruptcy. On the floor of the Singapore Stock Exchange, Davis said he felt relieved. "There is a temptation to see an IPO as the finish when it is only the starting post," he said. "Now we had to deliver for a bigger group of shareholders. There was a pressure you have that isn't there when you're a private company."

Encouragingly, Tiger had established itself as a brand in Singapore with the portion of its shares allocated to ordinary or retail investors eight to ten times oversubscribed. Institutional demand ensured the airline's IPO was over six times oversubscribed. In the end the original four investors only needed to put in $15 million of their $20 million budget. From $15 million the four investors including Irelandia had created an airline worth $500 million.

Tiger gave its pilots all a bonus after the IPO. "This was a mistake in hindsight," Davis said. "We paid them all at the same time and that caused a spike in people leaving to work in places like the Middle East. It was an own goal. We should have paid it out on different dates." But all told, the IPO was a success, as it gave Tiger the capital to fund its expansion, and proved the market saw the same opportunity it saw.

On 28 August 2010, Irelandia sold half of its 11.2 per cent stake in Tiger, grossing an estimated $30 million. Indigo Partners and Tony Davis also sold down their positions at the same time. In October and November 2011, Irelandia sold the remainder of its shares in several transactions. Gross proceeds across all of the share sales came to almost $70 million. For Irelandia, its full exit from Tiger marked a twenty-eight times return on its investment. "The amount of money the shareholders put into Tiger was miniscule," Davis said. "I think in terms of multiples we're Declan's best ever airline. Clearly he has made much more money elsewhere."

He said the company began to change quickly after Irelandia started to sell out. Within twelve months Davis was the only non-Singaporean on Tiger's board. He had worked closely with Irelandia and Indigo but now the board was full of local luminaries who he did not know as well. "The culture changed when we lost Dec and the Irelandia team," Davis said. "It was a shame as the approach that Dec brings in motivating management teams is unique. He gives a real clarity of purpose."

"Declan treats all his airlines as a form of offspring. There was always an emotional attachment and that inspired people."

Davis said his new board was not steeped in low fares. "There was a lot of re-questioning of our model. I wouldn't say the pure LCC model is naturally intuitive to Singapore Airlines. I think the secret to the success of Singapore Airlines has been the absolute opposite approach, which is the highest quality and the best of the best."

Davis started to think about moving on. "My skill set is probably more attuned to startups than a listed company," he

CHAPTER 13: IPO AND AN EXIT

said. "I found the increased bureaucracy a bit stifling. I had done it for seven years, and started to think was I the right person to do another seven?" Tiger was doing well in many markets, but it was struggling in Australia.

Davis volunteered to move to Australia to become its local chief executive after Tiger was temporarily grounded there. He told his board before he left that he did not think he should come back to Singapore afterwards. Australia proved impossible to crack. "We'd put so much effort into Australia," Davis said. "But it was a very difficult market." Tiger was in a death-fight with its rivals, and the subject of what it felt was a concerted drive to push it out of Australia. "It was classic Australian skulduggery," Ryan said. "They threw everything at us."

"We used Ryanair techniques against Tiger in Australia," Alan Joyce admits. "It did well in Singapore but it never really made any money in Australia." Joyce said the grounding by Australian regulators halted Tiger's momentum: "They never recovered after that. It became a bit of a train wreck in Australia."

One of the reasons Jetstar could fight Tiger so well was Conor McCarthy. Jetstar had hired the Dubliner in 2003 to help it set up the airline in response to rival Virgin Blue. McCarthy was still a shareholder in AirAsia, so he asked Tony Fernandes for his approval.

"Tony was worried so I said to Alan (Joyce) and Jeff Dixon (the chief executive of Qantas) at my first meeting that I can only help you if you're only doing this for domestic Australia and are not planning to move into AirAsia territory," McCarthy recalled.

103

Qantas agreed to this, so McCarthy started working with Joyce before Jetstar's launch in May 2004, so it was bedded in before Tiger arrived.

"It is first in, best-dressed," McCarthy said. "If you're first in you're able to offer fares that are lower than the incumbent by say 30 per cent. That is a significant cost saving so you win over lots of price-sensitive customers. If you're the second low-cost carrier, maybe you are 5 per cent cheaper again but this isn't enough."

Even when Tiger was cheaper than Jetstar it wasn't enough to make a big splash. Any misstep by Tiger was amplified by its rivals to suggest it wasn't reliable.

There was a feeling that somebody wanted to stop Tiger at any cost. John Goode was sent to Melbourne to help out, and Mason went down there also. So too did Ryan.

But McCarthy believes by then it was too late to turn things around. Jetstar was well-resourced and it was playing at home. Even cutting prices wasn't enough. "Tiger was very much built along Ryanair lines. A lot of Australian customers bristled at some of the very stringent rules on bags, various penalties and so on," McCarthy said. "Australia is a prosperous country so even though there's price sensitivity in the market it wasn't as acute as other markets. Customers were prepared to pay a little bit more to fly Jetstar."

Back in Singapore a local, Chin Yau Seng, was put in charge and it became obvious he was taking over the entire group. By the end of August 2011, Davis had resigned. "The board is appreciative of the efforts that Tony and the Australia management team had put in to get Tiger Airways Australia back in the air," Yau Sang said. Singaporeans were now in

CHAPTER 13: IPO AND AN EXIT

charge. Irelandia was out, and Indigo followed by selling down its shares and started another low-fares airline in the region.

In 2013, Virgin bought a 60 per cent stake in Tiger in Australia for AUD$35 million, with the option to buy the rest. The following year it exercised this option for AUD$1. The Singaporeans didn't want to slug it out in Australia anymore, and the same day they sold its Australian arm they increased their stake in Singapore-listed Tiger from 40 per cent to 55 per cent. Ultimately SIA ended up taking Tiger private and back into the mothership.

Joyce reflected almost a decade later that Tiger had made Qantas and its subsidiary Jetstar better operators. "Every airline in Europe went downmarket to compete against the low-cost carriers but we kept our full premium airline and set up the cost operator by miles in Australia. It forced us to operate at both ends of the market with different brands." He said this balancing act was hard to get right as usually carriers "cannibalised" themselves. "We had to walk a tightrope," he said.

Tiger was a catalyst too in Asia. It opened up routes to millions that had never been available or affordable before. It drove the liberalisation of a market that was previously comfortable in making travel hard and elitist. Davis had led the airline during this extraordinary period, but his departure was bittersweet. "Did I feel guilty about abandoning Tony at the time? I did," Ryan said. "But I felt it was the right time for Irelandia to sell, and Tony made a lot of money too."

"Tiger was the first time Irelandia set up an airline from scratch," Davis said. "We were the standard bearer for the Ryan family. Ryanair was a great success so there was a lot of pressure. It was clear fairly quickly you couldn't just take the Ryanair rule book and copy it. The market was different and the local culture was different. But in the end we succeeded. We floated the business and we changed how people flew."

"We achieved a lot with a small team," Davis said. "The scale of the network we built and our operating performance was fantastic. There were growing pains and lots of risk too. I'd be lying if I said that I didn't have regrets. It felt like the Tiger journey ended too soon, there was still so much we could have achieved. Maybe I do need to try and convince Dec that we still have unfinished business in Asia."

Davis joined Irelandia as a partner after he left, and he brought his operational prowess to bear in its other aviation investments.

Years later Declan Ryan met Alan Joyce for dinner. "He sits down and says: 'Thanks for fucking up the competition!'" Ryan recalled. "Qantas was a fierce competitor, but Alan is a great guy."

CHAPTER 14: LAS VEGAS AND THE DOGS

Maury Gallagher was looking for investors. It was 2005 and he had already co-founded two airlines in the United States – ValuJet and WestAir. He was battle hardened and had a young but experienced team around him as he sought to take his third airline, Allegiant, from bankruptcy to the stock market. Gallagher knew what he was doing but he was conscious of how easy things could go wrong. He wasn't just looking for money from investors, he was also looking for credibility. Gallagher was an MBA graduate from the University of California, Berkeley who had worked as an accountant before getting a job in late 1978 in the emerging aircraft-leasing arm of a company which specialised in renting out computers.

In 1979 Gallagher and some colleagues answered an advertisement in *The San Francisco Chronicle* for a 'management team' for a small airline in Santa Rosa California called WestAir. It was a tiny airline running half-a-dozen planes with a capacity of between eight and sixteen passengers. Gallagher took over the finances of the airline during a time of stagflation where the United States economy was experiencing both high inflation and little growth. "I realised that I had the 'stomach' for this type of problem, not uncommon in young, start-up companies," Gallagher recalled in his unpublished memoir. "I could sleep just fine even though I did not know where the funds were for the next payroll or to pay the gas bill in the next few days. Optimistically, I assume we would figure it out, that we would do what it took to make it through."

Despite its small fleet fuelled by gasoline, the management of WestAir was ambitious. It wanted to create a jet airline capable of taking advantage of the growing deregulation in the domestic US market. Terry Ashton came on board as chief executive of the airline.

Ashton was more experienced than the rest of the team and he'd previously worked as an executive with Hughes Airwest, a Westcoast airline backed by Howard Hughes, a colourful tycoon with interests in movies, casinos and aviation who famously died a recluse in 1976.

Ashton was smart and in his mid-forties with an understanding of low-cost airlines. He had the contacts to lead a $6 million funding round from venture capital funds and investment banks to get the new jet business called Pacific Express moving.

He also managed to close a deal to secure the airline's first jets from the British Aircraft Corporation. Ashton brought in Fred Cobb as head of operations and assembled a team to raise money on the stock market to fund the new airline. Gallagher was seen as the weakest link by the airline's bankers as he had least experience in airlines, but Ashton refused to push him out.

CHAPTER 14: LAS VEGAS AND THE DOGS

Pacific Express was ready to launch, but from the off things did not bode well.

"The company lost money in every way it could," Gallagher recalled in his memoir. "Through the first six months of 1982 it lost $8 million on $10 million of revenue; for all of 1982 it lost $19 million on $25 million of revenue."

Gallagher realised its BAC jets were too small with just seventy-eight seats versus its rivals which flew planes twice the size. This put the airline at a fundamental disadvantage compared to its rivals. Pacific Express was being beaten up on the one side by the much bigger United Airlines, whose then chief executive Richard Ferris said of fledgling rivals it was better to "kill the sparrow before it becomes a hawk". On its other side was Pacific Southwest Airlines, which had a leaner cost base, and which turned out to be a fiercer competitor than expected.

At board level, meetings became increasingly tense. A month after Pacific Express went public, Ashton was replaced as chief executive by Cobb, although he remained chairman. Gallagher didn't want to work for Ashton as he wanted to rationalise the airline by selling off non-core assets like its original business WestAir. Gallagher and Tim Flynn managed to buy WestAir and both left Pacific Express as a result when the deal closed in June 1983.

Cobb continued on with Pacific Express and in under a year, on 3 February 1984, the lead story in local Oregon newspaper *The Bulletin* was "Pacific Express folds its wings."

The paper reported that the airline went bankrupt so fast hundreds of passengers only found out at the airport as they waited for their flights. Eight hundred people working for the airline in five states were out of their jobs.

"Bottom line, the deck was stacked against the company – there was no chance it could have succeeded," Gallagher reflected decades later. He realised he had been lucky to escape with WestAir, which would become one of only two of the twenty-plus airline startups founded in California in the 1980s to survive.

Airline giant United Airlines started to court WestAir, which only had about 100 seats. United asked it to become a feeder airline and by 1985 the two airlines were closely affiliated, boosting the smaller airline's profile and prospects. WestAir grew from ten planes at the end of 1983 to seventy-two by the end of 1988. WestAir continued to add bigger and more modern planes and by 1990 it had grown revenues seven-fold from 1983 to $257 million. It had set up a subsidiary too on the East coast of the United States with the encouragement of United Airlines, to which it remained close. Everything was going well until Iraq invaded Kuwait, causing jet fuel prices to triple, and WestAir to start losing money. WestAir had expanded rapidly and it now found itself under pressure from its banks. It decided to sell its East coast subsidiary to right-size the business. After it did this, it received an unsolicited bid from Mesa Airlines, which was on the acquisition trail. WestAir was still losing money so Gallagher and Flynn decided to sell the business in 1992.

The deal was a bit of what Gallagher termed a "bear hug" as it was from a competitor at a low point in WestAir's fortunes. Flynn left the business after the deal closed but Gallagher went on to the board of Mesa to represent the pair's interests as shareholders. Gallagher clashed with Larry Risley, the founder of Mesa, who had re-mortgaged his home to found the company in 1982.

Risley was a micromanager who wasn't a fan of how WestAir operated, so there was friction from the start. Gallagher and Flynn ended up in a lawsuit against Mesa as they felt the contracts they had signed had not been honoured. Eventually Gallagher and Flynn won their case, but they were now out of WestAir. They had made some money and gained a lot of experience, and they were soon ready to go again.

Flynn and Gallagher moved to Las Vegas, and they went into business together. Gallagher was still interested in the airline business so travelled with a friend called Robert Priddy, a co-founder of Atlantic Southeast Airlines, a commuter airline in Atlanta.

In 1992, they went to Salt Lake City to see David Neeleman, later the founder of JetBlue Airways, to see if they could work with him on his first airline called Morris Air. Gallagher and Priddy were impressed by the margins Neeleman was able to achieve as well as his use of technology and ability to carve out a niche in the shadow of larger competitors. When they came back to Las Vegas they started to talk with Flynn about starting up a new airline. The plan was to pick off routes out of Atlanta by taking on Delta with a lower cost offering targeting the leisure market in the Eastern United States.

In 1993, Gallagher and his co-founders launched a new start-up airline called Valujet based in Clayton County,

Georgia. Valujet was innovative in its reservation system and allowed customers to buy tickets directly from the airline by phone before the internet was widely available. As a result, its customers didn't need a ticket. "Ticketless air travel was born!" Gallagher recalled in his memoir. "That meant that ValuJet did not have to depend on the travel agency community to distribute tickets – we could sell directly to our customers. The cost savings from this approach was dramatic. During its first full month of operation ValuJet generated $10 million of revenue with only three people in accounting."

In 1994, Andrew Levy, later an important figure in Allegiant and the chief executive of Avelo Airlines, joined ValuJet immediately after graduating from law school in Georgia. Valujet was initially successful, making a profit in its second month of trading by offering flights that were two-thirds cheaper than its rivals in the region. This was the fastest turn to profit in United States history.

With only one full quarter's results behind it, ValuJet went to Wall Street and floated on the stock market. Valujet's revenues tripled to more than $100 million in 1995. After only two years Valujet was worth $2 billion, ten times more than it had floated for. To capitalise on this growth, it ordered fifty new planes with a price tag of $1 billion. But there was serious trouble ahead.

The rapid growth in the airline industry was creating dangers. Between 1995 and 1996 there were four serious crashes, killing more than 100 people each time. One of the planes that crashed was owned by ValuJet. On 11 May 1996, Flight 592 had just taken off from Miami airport when a fire broke out in its cargo area. Hazardous material had been incorrectly

CHAPTER 14: LAS VEGAS AND THE DOGS

placed in the hold of the aircraft by the company's aircraft maintenance vendor. The aircraft plunged into the Everglades forest and all 110 passengers and crew were killed.

Other airlines that crashed during the mid-1990s came through it but Valujet didn't. The circumstances of the crash, a sad plunge into alligator-infested water in the middle of nowhere, ensured it stayed front-page news and it destroyed the airline's reputation. Valujet was criticised heavily, with the suggestion that low fares meant low safety. This was unfair as the accident was not due to any specific failure of Valujet or its aircraft but was instead found to be due to negligence by its maintenance vendor. Valujet remained responsible for overseeing this work, but it was an important distinction that was understandably lost amid the tragedy.

Valujet was grounded for an extended period and it lost $41 million in 1996, sending its share price plunging. Everyone involved in the airline was devastated by the accident and it never recovered. In 1997, Valuejet rebranded to AirTran Airlines and changed its business model. By then Gallagher and Priddy had left. "The emotional impact of these events are staggering for all concerned, particularly for the families and persons involved in the accident as well as the airline," Gallagher wrote in his memoir. "As a senior executive in this industry it has been something I have lived with for 40 years."

After Gallagher left Valujet, he invested in other businesses including a telecommunication firm, but he was drawn back to the aviation business despite the risks involved. A friend of his called Mitch Allee, who worked with him on the tech side of WestAir and Valujet, had co-founded WestJet Airlines, an airline in 1997 based in Fresno, California targeting the leisure market.

Another airline with a similar name objected, so Allee decided to call the new airline Allegiant, a play on his own name.

The airline bought old planes, which weren't ideal for the west coast, but it was still early days. In 2000, the dotcom bubble burst, impacting the US economy as oil prices rose. Weighed down with debt and with its planes inappropriate, Allegiant started to struggle. Gallagher loaned his old friend over $2 million to try and keep the airline going but it kept losing money. Allee tried to turn things around but Gallagher could see the airline was in a death spiral. He advised his friend to file for bankruptcy and to try to restructure the business. Gallagher was one of Allegiant's biggest creditors when it went into Chapter 11, and he risked millions more taking it out of bankruptcy and then moving its headquarters to Las Vegas.

Gallagher wanted to make it a low-cost airline that millions of Americans who lived in smaller cities dotted around the United States could use to access Sin City.

Gallagher asked Tom Mullins in Raymond James to raise external funding for Allegiant and prepare it for a flotation on the stock market. Mullins suggested he meet Declan Ryan.

Gallagher liked the sound of this as he knew the Ryan name would resonate with US investors who were now sitting on good profits from backing Ryanair.

The two men met in a hotel room in New York and immediately hit it off.

In his unpublished memoir, Maury Gallagher recalled the meeting:

CHAPTER 14: LAS VEGAS AND THE DOGS

"Declan, it's a pleasure to meet you," I said. "Thanks for coming to New York," said Ryan. "Based on what Tom Mullins has told me, I was interested in meeting you and hearing about Allegiant. I don't know if you know it, but we like to invest in early stage airlines, particularly ones who have a good growth curve in front of them."

"We have had a good programme for the last few years since we took over," I commented.

"I have gotten to know your operation at Ryanair and it appears we have a great deal in common. We have built ourselves first and foremost to be a low cost carrier focused on leisure traffic. And the best way to do that is by what we have termed 'basing', namely having all your aircraft, personnel and support in a particular city and having the aircraft go out and back from that city. It appears you have copied our model," I said to Ryan with a chuckle.

Ryan had a grin on his face after my remark. "Perhaps we have," he said, playing along with my remark.

"But we have found this to be a very sound model and that is part of the reason I am interested. We know this model works and you are doing a good job with it here in the States," he said.

Declan Ryan asked his father Tony to fly to Las Vegas to see Allegiant in action. Tony Ryan was not impressed, concluding it was "very boring". Tony Ryan didn't object when his son said he wanted to do the deal, but it didn't capture his imagination the way Tiger had.

Gallagher was inspired by Ryanair and Tony Ryan even before he met them. "We stole a chapter from Ryanair and took it to the next level when we started doing ancillary revenue," he said. Gallagher's father was half-Irish, so he felt a connection. "I really admire the Ryan family going back to Tony," he said.

Tony Ryan had worked for Aer Lingus in Chicago when Gallagher was growing up there. "I lived only a few miles from him but we never met. Tony was a brilliant guy. One of the things I got a kick out of was seeing the hard-ass nature of Ryanair and the Irish mentality in business in action," Gallagher said.

Declan Ryan could see the potential of Allegiant, and he was impressed by both Gallagher's ability and track record so Tony Ryan supported the investment. "They were pre-IPO, so they needed anchor shareholders," Ryan recalled. "We could see the opportunity."

Carragher went to Las Vegas on a due diligence trip. "We were blown away by Maury Gallagher and his team," he said. "It had the makings of a superb operation that needed the cherry-on-top, our low-cost carrier know-how and brand to assist with an IPO." Carragher recommended Irelandia make the investment, and Ryan agreed. "We wrote very risk-friendly legal documents with a share clawback structure if performance targets were not met," Carragher said. "But none of it was ever needed."

In early May 2005, Irelandia invested $7.5 million in Allegiant. It was part of a consortium that injected $39.5 million in fresh equity into the airline.

The other investors were PAR Investment Partners, a limited partnership controlled by PAR Capital Management, a Boston hedge fund founded by former airline analyst Paul A Reeder and Edward Shapiro.

Shapiro had previously worked as an analyst with Morgan Stanley and as an executive with Wellington Management Company, a huge investment management company. He was one of the best aviation investors in the United States and would later serve as an independent director at United Airlines.

The biggest external investor was the Comvest Group, a mid-market private equity firm based in Florida that put in $25 million. Comvest Group was co-founded by Robert Priddy, who was close to Gallagher from being in trenches with him running ValuJet.

"It was a good club to have prior to an IPO. They were strategic shareholders," Declan Ryan said. "Airlines love Irelandia coming in because we give them credibility. We drive them crazy as well, but they will get their costs down."

Irelandia had a 10.2 per cent stake in the airline. The next twelve months was about preparing the airline for flotation. "We helped them with the IPO, as we'd been there," Ryan said.

"Their IT system was quite bad, so we got them to relook at that. We got them to look even closer at auxiliary revenue. We got them to focus on their costs even more.

"For Allegiant, let's say they have a million passengers a year and their auxiliary revenue went from $2 to $20, that makes an enormous impact on their bottom line. Allegiant became one of the biggest resellers of hotels in the States because of Las Vegas."

Visitors tended to book their airline tickets six months in advance, and Allegiant had their emails. It knew what dates its passengers would be in Las Vegas, so it could retarget them with concert tickets, visits to the nearby Grand Canyon and so on. This all drove ancillary revenue.

"Allegiant are world-class at doing that," Ryan said. "Merely selling airline tickets became nearly irrelevant for them because they are selling so much of everything else."

Gallagher felt Allegiant was poised for success, but Irelandia gave him more surety. "Allegiant was profitable and growing but it was also consuming cash so raising the money was a safety net," Gallagher said. "In the airline business we sell ahead of time but the credit card companies for young carriers wouldn't give us all the money so we needed more working capital.

"Declan and Robert Priddy were really good endorsable airline people." Maurice Mason also joined the Allegiant board, and invested personally.

Ryan didn't go on the board, but he was influential, nonetheless. "Declan avoided boards if he was not needed," Carragher said. "But he controlled all our decisions."

Declan Ryan asked Paula Doherty, then only in her second year in Irelandia, to help out with the deal. She had impressed Ryan in her first year with her toughness and her attention to detail. Carragher had asked her to review every investment Irelandia had, and to prepare a fresh file on it.

Doherty had spotted that a well-known Irish person had taken an investment from Irelandia to buy a company but had never given it all the shares it was due. The sum involved was relatively small, but the principle was a serious one. After

CHAPTER 14: LAS VEGAS AND THE DOGS

being informed by Doherty, Carragher rang the individual demanding the issue be dealt with immediately. Carragher was assured it was just a mistake, but he didn't buy it. A legal letter followed and Irelandia got its money back.

Ryan wanted Doherty to sit in on the Allegiant deal, as he felt it would provide invaluable experience. "Declan and Anthony were very hands-on," Doherty recalled. "I was the junior person on the deal reading the documents, reviewing them, and listening in on meetings."

Ryan's interventions, she recalls, were brief, but effective. "The systems Allegiant was using were all these spreadsheets," Doherty said. "The information was there but everything was intertwined. I remember Declan telling them to streamline it. He knew ahead of an IPO an investor would be looking for the headline figures as opposed to too much detail."

Doherty was impressed by Gallagher and the team he had assembled. "They had a really strong management team," Doherty said. "Really young, enthusiastic go-getters."

Andrew Levy, who had worked for Gallagher as a young law graduate, was the talented president of Allegiant, but the person who most impressed Doherty was its CFO Linda Marvin.

Marvin had previously worked for Gallagher in a telecoms venture and she'd worked for him at WestAir.

Marvin joined Allegiant in September 2001, the same month as the September 11 attacks. Like Doherty, she was originally an accountant in KPMG. "I loved the fact that there was a woman on the executive team," Doherty recalled. "Being female was never an issue for me in Irelandia. Declan never made me feel any different to anyone else, so I can't complain. But most of the senior people in the industry were men." Up until Allegiant, Doherty hadn't worked on the aviation side of Irelandia's business but she did fall in love with it despite not being an aeroplane fanatic.

"The type of deals you do in aviation are bigger than anything most people would ever do," she said. "It was huge and fascinating." As Allegiant worked towards an IPO, Doherty and Carragher went along with the Allegiant team on its IPO roadshow. "Maurice was fielding questions," Doherty recalls. "A big thing was growth. Investors were wondering if there were enough niche growth markets for Allegiant to target. We now know there was, but back then it was brilliant seeing him in action."

In January 2007, Allegiant floated on the Nasdaq, raising $90 million. Its shares shot up by 46 per cent on its market debut. Trading at thirty-five times annualised earnings it compared well with its peers from the very beginning.

Allegiant offered non-stop flights from Newburgh, New York, Belleville, Illinois, and Allentown to Las Vegas and Florida. Only six of the seventy cities where it offered non-stop flights had a competitive service so it was opening up a new untapped market.

"I think the business model is an interesting one," Helane Becker, an equities analyst, told Reuters. "The type of equipment they are using, the markets they are flying to and from, and the fact that they don't have a lot of competition helps."

Allegiant used the IPO money to purchase additional aircraft, pay debt owed to Gallagher, and to grow its brand. Irelandia invested at $5 a share, and the company floated at $18. Irelandia sold out half its shares at the float, and then sold down the rest over the next year. Ryan was on the pricing

CHAPTER 14: LAS VEGAS AND THE DOGS

committee ahead of the float; there was some debate about whether to price it higher, but Ryan felt they should not be too greedy. "I'd had bad experiences with IPOs so I allowed them to move the price up by a dollar but for me the important thing in an IPO is to get it away," Ryan said. "You worry about the price after."

Irelandia sold the last of its shares at $32 a share, so it had made about seven times its money.

The share price went up over the next decade many times over. "That's a great example of getting out too early," Ryan said. "It was an extraordinary business and it still is. Maury Gallagher is one of the best."

According to Gallagher: "We went public at $18 and the shares touched $270 at peak. Now they've fallen back since but it is still up almost tenfold. Declan has said it might have been best to stay in but Declan's impatient.

"He wanted in and out and I can understand that. Often in airlines there is a parabola effect where they hit a peak and then go down. I can't think of one airline like us other than Southwest that has been able to keep broadly going up."

He added: "Very few start-up companies in the airline industry are successful. The journey claimed most because they did not have the proper strategy and leadership to survive."

"If you go in at $5, and it hits $35 it is hard not to take it," Ryan reflected. He'd learned the hard way often enough the dangers of clinging on too long to investments.

"We don't tend to look back too much," Paula Doherty admitted. "Obviously, we'd take a glance and could see how well Allegiant later did but we'd move on. When we are involved in any investment, we're constantly assessing it and reviewing it. But once we've sold out, our focus is the next deal."

After Irelandia exited, Tony Ryan read a headline in *The Irish Independent* saying that he had made $40 million from Allegiant. He rang his son that morning. "I see I got all the credit for your deal," Tony Ryan laughed. "Don't worry about it, you can keep the credit," Declan Ryan replied.

"Do you remember my comment about it being very boring?" Tony Ryan asked him. "Boring is good, Declan."

"Each of us knew that as long as the king was around, everyone would assume the king made the deal," Declan Ryan reflected. "And I was always happy to let him have the credit.

"But it meant a lot to me that he acknowledged I was striking out on my own, doing my own deals, having my own successes and making money for the family.

"As it turned out, he only had a few months to live, so I'm glad he got to see the success and that we could joke about it together."

CHAPTER 15: THE ORIGINAL AER DOGS

On 3 October 2007, Tony Ryan died after an eighteen-month battle with pancreatic cancer. He was seventy-one and passed away at 3pm in his beloved Lyons demesne in Kildare after receiving treatment in Dublin and Kentucky. "We are proud of Tony's many achievements, of his spirit of entrepreneurship which created enterprise and opportunity for many people in this country and abroad and, most especially, we are proud to have been his loving and loved family," the Ryan family said at the time.

Michael O'Leary said he would miss the "guidance, encouragement and friendship" of his former mentor. "We are all determined that Ryanair will continue to carry his name with pride and distinction," he said.

Tony Ryan was a trailblazer and pioneer in aviation leasing and in low-cost carriers in Ireland, Singapore, the United States and Mexico.

He was proud of Irelandia. In a letter to Anthony Carragher on 22 March 2007, he reflected on Irelandia's journey. "Irelandia is one of the country's quiet successes," he wrote.

"The transfer of low-cost airline technology is an inspired move and much needed by the aviation industry. Irelandia has a reputation and a world audience for such transfers."

Tony Ryan could see how Ryanair had inspired others. "I am amazed how popular the airline sector has become!" he wrote. Tony Ryan also advised against Irelandia taking too many risks as he was concerned about the economic outlook. "This may be a time to be cautious. Trees do not grow to the sky."

In his 2013 biography of Tony Ryan, the historian Richard Aldous said: "What did make Tony exceptional was that he turned the dreams he shared with his generation into reality. That came about not because he wanted to make a fortune – although he was happy when he did – but because he had the vision to see where the market was imperfect, the courage to stake his claim and the tenacity to see the job through. In that regard Tony was the epitome of what it meant to be an entrepreneur."

Tony Ryan was the original Aer Dog. Within weeks of his passing, Cathal Ryan died on 18 December 2007. He was just forty-seven, and also fighting cancer.

Paula Doherty recalls being in New York sitting in a taxi with Declan Ryan after he had lost his father and brother. She was then one of the youngest in Irelandia's team and not as close to him as the likes of Carragher. "He was quiet and I just … I didn't know what to say or do. I honestly don't know how the Ryans made it through those months, to not crumble under that pressure. Maybe Declan did behind closed doors but to us he was strong. Maybe he had to hold it together for the rest of the family and for us," she said.

CHAPTER 15: THE ORIGINAL AER DOGS

Declan Ryan recalled: "When Cathal died in 2007, Mom turned around to me at the funeral and said, 'All the humour in the family is gone.' I said to her, 'Mom that's the perfect line.'" As the middle child, Ryan had grown up idolising Cathal Ryan, who had protected him in school. He had helped him discover his own strengths in trying to impress his brother. Cathal Ryan was the pilot, an original co-owner of Ryanair and investor in Irelandia. His intelligence and sense of fun had been a glue that kept the Ryan family together. In just sixty-six days Tony and Cathal Ryan were gone, and now the remaining dogs would have to hunt without them.

CHAPTER 16: THE GOODE YEARS

Tony Ryan's warnings about the Irish economy before he died in 2007 would prove to be true. The subsequent financial crash was a formative experience for John Goode, who would later become head of the aviation arm of Irelandia. Goode grew up in a small village called Kiltormer in Co. Galway on the west coast of Ireland, the second oldest of five children. His mother Paula ran a post office and a shop with his father, John Sr. Growing up, John Goode's passion was hurling, and his father managed the local hurling team. "We were very competitive and we played in many county finals, usually losing, so that makes you battle hardened," he said.

Goode studied Economics and Social Studies in Trinity College Dublin, and he recalls Michael O'Leary coming in to give a guest lecture about Ryanair. O'Leary began his talk by saying: "I'd like to touch on the idea of setting up an airline. Don't because if you do it in Europe, we will fucking kill you!" Goode had no interest in airlines at the time, but O'Leary's drive stuck with him.

CHAPTER 16: THE GOODE YEARS

Goode wanted to work in investment banking, but he left it too late to apply for graduate jobs, so he got a job in construction instead in Dublin. In January 2006 he moved to London and got another job in the building trade. His boss hired him with the condition that he played Gaelic football for Neasden Gaels, a north London club. A teammate was Barry Comer, the son of builder Luke Comer, and he suggested he apply for a job in Anglo Irish Bank, then seen as Ireland's most dynamic lender. Anglo offered him a job, but Goode's uncle Gearóid Hardy, a lecturer in UCD, suggested he look at a new Dublin finance house called International Securities Trading Corporation (ISTC). ISTC was founded by a former Anglo banker called Tiernan O'Mahony, and it had raised €165 million from high-rollers.

Goode started in June 2006 with ISTC, in a modern office block on Adelaide Road in Dublin 2. He was the youngest in the office, so he ended up helping out wherever he was needed. Investors loved ISTC. It was profitable and tipped to float on the London Stock Exchange.

But, in July 2007 two hedge funds run by Bear Stearns collapsed at a cost of $1.4 billion, sending a shiver through Dublin.

Goode met some colleagues in the pub after the Dublin Horse Show in August 2007. They were a little worried but concluded: "ISTC should be fine." It was the first time Goode considered ISTC was in any risk.

Goode's task was to monitor some of its investments. He watched "blip" after "blip", as pools of loans ISTC had invested in started to default. O'Mahoney rang him for an update.

"Do you want to know in percentage terms or money how much we're down?" Goode asked. "Money, John, money, money, money. I only care about the money," O'Mahoney replied.

There was panic in the market, and ISTC faced ever bigger margin calls. Nobody knew if it was a temporary liquidity issue, or more serious. In October 2007, ISTC announced it was issuing a new bond underwritten by a company controlled by the billionaire Irish financier Dermot Desmond. ISTC said it was now "robust". But then more ISTC investments were downgraded. It had to tell Desmond, and wisely he pulled out. "Once that happened we knew we were going to have to make very difficult decisions," Goode recalled. ISTC's shares on an investor grey market were suspended. Downgrades were now daily.

ISTC tried to do a deal with its twenty-five banks, but it was too late. An examiner was appointed to the business, but then another downgrade happened. "That was the final nail in the coffin for ISTC," Goode said.

The fall of ISTC was the greatest corporate bankruptcy in Irish history, causing a loss of €820 million. It was a record it would hold for only a short time, as all of Ireland's banks collapsed within a year. The experience of ISTC would stand to Goode, in what was ahead.

"I learned in ISTC that there are two types of people in a crisis: there are rabbits in the headlights and there are people who roll up their sleeves and say what can I do today," Goode said.

In March 2008, Goode joined the stockbroker Goodbody. He was twenty-three, and assigned to work with Joe Gill, a respected aviation analyst. Six weeks after he arrived, Gill announced he was leaving to work for rival Bloxhams.

CHAPTER 16: THE GOODE YEARS

Unexpectedly, Goode was asked to report on airlines, an industry he knew nothing about. Goodbody's parent company, a bank called AIB, was on the brink of falling, so it didn't have the time to find anyone else. Goode started writing about airlines during an interesting time. Ryanair had just bought 29.92 per cent in its rival Aer Lingus after a stock market dawn raid.

The European Commission then stepped in and blocked Ryanair taking over its old foe.

Ryanair's share price had been knocked back by the financial crisis. But Goode made a judgement call that it was going to recover quickly, once the market realised how resilient it was in the banking crisis. "People started listening to me a little more after that," he said. Goode loved Ryanair's model, and he was convinced it was made for hard times. His star rose as Ryanair became the second biggest stock in the Irish market. In January 2009, Goode got an email out of the blue that would change his life. It was Declan Ryan asking to meet him for coffee. Joe Gill, his short-lived boss, had recommended him. "I'd never heard of Irelandia," Goode said. "It was only later that day that the name Ryan pinged." Irelandia didn't even have a website, so he went to meet Ryan knowing little enough about him.

John Goode met Ryan and Maurice Mason in Irelandia's office in the Irish Financial Services Centre in North Dublin on a scorching day. He was wearing a pristine suit and tie, but Ryan insisted he take his jacket off. "I was immediately struck by how laid back the conversation was," Goode said.

Ryan asked him what Ryanair should do differently. Goode said it should hedge against fuel and currency movements.

Mason disagreed, but Goode put up a good argument, impressing his interviewers. Goode told them about working in ISTC when it went bust. "We like people who have scar tissue," Ryan said. He offered him a job. Goode had a secure position in a blueblood broker founded in 1876 when his peers were losing their jobs or emigrating. "Declan said something that got me hooked: 'What would you say if I needed you to go to Monterrey for three to six months?'" Goode later had to Google where Monterrey was to find out it was a city in north Mexico. But in the moment he replied: "No problem."

CHAPTER 17: VIVA MEXICO

Irelandia was looking to bring its low-cost DNA to the world, but it knew this needed a lot of money and it was risky without good local partners. Mexico's biggest bus company, IAMSA, knew its business was under threat because of low-fares airlines, but it didn't have any expertise in the area. In Brazil an airline called Gol had been founded in 2001, and its origins were in a conglomerate involved in various transport businesses including a long-distance bus company. IAMSA could see this airline appeared to be growing fast, and it wanted to follow suit.

In May 2005, IAMSA started looking for a joint venture partner to help it develop a new airline that would dovetail into its vast bus network. "Mexico was an obvious market. It was screaming for a good low-cost carrier," Maurice Mason said. "It had a large domestic market that was underpenetrated in terms of airlines. Finding the right partner however was critical." Irelandia was approached by a wealthy young Mexican to start an airline. "He was a nice guy but just a kid with an idea," Mason recalled. Looking at this deal brought Irelandia to Mexico, where it met a broker looking for a partner for IAMSA. "I had spent six months in Mexico kicking tyres," Mason said. "This was the last tyre left to kick so I agreed to meet them." Mason met Rafael Herrera Fernández in Camino Real, a five-star hotel in Mexico City.

Fernández was the president of IAMSA. He reported into a dozen families that owned the group which carried 250 million people a year on buses. "Rafael didn't say a lot but he was steeped in the bus industry," Mason recalled. Also, there was Roberto Alcántara.

Alcántara's father founded a huge bus company called the Toluca Group, which merged in 1990 with rival the Flecha Amarilla Group to form IAMSA. "Our conversation was translated but we fell in love," Mason said. "I felt these guys totally get what we're trying to do."

IAMSA had already tried and failed to partner with various airlines. It had spoken to Brian Dunne, a former chief financial officer with Aer Lingus, about setting up a regular airline with Air Canada. IAMSA didn't know what type of airline it wanted to create yet. Mason came back to Dublin to discuss it with Declan Ryan. "It took a while to warm him up to it," he said. Irelandia's partners in Tiger were investor royalty, but this was different. "Our partner wasn't Singapore Airlines, it was a Mexican bus company. These guys were tough hombres," Mason said. Mexican ownership rules meant Irelandia had to be a minority shareholder, so Irelandia was wary of getting dragged into something they couldn't control.

Ryan agreed to meet IAMSA in New York. "We had their business plan, and it was the same as our business plan in many ways," Mason said. "They had reached the same

CHAPTER 17: VIVA MEXICO

conclusions, but they just needed someone who could do it and wanted to do it."

When Ryan met IAMSA he quickly warmed to them. Intuitively, he could see the combination of a bus company and a low-fares airline was a winning one. Ryan convinced them that low fares was the only way to go. Despite Mexico's share ownership rules, Irelandia was prepared to live with it as it warmed to IAMSA and the opportunity.

In a move out of Irelandia's playbook, Ryan insisted the airline was based in Monterrey, and not Mexico City. It fit perfectly: a point-to-point service using a single aircraft fleet offering low fares to locations it believed were underserved or overpriced. Ancillary products were an important part of Irelandia's game plan but having IAMSA as a partner gave them a new product selling tickets that connected bus journeys directly to planes. "IAMSA was the perfect partner," Carragher said. "It echoed the Gol path in Brazil. We had a great relationship, and the trust and rapport with Roberto (Alcántara) was key." Seeking to launch the new airline quickly, Irelandia brought Conor McCarthy and his team in PlaneConsult in as consultants.

Irelandia also asked Michael Lillis to help it. Lillis had helped negotiate the Anglo-Irish Agreement, a 1985 treaty between Ireland and Britain that was the bedrock to an eventual peace agreement in Northern Ireland. Lillis was well-connected in the region. He had shared cigars and rum with President Fidel Castro in Cuba, and he had worked with Tony Ryan as managing director of GPA's Latin American division.

After GPA went broke, he worked for its new owner, GECAS, repossessing planes in the region. "IAMSA and Mick

Lillis brought the local politics and nous, while we brought the LCC magic," Carragher said.

Despite rapid progress, the would-be airline still didn't have a name. Tony Ryan wanted to call it Ryanmex.

"I had tested the idea with our Mexican guys and they were really excited about it," Mason recalled. A logo was designed and a press release was prepared. It was now time to fly to Mexico to announce the new airline.

But then Tony Ryan rang Mason: "I don't think Dec is going to agree to this." His son had vetoed the name. "It is hard enough for our family to go on holidays with our name in Europe," Declan Ryan said. "We don't want to become famous in Mexico as well."

There was now a scramble to find a name. Tony Ryan and Mason suggested Aerobus, but IAMSA said it had a bus firm already using that name.

"How about VivaAerobus?" Irelandia fired back. VivaAerobus it was.

Declan Ryan recalls flying down to Mexico to see his father for his sixty-ninth birthday in a beach house he was renting in Los Corrales, Jalisco. "In the taxi from the airport, I was talking to the driver, who had better English than I had Spanish, and he started telling me about how he'd flown to the US on an American low-cost carrier," Ryan said. "'How did you buy the ticket?' I asked him. 'I texted my brother in LA,' he replied. And it was like a lightbulb going off. Internet access was an issue in a lot of places and we had to find a workaround. So when we set up VivaAerobus, we made it so anyone could stop by their local Oxxo minimart to get a flight ticket as easily as picking up a pack of Tecate Light beers.

CHAPTER 17: VIVA MEXICO

Karma, the chance encounter, call it what you like. Don't ignore them. Sometimes the best ideas come from the most unlikely sources."

VivaAerobus' first commercial flight was from Monterrey to Tijuana on 30 November 2006. By 11 October 2007, it had carried one million passengers, but then oil prices spiked.

It was making serious losses, and Irelandia was concerned its first chief executive, Mike Szucs, wasn't responding enough. Szucs was a former chief pilot of British Airways' Gatwick operations and an ex-chief operations officer with Easyjet. He was operationally strong and wanted to keep growing despite fuel costs to win more market share. Irelandia didn't want to keep losing money.

"VivaAerobus had already run through its capital," Mason said. "I was angry with Mike as I felt he should have been scaling back more."

VivaAerbus had left it too late to hedge against oil. "Mike knew his stuff and he felt we should absorb the losses. I felt we're losing our shirts," Mason recalled.

Declan Ryan moved to Acapulco, a city on the Pacific coast of Mexico, to get a handle on things. It was no holiday, as Ryan got stuck into the detail of trying to turn around the airline.

"Dec said this is really tough and it may not get better so we need to consider shutting down temporarily," Mason recalled. "We had a strategy to salvage things and turn them around, but we couldn't put any more in." Irelandia wanted to wait for oil prices to fall back before trying to grow again. "But if you shut off the blood supply entirely, it would be hard to resurrect such a young airline," Mason said. "So we were examining all our options."

IAMSA intervened and agreed to cover the airline's fuel bills. It could have diluted Irelandia's shareholding, but it didn't.

"IAMSA said we want you with us. We understand it is frightening, but we will get through this. They were really honourable and they brought us through that 2007–2008 period," Mason recalled.

IAMSA thought long-term. It was worried Irelandia could pull out when it needed its expertise, but Ryan said he would sit tight. In May 2008, VivaAerobus launched a VivaBus shuttle service connecting bus stations to airports, and millions of passengers started to arrive.

In 2009, VivaAerobus established Guadalajara as its second operating base. In March and April 2009, swine flu hit Mexico, killing 400 people. VivaAerobus lost money as a result of the flu, but when rival Grupo Mexicana was forced to suspend operations, it allowed VivaAerobus to enter Mexico City. John Goode recalls going into a VivaAerobus board meeting in 2009 not long after he joined Irelandia and being struck at how optimistic its projections were: "We'd just had a horrible twelve months, and now we were projecting a return to profit. I said to Maurice Mason and Anthony Carragher, 'I don't think we will accomplish this.'"

In September 2009, VivaAerobus launched ten routes out of Mexico City Airport, and because it was taking up another airline's routes it got them at no cost. VivaAerobus was now gaining real traction. In 2011, VivaAerobus's concession to operate an airline in Mexico was extended by thirty years, securing its future.

The Irelandia team were pleased at how well things were going. "There was an emotional connection with Mexico,"

CHAPTER 17: VIVA MEXICO

Mason said. "Declan said to me at one point I could do this all my life (invest in Mexico) and I said so could I. I could see VivaAerobus being a lifetime investment." As its rivals retrenched, VivaAerobus grew. "Hard times are always relative," Mason said. "You have to work out how to endure."

A dozen airlines in Mexico had started and then failed, but VivaAerobus was working. Goode did up a slide with the title the "Grim Reaper" listing all their rivals who went broke. "Thankfully we weren't one of them," Goode said. "But it showed how tough it was."

By February 2012, VivaAerobus had carried twelve million passengers, and in August it relaunched its website.

In May 2013, Monterrey Airport built a dedicated aircraft hangar exclusively for VivaAerobus to support its maintenance operations, and in June 2013 it added a new base in Cancun. Mexico City Airport became a "virtual base" by relocating aircraft and crews to more low-cost Cancun, giving VivaAerobus a crucial cost advantage to its competitors. VivaAerobus was flying.

CHAPTER 18: THE MAX FACTOR

Sitting in KPMG's offices on Harcourt Street in Dublin 2, Steven Maxwell listened to senior partners discussing the biggest deals it had worked on in early 2010. It was the usual big names – firms listed on the stock market in Dublin or multinational corporations. Then, someone mentioned a company he had never heard of, Irelandia, as one of KPMG's top ten clients. "I remember thinking, who are those guys?" Maxwell would later recall.

Tiger had just listed, and the flotation had generated huge fees for the accountancy firm. Irelandia piqued the interest of Maxwell, a Dublin-born UCD graduate who was the son of a telecoms manager. Later that year, Maxwell was asked to help out with the Irelandia audit.

He met Anthony Carragher, but not Paula Doherty, as she was on maternity leave. He remembers the buzz in Irelandia's office, which was then in a restored warehouse on Barrow Street in Dublin 2. Audits are usually boring, but Maxwell recalls being ushered into a room called Rosanna to go through Irelandia's books. The inspiration for the naming of the room

CHAPTER 18: THE MAX FACTOR

was a former Miss World that the developer of the building Johnny Ronan had flown with to Morocco in the middle of the Irish financial crash.

"It was different," Maxwell said. "It didn't take itself too seriously." Maxwell started to move up in KPMG. He worked on the audit of Kingspan, a stock-market-listed insulation board manufacturer. "This got me up to speed on what happened in public companies," he said. It was the summer of 2013, and Maxwell wanted to travel. An old friend was going to Australia so he decided to join him. Then the friend pulled out, so he went down alone. The first two months were spent surfing on Manly Beach. But then his old boss Colin O'Brien, a partner in KPMG, rang him. "Would he interview for a job in Irelandia?" Maxwell had just signed a contract with EY, but he agreed to a Skype call with James Muldowney, who then co-led the aviation side of Irelandia's business along with Tony Davis.

Muldowney wore a t-shirt as he grilled Maxwell. Maxwell felt sure he hadn't got the job. A few days later, Muldowney rang him and told him to come to Mexico for another interview. Irelandia was just about to sign the biggest aviation contract in Mexican history, so Maxwell figured why not.

It was October 2013, when Maxwell left Sydney at 6pm on Sunday for Los Angeles, and then a flight to Mexico City. He was due to arrive at 8pm that night local time, leaving plenty of time before his interview with Irelandia at 7am the following morning.

But his flight to LA was cancelled, so he went to Hawaii, San Francisco and then Los Angeles to Mexico City. His bag was lost, and he was bedraggled when he arrived at the upmarket W Hotel off Reforma Boulevard at 6am. At the desk his debit card bounced, as he'd spent all his savings on new flights. By chance Declan Ryan was behind him checking in. "I'll take care of that," he said. Ryan said don't worry about the interview but make the ceremony at 9am. Maxwell had nothing to wear, so he had to borrow a white shirt from the hotel's receptionist.

As Maxwell approached the 200-metre-long red tezontle façade of the historic National Palace in Mexico City it was impossible not to be impressed. The president of Ireland, Michael D Higgins, was in town to witness the signing of a $5.2 billion contract between VivaAerobus and its new aircraft supplier, Airbus.

The president of Mexico, Enrique Peña Nieto would be there too. Even for a country the size of Mexico, VivaAerobus ordering fifty-two new planes was a big deal. Irelandia had nearly gone with Boeing, but Airbus had come back at the end with a knock-out deal.

Maxwell, hoping that nobody would guess the W monogram on his shirt was that of his hotel, watched as Declan Ryan signed a nine-zero deal with Airbus North America chief executive Barry Eccleston and IAMSA's Roberto Alcántara Rojas.

"We couldn't understand why [low-cost airline] Southwest in the States had never been into Mexico so we thought there was an opportunity. It took us a year to find IAMSA," Declan Ryan told *The Irish Times* at the time.

"It has gone phenomenally well. The Mexican market is booming," he added. Asked for advice for anyone thinking of investing in Mexico he said: "Pick your partner carefully."

Afterwards Steven Maxwell began to be interviewed by

CHAPTER 18: THE MAX FACTOR

each of the Irelandia team in turn. It was Tony Davis, James Muldowney, John Goode and then Alan Bird. Bird was a few months in the job as CFO of VivaAerobus. He'd taken over after Mauro Castillo left the airline when it moved its headquarters to Mexico City.

"Alan is pure low-cost," Maxwell said. "He wanted a number two, a financial controller." Maxwell thought his interview was for Irelandia, but it turned into one for VivaAerobus.

During the trip, Maxwell bumped into Barry Napier, the chief executive of Cubic Telecom, who was having breakfast with Declan Ryan at a function organised by Ireland's inward investment agency the IDA. Napier knew Maxwell's father. "Four or five years later, I remember Dec telling me he asked Barry: 'What's your man like?' And Barry told him: 'I have no fucking idea but his Dad's pretty good.'"

Halfway through the week, Bird asked Maxwell to help out in VivaAerobus for two days. Bird gave him the airline's business model and projections, and asked for a critique.

"I was absolutely wrecked at this point," Maxwell said. He knew nothing about airlines, so felt the only thing he could do was check all the calculations. "I spotted a number of errors," Maxwell recalled. "And Alan was like this is going to analysts next week." Bird now wanted to hire him.

On the second last day of the trip, Irelandia asked him to move to Mexico for five months to help VivaAerobus prepare for an IPO. Bird was under pressure, so it offered to pay Maxwell's salary. "There was no way then I wasn't going to recruit him," Bird laughed.

Maxwell agreed to move to Mexico, but the last thing he needed to do was to be interviewed by Declan Ryan on the Saturday morning before he left.

"Dec's Dad had a reputation for being tough so that is what I was expecting," Maxwell said. Instead, the interview lasted only five minutes. "Dec clearly trusted his team, so he'd made his mind up," Maxwell said.

A week later, Maxwell was living in Mexico City, and a financial controller in VivaAerobus. Deloitte was advising on the IPO, and his job was to supervise it. "I knew how to do it from Kingspan," Maxwell said. KPMG, Barclays and the law firm Cleary Gottlieb were all working with him. "It was typical Irelandia, sink or swim," Maxwell said.

CHAPTER 19: INDIA TO TURKEY

After investing in VivaAerobus in Mexico, Declan Ryan thought about setting up a private equity fund like Bill Franke's Indigo Partners to give him more firepower to take greater risks. But he also knew that raising institutional cash would mean more bureaucracy. Ryan had preferred working with a tight handful of people he trusted. He knew he would have to scale his team dramatically if he was to go down the private equity route. Ryan was conscious that investors had their own motivations and investment time horizons, something he feared could force him to make the wrong decisions. Irelandia had used its capital efficiently by partnering with strong local investors, so he decided against raising money from external investors.

Ryan had created a global platform that was competing for deals in multiple continents simultaneously despite its relatively small size. Declan Ryan thrived on the challenge of running Irelandia, and he was glad his father had witnessed its success after Ryanair.

"I know Tony was glad that I was driven to do something with my life," he said. "I could have hit Nassau, played golf every day in the sun, drunk too much. But I still wanted to prove myself further, to do things on my own terms. I understood I was still in the shadow of Ryanair. People close to the airline like Michael (O'Leary) and (David) Bonderman would give me credit for it. But a lot of people still saw me as Tony's boy, not an entrepreneur in my own right. Sometimes I felt that even if I went public with an airline flying new Concordes across the Atlantic for $99, I would still be 'Tony Ryan's son.'

"Still, I knew the low-cost model could go to other places and I wanted to try it. If Tiger had failed, I like to think I still would have had the guts to give it another go. But once it became a success, there was no going back. Financiers in the industry began queuing up to invest. It was new frontiers all the way. There's not much like the thrill of that kind of success."

Ryan was taking big risks, but he was also cautious. He never gave personal guarantees, as he had seen how this had almost destroyed his father, and damaged friends when Ireland's economy crashed in 2008.

Irelandia was also prepared to walk away from deals if it didn't feel right.

For example, in the mid-2000s, Irelandia was on-and-off travelling to Bangalore in India trying to do a deal with Captain Gorur Ramaswamy Iyengar Gopinath, an ex-Indian army officer.

Gopinath was born in a remote village in the southern state of Karnataka to a farmer-teacher father and a stay-at-home mother. He had founded a private helicopter charter company, and after a trip to the United States in 2000, decided to set up an airline.

CHAPTER 19: INDIA TO TURKEY

"I came back to India possessed by the idea that the common man must fly in India too," Gopinath once told the BBC. In August 2003, Air Deccan was founded with a fleet of six forty-eight-seat turboprop aircraft connecting Hubli to Bangalore. Gopinath grew the airline explosively, tapping into India's huge population until it operated some 380 flights a day from sixty-seven airports through a fleet of forty planes.

In 2005, Irelandia first met with Gopinath to see if it could bring order to his sprawling, yet loss-making, airline by turning it into a low-fares carrier. "Gopi had massively overexpanded," Maurice Mason recalled. "Dec and I and the team went down to see if we could bail him out. But it was like sand, it just kept slipping through our fingers as he had gone in so many directions. Nothing he was doing was economical. They couldn't tell us a single route that worked."

Despite this, Mason liked Gopinath and at one stage the Indian offered Irelandia part of his business for free just to save it. "He says 'Tell you what, I will give you the jet business'," Mason recalled. "I said 'Gupi I can't take it.' I would just have to shut it all down. He said 'Oh don't say that!'" There was no part of Air Deccan that was making money, but it was very popular, so Irelandia decided to take a harder look along with rival Indigo Partners to see if there was the potential to invest. Both sent teams to Bangalore to do due diligence.

"Air Deccan was looking for $50 million. Indigo had around ten guys in suits, while it was just me and Maurice," Anthony Carragher recalled. "We were going through route profitability and everything was red."

"I'm doing back-of-the-envelope figures and I said, in six months $50 million will be gone, and not much will have changed." After half a day, Carragher and Mason called it quits and left for a swim in their hotel.

Suddenly, a flustered Gopinath arrived, catching them in their swimming trunks. He begged them to return to the process. "Not a chance," Carragher told him.

Irelandia turned down the deal, as too eventually did Indigo, but Mason stayed in touch with the likeable Indian.

Two years later Kingfisher, a beer company owned by Vijay Mallya, who also owned Kingfisher Airlines, tried to buy his airline. "Gupi asked me what I should do," Mason recalled. "I said: 'Take it. Take it.'"

Three months later he had sold his airline. "He never listened to me before but he did this time," Mason said. "It was the only offer on the table, so he had to take it."

Known as the 'King of Good Times', Mallya was a great salesman, but not an airline operator.

He closed his airline in 2007, and later his entire business empire went bust. Mallya fled to Britain and, as of 2022, was still fighting attempts to extradite him back to India to face charges of alleged fraud.

Air Deccan was not the only Indian deal looked at by Irelandia. It considered investing in SpiceJet, a low-fares airline founded in 2005, as well as GoAir, later rebranded as Go First, which was based in Mumbai. SpiceJet would go on to become the second biggest airline in India, while GoAir became its fifth biggest airline. Irelandia passed on both deals, but it kept looking at India.

It met IndiGo, a low-fares airline in Gurgaon, a city in the state of Haryana in North India as it prepared to float. The co-founder of the Rakesh Gangwal was in Washington so it

CHAPTER 19: INDIA TO TURKEY

flew to meet him. "It was more to ask to be involved. They had such a fantastic business," Mason recalled.

"They said you can come in, it would be nice. It was pre-IPO and he said this is the valuation we are talking about. I said 'Oh it is very high and it was tough so we just let it go.'"

IndiGo successfully listed in 2015 and went on to become the largest airline in India, with a market capitalisation in June 2022 of over $8 billion.

Irelandia ultimately didn't find a deal in India. It walked away from airlines that became valuable, but equally it had avoided other disasters.

At the same time as India, Irelandia was looking at Turkey, which was seen as getting ever closer to the European Union. Irelandia started talking to a Turkish billionaire called Ali Sabanci about his plans to launch Pegasus Airlines. Sabanci's grandfather Haci Omer Sabanci had started life as a cotton picker before becoming rich from vegetable oil and banking. His family set up Sabanci Holdings after he died, a vast conglomerate in financial services, cement, retail, property and industry.

Ali Sabanci was part of this multi-billion-dollar dynasty, and he wanted to make his own mark by founding an airline. But a deal couldn't be reached. "They loved the Ryan name, but they didn't want our money, and they were certainly not going to be influenced or controlled by anyone," Mason recalled. Ali Sabanci was ex-Morgan Stanley, so he felt he understood the capital markets, and only wanted Irelandia's operational expertise. "Ali wanted advice but not to give up any control," Mason recalled. Irelandia decided the deal wasn't for it. Pegasus would eventually float in 2013 with a market capitalisation of $1 billion.

Irelandia had become a go-to firm for anyone thinking of starting an airline. "People wanted the Irelandia name. They wanted the money," Mason recalled. "But they often did not want the terms and conditions and type of engagement we wanted."

Irelandia wanted to back airlines where it could make a difference, rather than just giving its brand. It was small so it could be nimble, and it understood the start-up airline mentality. But it had to be careful as the amount of capital required to run an airline could quickly become overwhelming if anything went wrong. Irelandia was hungry, but nothing felt right. Then a spiral-bound business plan from Colombia arrived.

CHAPTER 20: THE MEDELLÍN CARTEL

In October 2010, an investor presentation landed on Declan Ryan's desk in Dublin. An executive in Airbus had passed it on to him to take a look at as he felt it looked promising. The presentation was more than 100 pages long and it outlined a plan to create a new low-fares airline in Colombia. Irelandia had already looked at various markets in South America, but it had passed. Charlie Clifton, who helped set Tiger up, had examined a deal with them to invest in a family-owned Brazilian airline called Webjet. Irelandia had passed as it felt it was too difficult to turn into a low-cost carrier. Clifton believed in it, however, and joined its board and became a full-time adviser. He parted ways with Irelandia, and eventually helped sell the business to another local airline, Gol, in 2011.

Along with Brazil, Irelandia had also looked at a Colombian airline being promoted by a group called Aires. "An interesting story but not the right guys," John Goode concluded.

But this new approach was different, combining some experience and a lot of energy.

William Shaw was a tall blond Mexican with a Scottish mother who had worked for British Airways before going to study in Stanford.

In the business school in September 2007, he met Gabriel Migowski, a Brazilian ex-aviation analyst.

Migowski was studying how Avianca had merged with regional airline ACES in the wake of the September 11 attacks. He concluded Colombia was underserved by airlines and started to work on a business plan with Shaw called *La Nueva Aerolinea* or The New Airline.

Despite its rising middle class, they could see there was no real-low fares airline domestically in Colombia. The Medellín–Bogotá route was the busiest route in the region and it was regularly overbooked.

A few years earlier Migowski had worked with Juan Emilio Posada, then Avianca's chief executive, on a plan to bring the airline out of Chapter 11, a restructuring process. Posada left Avianca in 2005 to run a private airport on the northeast coast of Colombia, so Shaw and Migowski asked him to chair their start-up. Posada knew Fred Jacobsen. He had previously run Challenge Air Cargo in Venezuela, before managing Colombia's biggest cargo company, Tampa. The latter had been bought by Avianca in 2008.

The four co-founders raised $500,000 from a group of investors that ranged from Luis Carlos Sarmiento Jr, whose father was a billionaire banker, to Jacobsen's parents.

Investment bank Lazard was hired to prepare a pitch to potential investors for the group, which was now called Fast – an acronym for 'Fun Affordable Safety Tech-savvy'.

Migowski had a contact in Airbus who introduced him to

CHAPTER 20: THE MEDELLÍN CARTEL

Irelandia. "Other than Mexico and Brazil, Colombia was the next standout market opportunity in Latin America," Mason recalled. "In my mind it was better than Brazil as it was more open to investment. The rule of law was good. The founding team was a little edgy, but that was okay.

"Juan Emilio Posada had a track record. Gabriel Migowski was very bright. William Shaw got on with people. Fred Jacobsen was an operations guy. It seemed to be a balanced team."

Ryan, Mason and John Goode flew to Colombia, asking Garret Malone, an Irish businessman who spoke fluent Spanish, to accompany them. Malone was from Cavan and ex-Ryanair so he had valuable operational experience.

The Irish group dined with Posada in his home, following it up with scheduled meetings with various influential Colombian businessmen who were advisers to Fast.

One was Miguel Cortés, the chief executive of Grupo Bolivar, a financial conglomerate in Bogotá. At one point Cortés asked to speak to Ryan alone, where he confided he was worried about the risk of investing in an airline. Ryan told him about Irelandia's track record, and this convinced him.

Ryan asked Mexico's IAMSA to invest too, as he was already thinking ahead to the two airlines working together. Goode and Mason then visited various local airports. The more they learned about Colombia's mountainous terrain and fast-growing economy, the more they liked it. Colombia had been held back by decades of violence caused by narco-terrorists, and both left and right wing militias. It was still a dangerous country, and six years away from a peace agreement with its largest militia, FARC. But the country was going in the right direction, and Irelandia was prepared to bet on it.

Irelandia took a quarter of the new airline, with its remaining shares split evenly between Grupo Bolivar, IAMSA and the four co-founders of Fast with their seed investors.

Back in Dublin, Anthony Carragher and Paula Doherty drew up the contract between the four parties. The four founders (the Fast consortium) were worried about being diluted, but eventually a deal was reached on 31 January 2011. Now it was time to launch an airline. Nobody liked the Fast name, so the airline was rebranded as VivaColombia, a reference to VivaAerobus in Mexico.

A logo was quickly chosen that was based on the colours of the Colombian flag using a series of symmetric circles that was similar to the branding of VivaAerobus.

Now the airline needed a chief executive. Shaw was fiery and understood how to attract headlines, but he had never headed up an airline. "He was a good communicator, but no CEO," Ryan felt.

Posada had led an airline, but Irelandia favoured Jacobsen.

"I wanted to be CEO, it sounded logical – I felt I had already changed my paradigms but you know I didn't have enough experience to contradict Declan," Posada said in *The Viva Effect*, a book about the airline.

"People in Hermés ties cannot run a low-cost airline," Ryan said. He feared that Posada's experience running Avianca would stop him fully embracing a low-cost model. Jacobsen

CHAPTER 20: THE MEDELLÍN CARTEL

was from a cargo background, so he was used to thinking about margins, costs and competition.

Ryan also insisted on a change to VivaColombia's business plan. It could not be based in Colombia's capital Bogotá, where its rivals were. "The last place you would base Ryanair is in Heathrow. So we said: 'You go to Medellín', which is the Manchester of Colombia," Ryan said.

Medellín was a city made infamous as the home city of Pablo Escobar, the late drug lord and narco-terrorist, but it was a place that also took pride in its work ethic. It was the right home for Viva.

CHAPTER 21: MO' EXITS

As he fielded questions from the media about his new airline in March 2011, Fred Jacobsen was surrounded by microphones. Nobody could understand how his new airline could hope to sell airline tickets for just COP29,000 ($16 at 2011 exchange rates). "From the beginning we were born as other low-cost airlines have started: direct flights, standardisation of the fleet, of operations, simplicity," he explained.

Local newspaper *El Espectador* said the airline was "the best-kept secret of Colombian aviation."

In a side room, Declan Ryan sat quietly. Ryan disliked the spotlight, but on the sidelines he told *El Espectador*: "There is still a huge opportunity to sell air tickets at really low prices and that is what VivaColombia is going to take advantage of.

"I am not worried about Aires (a competitor) since it is owned by LAN (the Colombian subsidiary of Chilean group LATAM) and this airline is not a low-cost airline."

El Espectador said that after the press conference the investors in Viva had gone to a local restaurant. "Each one

CHAPTER 21: MO' EXITS

toasted with the liquor of their country, that is, whiskey for the Irish, tequila for the Mexicans and beer and brandy for the Colombians," it said. "But in the end everyone took everything. That is VivaColombia."

After fanfare, it was back to reality. Viva realised that it couldn't offer the low fares it promised. Colombia had a fuel surcharge dating back to the 1990s, which was effectively a tax.

It protected legacy carriers whose high ticket prices could absorb it but held back low-cost carriers. Ryan spoke to the President of Colombia, Juan Manuel Santos Calderón, and argued the tax should be scrapped. More people being able to fly he said would have a multiplier effect. The President helped Ryan to convince the aviation authority Aerocivil, and the surcharge was removed on 1 April 2012. Viva hired its first 150 pilots, crew and support staff, and it trickled five Airbus A320 planes into the market. It was now getting ready for its first flight in May 2012. In Mexico, however, there were other concerns. Tony Davis was spending more time down there for Irelandia, and he asked his old friend Alan Bird to prepare a short report in January 2012. Three months later Bird's report arrived. It found issues with flight performance metrics and some aspects of financial reporting. The report highlighted some issues, but it also said that they could be fixed.

"The classic thing about consulting is there are a lot of deep breaths at the start, but you also offer solutions," Bird acknowledges. As Irelandia was considering the Bird report on Mexico, there was much worse happening. The Colombian airline's chief executive Jacobsen's daughter Dani was diagnosed with a terminal disease. He was heartbroken, and as she weakened, he moved to Texas to be with her.

Posada stepped up to become executive president on 26 February to give Jacobsen time with her as she died. On 4 May, Dani Jacobsen passed away. She was only sixteen. All of the Irelandia team were fond of the Jacobsens and felt for them and their terrible grief. Around this time there was a row between Maurice Mason and Declan Ryan. Maurice Mason wanted to go on a business trip to Airbus to discuss new planes, but Ryan said there was no need. He told Mason he had visited Airbus only a few weeks earlier and didn't think a second trip was justified. Mason said he was going to go. After Dani Jacobsen died, Mason wanted to go to the funeral in Colombia, but he realised he hadn't been invited by Irelandia.

"Dec had a group going to the funeral and I wasn't in it. I knew Fred way too well not to go. I just flew in myself, went to the funeral, and left again," Mason said. "It was a real recognition to me there was a divide."

Ryan and Mason had been working together for nine years, but Mason was always a little apart. He would invest alongside Irelandia and do his own deals. There could be friction.

A few days after the funeral, the row in relation to the Airbus trip flared. "It's just a waste of money at this time," Ryan said in an email on 10 May. It wasn't just the cost that annoyed him. Irelandia's relationship with aeroplane manufacturers was crucial to Irelandia's success. Ryan couldn't understand how he was only finding out days before the trip, which Irelandia was due to pay for, that Mason was going to visit Airbus so soon after he had.

Later that morning, Anthony Carragher sent an email to Maurice Mason, John Goode and James Muldowney, the

CHAPTER 21: MO' EXITS

trio in the Irelandia aviation team. The subject line was: "Communication."

Carragher said he was disappointed that two trips had been organised, with each not knowing of the other. Carragher also complained about a business report about Colombia taking two months to reach him and Ryan.

Mason retorted that the report had been sent on as soon as he received it, and the delay was not his fault. "I take responsibility for the Airbus issue and will cover the costs personally," Mason said. "There clearly is a communication problem and it is not restricted to the IA (Irelandia Aviation) Dublin team."

"It is no longer my concern but I strongly suggest a formal communication of activities on at least a weekly basis if not more frequently."

It was a terse exchange, and not that bad a bust-up. But it grated. The loss of Dani Jacobsen had hit them all hard, and emotions were heightened.

Maurice Mason went into Irelandia's office on Barrow Street later that day. "At this stage I was ready to go," he said. "Dec said 'We need to talk.' I said: 'Let's not. Let's just call it quits.'" Mason got up and walked out. A few days later he came back and cleared his desk. "We needed space between us. He needed to move on. He had moved on. That was it," Mason said.

The next day, Ryan sent a note to Irelandia saying Mason had become a consultant. "This move has been on the cards for a while & more importantly lets him do a lot of other things that he wants to pursue. Being a partner in IA is both demanding and time consuming," Ryan said.

"With Anthony, Mo has been one of the pioneers of IA and

in some ways an 'Unsung' hero of the LCC industry. Look at some of the deals he's been involved with for us – Tiger Airways, Allegiant, both Vivas. He's been in aviation since the 1980s so his knowledge is immense."

Ryan said Mason would be predominantly working on VivaAerobus with a view to an IPO or other capital development. "He leaves IA in a very strong & vibrant state ... For that and many other things I genuinely thank him for his guidance, knowledge and real achievements."

"My work with you and the team you have assembled has been hugely rewarding in every sense of the word," Mason replied. "I greatly appreciate the opportunities and friendships it has brought."

John Goode wrote to Maurice Mason afterwards. "From a personal perspective, I know the learning curve will undoubtedly flatten without your presence," he added. "I think the thing I learned from you that I value most is an improved ability to consider a variety of options/viewpoints regarding a specific topic or situation (I don't think I've ever met someone as good at that as you)."

"While I'm sorry to see you go, I look forward to sending you off on a blockbuster note when we go 4-0 with Viva and make a ton o' money for all involved!"

"It's working with curious people like you that make it all the more interesting and challenging," Mason replied. "We won't be strangers…"

Mason was no longer involved in anything new Irelandia did. He did some work in Mexico, but he got more involved in other businesses. He tried setting up an asset management business start-up with some other Morgan Stanley alumni, but

CHAPTER 21: MO' EXITS

it didn't get going. He invested in other airline companies, and became a non-executive directorship of Flyr, a new Norwegian airline founded by Eric Braathen. But he was now leaving the Irelandia departure lounge.

I am sitting outside a coffee shop at the top of Barrow Street in Dublin 4 interviewing Maurice Mason in July 2021. It is just around the corner from Irelandia's office. By chance, Declan Ryan calls in to pick up his morning coffee. He greets Mason in a friendly way, but doesn't stop.

Maybe he doesn't want to disrupt our interview, but Mason tells me the two are not often in contact.

"I value the years working with Irelandia enormously. I really do. There were far more good days than bad," Mason said. Looking back, why does Mason think it ended the way it did? "I got the sense that Dec thought I was taking things for granted. I was coasting or something," Mason said. "I think there was an accumulation of things that got him thinking." After his success in Tiger, Tony Davis had joined Irelandia to co-lead its aviation division. He had operational experience unlike Mason, and he was close to Ryan.

"My relationship with Tony (Davis) wasn't brilliant at that stage," Mason admitted. "Dec has a thing which I would call a highly distributed intelligence. My intelligence is located in my head and his is in his gut. The gut is always ahead of the game. There is friction in friendship. Sometimes you need to move apart."

CHAPTER 22: A KIDNAP ATTEMPT

Three weeks after his daughter's death Fred Jacobsen was back to launch Viva. For its inaugural flight, its first aeroplane was renamed Dani. William Shaw was the public face of Viva, and he ran cheeky advertising campaigns and used social media to give the airline an irreverent character. One of its early slogans was "Medellín–Bogotá for the price of two hamburger combos…"

There were lots of early issues. A volcano exploded, delaying flights. Its regulator Aerocivil increased the number of hours that pilots needed to fly before being qualified, a move that hurt the new airline. Viva launched a route to the Caribbean coastal city of Apartado only to discover its planes were too big for the runway. Bolivian entrepreneur Germán Efromovich, the largest shareholder in Avianca, predicted it would fail. "You don't have to be a science fiction scientist or a PhD to understand that it is impossible to pay the costs of an air operation, at a bus price," he told a Colombian website called Minuto30. "I don't know how they do it … We should not confuse low-cost with a kamikaze or suicidal company, when

CHAPTER 22: A KIDNAP ATTEMPT

the ticket is sold at a third of its value. To achieve this, you have to suppress services, and make very short flights because they are practically seated in a foetal position."

Despite the naysayers, Viva carried 52,000 people on 400 flights in its first summer. It created a new market by targeting passengers who had previously travelled in local buses called chivas. This earned it the nickname ChivaColombia. The name was intended as an insult, but it became a source of pride.

At Viva's August board meeting Fred Jacobsen, still reeling from the loss of his daughter, said he would like to step down to spend more time with his family.

William Shaw was generating lots of publicity, but he was also falling out with his co-founder Gabriel Migowski who was CFO and responsible for paying for his antics.

Shaw convinced Irelandia to hire a new CFO, but Migowski remained a non-executive director.

This meant that Viva now needed to find both a CEO and a CFO. Jacobsen had led Viva as it carried 400,000 passengers in its seven months, but now Irelandia worried it would lose ground.

Viva needed to find a leadership team quickly. In December 2012, it appointed Mike Szucs, a former VivaAerobus chief, as chief executive. Another VivaAerobus alumni, Ciprian Rodriguez, was retained as CFO.

Szucs was, Irelandia knew, operationally strong, as he had restructured an airline in Spain called Spanair. But after a deal with Qatar Airlines fell through, he needed a new job. He moved to Medellín, but his family stayed in Barcelona.

Rodriguez was an accountant, and prior to Viva convincing him to return to aviation was running a cosmetics business with his wife. While not chief executive, Shaw in many ways acted as such.

He picked a fight with a local jet fuel supplier to try and get a lower price. The supplier called his bluff, causing Viva to scramble to find a new one.

After six months, Viva told Szucs it needed him to spend more time in Medellín. His family didn't want that, so he decided to leave.

Irelandia soon afterwards identified a possible replacement: Barry Biffle, the chief marketing officer of Spirit Airlines in Florida. Biffle was an old friend of Tony Davis, and he was eager to get chief executive experience. Like Shaw, Biffle knew how to attract attention. He had been responsible for an ad campaign for Spirit promoting MILF tickets – which Spirit said stood for Many Islands Low Fares.

Another campaign at the time of the BP oil disaster had the tagline: "Check out the oil on our beaches." The ads were juvenile, but not unlike similar Ryanair campaigns in Europe, they had worked. Biffle was a rising star, and Irelandia wanted him. Ryan told Rupert Stebbings in *The Viva Effect*: "He was the legs of Spirit and the test of that is its decline after he left."

Biffle moved with his family to Medellín and made an impact. He shut down loss-making routes, and moved Viva into profit, a rare achievement for an airline a little over a year old. Biffle decided to set up a second base in Bogotá, because, as he put it: "If you're going to rob a bank, go to the bank."

In December 2013, Viva announced international plans by flying to Lima in Peru. Biffle was having fun; when a pet hamster called Miguelito escaped a customer's handbag and

CHAPTER 22: A KIDNAP ATTEMPT

ran around a plane leading to rumours of rats, he defused the situation with good humour.

As Ryan had predicted, Viva was acting as a catalyst for travel in Colombia. Passenger numbers overall rose by 47 per cent, and Viva had 8.7 per cent of the market, allowing it to pass out Panamanian carrier Copa (it remained well behind Avianca and LAN). As 2014 finished, Biffle invited his in-laws to visit Colombia for a holiday in an old colonial-era town called Santa Fe de Antioquia, a few hours' drive from Medellín.

On their way back to Medellín, Biffle's vehicle was boxed in by other cars at a red light. Motor bikes with pillion passengers carrying guns surrounded his family. They banged on the window, demanding valuables, and possibly wanted to kidnap its passengers too.

A gun was stuck inside the car, and Biffle was told to hand over his watch. It was thrown back at him when the thief realised it wasn't valuable. Just then the lights turned green, and Biffle managed to accelerate into an inside lane and escape.

But he then ran into traffic again, and fearing he was being pursued, Biffle and his family hid in a local college. They waited there until dusk, when a local student guided them home. Viva's Mexican shareholders, IAMSA, were shocked Biffle didn't have an armed guard. Irelandia couldn't be sure if the attack against Biffle was random, or if he had been targeted. Viva hired more security, yet Biffle's wife suspected she was being followed in a supermarket. There were signs also that a criminal gang was tracking them.

Biffle went back to the United States for Christmas, and, even after Davis tried to talk him out of it, decided not to return. "Barry was in the wrong place at the wrong times,"

Ryan said. "If his in-laws and his little kid weren't in the back seat maybe it would have been okay. But his father-in-law told him when he got home that his daughter was not staying in Colombia. Barry didn't have a choice, and I understand why he left."

Paula Doherty also accepted his decision. "Nothing is worth your family," she said. "None of the rest of us ever had these incidents but maybe they saw him as a foreign American CEO and thought he must have lots of money."

Biffle joined Frontier Airlines, which had just been taken over by Bill Franke's Indigo Partners after leaving Viva. He would go on to great success there, but in his ten months he impacted Viva for the better.

"It was a real disappointment," Maxwell said of his departure. "He did a lot of things that set the business up for an excellent year after he left." Biffle left Viva making money and ready to grow. However, it was now looking for its fourth chief executive in less than three years.

Dr. Tony Ryan. © David Levenson

Brian Mulvihill infront of the A320, named Kiltomer 92, at the first delivery of Viva's new fleet in Airbus, Toulouse, 12th October 2018.

The sun sets on the Aer Dogs Viva Chapter.

John Goode signing the Viva Air purchase agreement.

Orla and Steven Maxwell attend a delivery.

Maurice Mason.

Francisco 'Pacho' Lalinde former COO and interim CEO of Viva Air.

Tom Lyons and Richard Aldous.

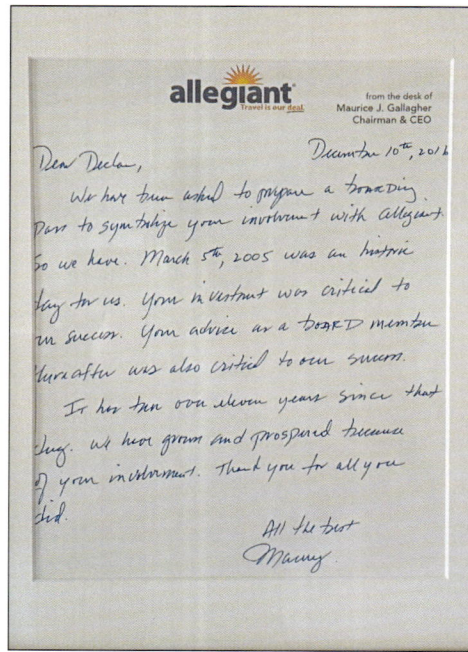

Dear Declan,

We have been asked to prepare a boarding pass to symbolize your involvement with Allegiant, so we have. March 5th 2005 was a historic day for us. Your investment was critical to our success. You advice as a Board Member thereafter was also critical to our success.

It has been eleven years since that day. We have grown and prospered because of your investment. Thank you for all you did.

All the best

Maury

Dated December 10th, 2016.

The Irelandia Team, May 2022 in Miami.

4 Aer Dogs let loose in Miami!

Paula Doherty, former CFO of Irelandia.

Viva Air's inaugural flight, flying over downtown Medellín.

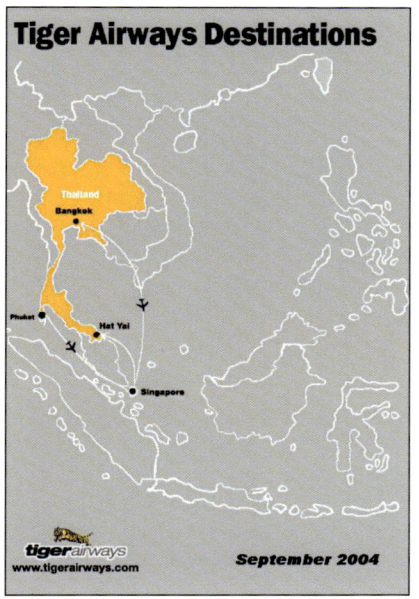 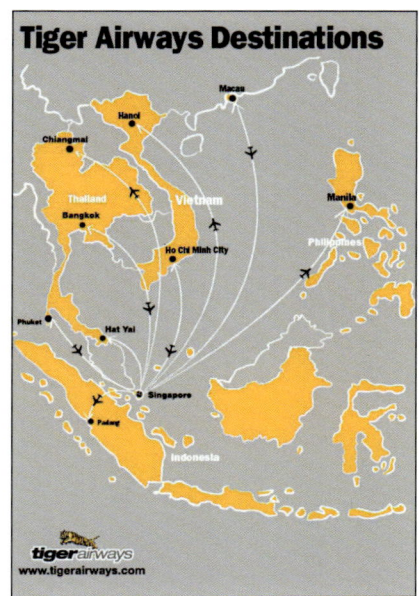

Left: September 2004. Right: June 2005. Tony led Tiger Airways during the expansion of their routes. He had to navigate the challenge that Malaysia and Indonesia wouldn't allow Tiger to fly to its two neighbouring countires - so Tiger had to be creative with their route development.

The passengers on Tiger Airways inaugural flight to Perth are entertained by a professional violin player.

The last GECAS redelivery, post covid, departs Colombia.
This was Summer of 2020 in the middle of Viva's restructure.

Tony Davies on the frontcover of January 2008's issue of Low-Fare & Regional Airlines.

Tony Davies in 2005 - the launch of Tiger services from Singapore to Chang Mai.

CHAPTER 23: THE END (AND START) OF AN ERA

Back home in Dublin, Anthony Carragher was moving on from Irelandia. He had immersed himself in the business since 1996. After seventeen years, he was exhausted. "I was burnt out," he said. "I was never in love with aircraft, but I did love being in Irelandia to bits." He first thought about leaving in 2011 when Ryan had asked him to move to Brazil to oversee a potential investment in an airline called Webjet. Webjet was too risky to invest in, but Irelandia said it would bring its expertise to the table in return for 10 per cent. "They didn't like this offer," Carragher said. "Maybe I was too aggressive, but you can't do crazy stuff without getting well rewarded for it." Carragher told Ryan if they got involved in Webjet he was not prepared to live in Brazil as he had young children. "I love Brazil, but I'm a home bird and would have missed them too much," he said. Carragher stayed with Irelandia until June 2013 when he resigned to become chief investment officer with Staycity, a serviced apartments group that managed a portfolio of thousands of apartments.

Irelandia was an investor in the business, which began in a former U2 studio turned apartment in Dublin's Temple Bar in 2004. The business was co-founded by Tom Walsh before Airbnb existed, and Irelandia had helped it grow internationally. "I led our original investment, so I knew it inside and out," Carragher said. "Declan is always looking for an underserved market that can grow. Short and long stay apartment stays were very big in the US, very big in Asia, but there was hardly anything in Europe. He could see a gap in the market just like he could see with low-cost carriers."

Ryan was prepared to invest in Staycity because he believed Europe would have to catch up with America and Asia. "That was always one of Declan's principles – the world is becoming more connected over time," Carragher said.

The other reason Carragher left was because he had his own ambitions which had been subsumed by Irelandia. He had a first draft of a novel he wanted to finish, and he had an idea for a book about his beloved Liverpool FC. It was time to move on. "Declan is my friend and I am very fond of him," Carragher said. "But I just got a sense Declan too wanted to move on from me, not in a bad way.

"I know Declan probably as well as most people in the world know Declan. Declan loves new things and new people – they inspire him and he gives inspiration to them.

"It was time for John Goode to step up and be the new aviation guy, and it was time for Paula (Doherty) to get her chance as CFO. It was right for everybody. I didn't want to ever do it forever."

He added: "I was in love with the idea of winning but I never wanted to be the boss of a company. I was always happy to be

CHAPTER 23: THE END (AND START) OF AN ERA

the number two. We'd gone all over the world trying to find deals. You'd find people who'd say they were running a low-cost airline, but they were not. Declan knows what it takes.

"If you don't know how to run a low-cost carrier, you'll get it wrong. There can be no let up. Everybody has to think about costs all the time. Everything must be low-cost.

"Every board meeting I ever went to with Declan for any of the airlines ... He was like a dog with a bone on costs."

Looking back, Carragher said he would travel with Ryan for many hours on planes. "He'd spend the whole time thinking, 'where can we chip away at cost'," he said. "The biggest obstacle Declan had in trying to make deals successful was teaching other owners, other investors, staff, that this was the only way."

Irelandia, he said, always looked to set up its base in secondary locations rather than the capital. "You build your fort. You protect it, and from there you grow," he explained.

He added: "Anybody can read a book on how to set up and operate a low-cost carrier. Irelandia had the ability to do it. It takes a maniacal everyday focus on driving down costs and stimulating growth.

"Many other LCCs failed because of the misguided belief that profitable growth could be bought through buying aircraft or landing slots – land grabs.

"Irelandia also succeeded because of the Ryan brand. The surname brought credibility and a belief from banks, institutions, capital markets, aircraft lessors and manufacturers. Investing in airlines is a surefire way to lose money, but the Ryan brand made people feel more comfortable and secure."

Carragher said he had grown to love Tony Ryan, but he said

being his son wasn't easy for Declan Ryan. "Tony's success was underrated," he said. "The people who worked for him are captains in the airline industry, and many have become rich.

"Ryanair may be the most successful airline ever. By successful I mean profitable, sustainable growth. There are bigger airlines than Ryanair but they are bigger because they have the support of governments funding them and subsidising them. "Ryanair fought to grow despite huge kickbacks by governments. Declan in some ways surpassed Ryanair with what he did next. To take that Ryanair model and to build successful airlines in nearly every continent in the world is unheard of."

According to Carragher, Bill Franke in Indigo Partners was the only person who had achieved something similar, but he did it with more money behind him from multiple investors.

"Declan did it on his own repeatedly under the pressure of being his father's son and not failing," Carragher said. "It took a lot of balls, but I never heard a word of fear or worry from Declan."

Did Carragher miss Irelandia when he left? "No," he replied. "I loved it, but I don't miss it. I couldn't do it anymore. I had given it everything."

After Anthony Carragher left, Declan Ryan approached Paula Doherty to see if she would take over as chief financial officer. Doherty was used to leading non-aviation investments by Irelandia, but she had only helped with its aviation interests. Now she was being asked to move into the

CHAPTER 23: THE END (AND START) OF AN ERA

heart of Irelandia by taking responsibility for all three sides of the business: aviation, investment and philanthropy.

Ryan was friends with Doherty, so he asked Colin O'Brien from KPMG to interview her for the role. O'Brien asked if she wanted the role. "I had to think about that," Doherty said. "I was not sure I did want it. It was a lot of responsibility and I had two kids at that stage and I wanted more." The more Doherty thought about it though the more she realised she could do it if she could have certain reassurances. "I had an honest discussion with Declan about it," Doherty said. Ryan asked Doherty what she wanted in life. "A house in the country and horses," she replied. Ryan said: "Stay with me, and you'll get that." Doherty said: "I also want more children." Ryan said: "I knew that. Of course." Doherty felt a weight lift as she was worried Irelandia had such a small team it might prove impossible to take maternity leave. Doherty became CFO at the age of thirty-six. She said she would only do it for four or five years at most. She had two young children and wanted more. Doherty had seen how the role had consumed Carragher and hoped it would not also happen to her.

CHAPTER 24: SHAW BITES THE DUST

Back in Colombia, Juan Emilio Posada now made his move. Medellín was his hometown, and he had run an airline before, so he wanted to be chief executive. Irelandia finally backed him.

"Barry Biffle had the building blocks in place for the medium term, it was impossible to screw it up," Ryan said. To keep an eye on costs, Ryan became chair. The relationship between Posada and Irelandia could shift between cordial and tense.

"Juan Emilio was charming but he was political," according to Paula Doherty. Posada owned a ranch overlooking Medellín and Doherty recalled being invited out there: "He had a horse ranch and after one of our board meetings he invited me out to ride his dancing Spanish horses." The Paso Fino or 'fine step' horses were originally bred to be ridden on plantations because of their endurance and comfortable ride.

Instead, Doherty found herself riding one around a big arena where Posada kept his horses on the grounds of his home. On another occasion Posada invited Doherty, Brian Mulvihill, Steven Maxwell and Stephen Rapp to join him for drinks in

CHAPTER 24: SHAW BITES THE DUST

the bar in his home. He then sent the trio into the mountains with hip flasks of rum and coke to make their way to another bar on top of a nearby mountain.

"Steven (Maxwell) had never ridden a horse before," Doherty recalled. "He went to get on his horse and the stirrup broke. But it was a great craic. We got to the top of the mountain and there was a bar opened up just for us … it was surreal looking at the most beautiful view of Medellín you've ever seen on horseback."

Despite these enjoyable times there was still distrust. "Juan Emilio would have been a great politician," Doherty said. "He wasn't always aligned to our views about strategy or the potential to grow more."

Posada took over as the price of jet fuel rose, and as the Colombian peso devalued by a quarter against the dollar. Meanwhile, Avianca and LATAM were now taking Viva seriously, and attempting to squeeze it on key routes. In June 2014, Viva took its first bookings for Panama. It wanted to fly to Tocumen Airport in Panama City but couldn't get any concessions. The airport was the headquarters of local champion Copa, and Viva suspected this was why it was being blocked. This was denied by all sides, but Viva was still locked out.

Instead, Viva decided to fly out of Pacifico, an old United States military base best known for its role in counter drug operations, on the far side of Panama City. In August 2015, Tocumen Airport took over operating Pacifico. It doubled airport fees and added a new security tax, taking away Viva's cost advantage.

The competition was intense. Copa launched a low fares rival called Wingo in October 2016, which also flew out of

Pacifico. Another airline called Air Panama started flying from Medellín to Albrook, another old US air base in Panama. In May 2018, Viva pulled the plug on Panama as it was losing too much money. Viva was experimenting trying to expand internationally by flying to places like Lima in Peru and Quito in Ecuador, and again facing competition and currency issues.

In Colombia, however, things were better. In its first two years it had carried 3.3 million people, and was growing fast. Shaw was, however, grating against Posada. After the threats against Biffle, Posada had been given a full security detail. Shaw wanted the same as he had the higher profile. "I understand that we are very busy, but we must take care of our main asset – our people," he said in an email in late 2014. Posada did not respond for a week, but then agreed to meet him. Posada said he would protect Viva employees at work, but not in their private lives. This was a jab at Shaw, who liked late nights and socialising. Shaw sent another email claiming: "My safety is of secondary importance."

Viva hired security consultants, who said there was no firm evidence any gang was targeting Viva and advised Shaw to exercise more caution in his private life. Posada wrote to Shaw telling him to follow the consultant's "suggestions". If the Mexican was worried, he said he should lower his profile by making fewer public appearances as the face of Viva. Shaw was not amused. He bought a bullet-proof car and decided to oust Posada. Shaw knew that Posada was paid more than he was, and he was due a bonus. He and other directors pushed for Posada's bonus to be reduced, which he agreed to.

CHAPTER 24: SHAW BITES THE DUST

Shaw then asked for a pay rise for himself. Posada refused, and Shaw resigned on 25 November 2014, giving four months' notice so he would be able to collect his own 2014 bonus. John Goode asked Posada to win Shaw back by increasing his pay, but Posada dug his heels in. By March 2014, Shaw was gone from Viva, but was still advising Irelandia on creating a new regional airline headquartered in Panama. Viva itself had now lost three of its four founders.

CHAPTER 25: MEXICO NOT LOVED IN NYC

The former headquarters of Lehman Brothers in midtown Manhattan is infamous. It was where, at the start of the financial crash, hundreds of workers spilled out onto the streets carrying cardboard boxes carrying their personal items after they were fired.

Declan Ryan was ascending to the top floor, of this building, now occupied by Barclays, in February 2014 as he hoped to float his Mexican airline VivaAerobus. John Goode, Steven Maxwell, Maurice Mason, James Muldowney and Paula Doherty all accompanied him. Doherty was seven months pregnant with her third child Amelia, but she wanted to be there. Juan Carlos Zuazua, the chief executive, and Alan Bird, the chief financial officer, were also there. Roberto Alcántara, the chair of Irelandia's business partner Mexican bus company IAMSA, was also with them along with some of his team.

Ryan and his entourage came out of the elevator and headed towards their assigned executive meeting room on the thirty-eighth floor. As they walked in, they noticed bottles of champagne and glasses being wheeled out. It was not a good sign.

CHAPTER 25: MEXICO NOT LOVED IN NYC

A Barclays banker advising them closed the door. He came straight to the point: "My recommendation is to pull this."

VivaAerobus and the Irelandia team had been working for six months on a road show trying to raise support for an IPO on the Mexican stock exchange. Many of the meetings went well, but now the market was not prepared to invest in the Mexican airline. The dream of a fourth successful IPO was dead.

Only months earlier it had all looked so promising. Irelandia was coming up to seven years into its investment in VivaAerobus and had made a profit in five out of those years. It wanted an exit and its Mexican partners IAMSA were supportive of a flotation. In June 2013, Irelandia, IAMSA and its adviser held a meeting on the project, code-named Victoria, to prepare for an IPO.

More than thirty people were at the meeting. In a note to Irelandia afterwards, James Muldowney said its advisers Barclays and Raymond James felt they could position VivaAerobus as the "most proven ultra-low-cost carrier" that "had coped well with lots of issues over the last few years and was always able to come out profitable". The airline, he noted, had "good growth (but conservative) and increasing margin in the future".

VivaAerobus's chief executive Juan Carlos Zuazua did a "great job," Muldowney added. Zuazua, known as JC, was only in his early thirties, but he was three years in the job and talented.

Alan Bird was less charismatic, but Tony Davis advised his grey hairs were important. Bird had the technical know-how to field any tricky financial questions, and he had experience from preparing Tiger for the market. Mason agreed: "We can get (Alan Bird) there with coaching. With such a young CEO leaves us too thin."

Rival airline Volaris, which was backed by El Salvadorean billionaire Roberto Kriete, had successfully gone public in September 2013. VivaAerobus felt it had to follow.

Volaris, like VivaAerobus, was founded in 2006, and it had raised $345 million from investors in an IPO that was three times oversubscribed.

International equity was pouring into Mexico at a greater rate than ever before. In the first seven months of 2013 Mexican companies raised $9.1 million more than any previous full year, according to Thomson Reuters.

Irelandia felt that VivaAerobus needed access to the capital markets to keep up. VivaAerobus was smaller than its rival, but Irelandia felt it was better managed and more profitable. "We had, we estimated, an over 30 per cent cost advantage over Volaris," Steven Maxwell said. "Volaris was saying it was the low-cost carrier in Mexico when we were."

Barclays, HSBC and Raymond James were advising on the IPO and on 24 January 2014 an offer memorandum for investors was completed. This memo provided an insight into what VivaAerobus had achieved.

Since launching in November 2006, VivaAerobus had grown from a fleet of two to nineteen aircraft. In 2012 it carried 3.8 million passengers, and it operated forty-nine domestic routes and had one route to the United States.

"We have the lowest cost base of any publicly-traded airline in the Americas, with the lowest cost per seat and the lowest stage-length adjusted cost per available seat per kilometre for the twelve months ended September 30, 2013," VivaAerobus said in the memo.

"We focus on operational simplicity and profitability, based on a business model that has been successfully deployed by other ultra low-cost carriers, such as Ryanair and Spirit."

VivaAerobus's focus was the growing Mexican market of price-sensitive leisure passengers visiting friends and relatives around the country and business travellers working for small and medium enterprises who wanted the convenience of flying but at a low price.

Having IAMSA as an investor gave a "strategic advantage" as it offered its hundreds of millions of bus passengers the option of flying in over 300 bus stations, the airline said.

Passenger traffic for VivaAerobus had grown at a compound annual growth rate of 24.3 per cent from the end of 2007 until the end of 2012. At the end of 2012, revenues reached $300 million and net profits stood at $19.1 million.

VivaAerobus had a stable senior management team combining youth and experience. The deal Irelandia had negotiated with Airbus was another edge, as Irelandia knew it was one of the most competitive in the world. From 2014 on VivaAerobus was transitioning away from its old Boeing planes to fifty-two new ones from Airbus. The first twelve of these were fitted with the best existing engine options, with the forty after that kitted out with a new even better engine option. All fifty-two planes were more fuel efficient, and they could carry 180 passengers, 21 per cent more than Boeing.

Irelandia felt VivaAerobus was compelling. On 20 December 2013, Muldowney gave an update on the investor roadshow saying the airline had a "differentiated story" because of its IAMSA link and provable low-cost model. Muldowney said the challenge was "capacity additions" by rivals that could lead to overcapacity in the market. Another problem was

VivaAerobus was floating for less than a $1 billion, so was too small for some investors. Finally, he said the "sustainability of low costs" could never be certain, if fuel spiked. Muldowney said it was still "full steam ahead". On 5 February 2014, Muldowney updated again saying: "Roadshow continues to go well…" A big Mexican pension investor called Afore XXI Banorte had agreed to take 10 per cent of the offering. "Book is building … local demand for the stock," Muldowney added. The pension funds offer was below the price he wanted, but its advisers felt pricing would move up nearer the IPO. Perceptively he said: "Markets are still choppy/mixed with volatility edging higher."

Juan Carlos Zuazua went to an investment banking conference in New York, and again shone, according to Steven Maxwell. "I remember sitting beside a US investor, and JC got up and did his presentation. He was brilliant, and the guy said to me: 'When can I invest? This is perfect,'" Maxwell recalled. "It was all really encouraging but as we were putting things together I could see the latest numbers coming in were slowing."

As the IPO neared, Alan Bird recalls taking a private jet to carry out a series of tightly scheduled meetings with prospective investors from huge investment funds in New York, Boston, Chicago and San Francisco. A final meeting in Los Angeles was cancelled, so Bird suggested to JC, half in jest, they go to Las Vegas. "What we're doing here is gambling so we may as well go," he said. "I was sorting of testing JC, but I'd have gone if he'd been up for it."

JC didn't want to go, so they flew back to Chicago instead. Bird recalls going out with JC that night to a karaoke bar.

CHAPTER 25: MEXICO NOT LOVED IN NYC

They were optimistic. "We were in a good place. We thought the presentations had gone well," Bird said. "There was a lot of interest, but looking back we never closed. Nobody committed to investing in the same way they had in Mexico."

In February, markets worsened. VivaAerobus had two-thirds filled its book with Mexican investors. It had local retail interest too, but it now couldn't convince North American institutional investors.

Volaris' share price had fallen in the months after its flotation. VivaAerobus had a better story but it was seen as similar by investors thinking of where to allocate capital.

"Volaris had gone out with a big upsell message when it floated," Maxwell said. "We had a similar story. We were partners with Mexico's largest bus company with 10,000 buses transporting 260 million passengers a year. Our bus partner was better and we had a lower cost base, but for investors they didn't see how we were different."

Bird agrees with Maxwell. "We were naïve," he said. "We had gone on a roadshow telling everybody Volaris, who had gone public, were not as good as us. We ended up talking down our price by talking Volaris down," Bird said. Financially, VivaAerobus's growth was slowing. In part this was seasonal, while the airline was also waiting for new planes to push it on. But for investors only looking at the numbers, it was enough to make them hesitate. Finally, the float at $400 million was too small to attract big investors prepared to take on more risk. VivaAerobus was only listing in Mexico, so investors didn't want to get caught in a relatively small company not listed in the US. "We just weren't big enough for many investors in the United States," Bird said.

VivaAerobus could have still floated, until in February 2014 Russia invaded and seized control of Crimea in Ukraine. This really spooked all investors in emerging markets. Mexico was ten thousand kilometres away, but it was seen as the same thing within the investment community.

"The way that big American fund managers think is that they have an exposure to America, an exposure to Europe and then there's an emerging market bucket ... possibly a China bucket," Maxwell said.

"If something is going squeaky somewhere in emerging markets like Ukraine, they get nervous about all emerging markets. That was a big reason why the IPO failed and we just couldn't get the valuation we needed." Doherty felt Barclays had taken things to the wire without much warning that the float might fail. "To pull it so late was disappointing," she said. "It was a big shock. Barclays should have called it sooner."

After the float failed the Irelandia team and their Mexican partners went for a meal in a New York steakhouse. Irelandia was despondent as they'd worked so hard on the deal. Muldowney had led it, and he left Irelandia a few months later. "We had a great story. We had a great partner," Maxwell said. "We'd gotten a great aircraft deal from Airbus that was the best we'd ever done. Our initial response was 'How is something that's happening in Ukraine affecting Mexico?'

"I just don't think we grasped how much Mexico was seen as an emerging market versus Ryanair which was in London, Tiger in Singapore, and Allegiant in New York."

Roberto Alcántara, however, was pragmatic. His experience was in private companies, and he knew VivaAerobus was a good business that complemented IAMSA. He took a

CHAPTER 25: MEXICO NOT LOVED IN NYC

generational approach to investing and knew VivaAerobus would come back. He rose from his chair and addressed the room. Alcántara spoke from the heart, about why they all could be proud of VivaAerobus. The IPO had failed, but they still had a great airline.

"It gave a lot of lift to the Irelandia team hearing him say that," Maxwell said. "Dec was still disappointed, but we knew we had to brush it off." "It hurts when an IPO fails - in your pocket, for sure, but also to your pride," Ryan added. Paula Doherty remembers feeling unease. "I remember thinking the Mexicans didn't want to do this," she said. "They wanted to keep the airline private and in the family."

Instead of an IPO, JC, Bird and Juan Soto, the airline's head of treasury, worked on raising an $80 million credit line. It was roughly what they'd hoped for in the markets, but with an interest rate.

"We needed the cash to pay for aircraft orders and fleet transition" Maxwell said. VivaAerobus raised its fresh debt borrowed against revenue generated from credit cards. IAMSA had used this form of finance many times before, so its reputation and experience ensured the raise went smoothly. While the IPO hadn't happened, VivaAerobus was now in a solid position.

CHAPTER 26: A NEW AIRLINE FOR LATIN AMERICA?

After VivaAerobus closed its debt financing, Steven Maxwell and John Goode moved back to Ireland. VivaAerobus hadn't floated, but it was stable and it was growing. "There was no time for wallowing in self-pity," Paula Doherty recalled. "We came home and we weren't that down about it. Declan just said, 'Right, what do we do now?'"

John Goode was moving to the fore in Irelandia's aviation arm, and was considering whether to co-invest with Icelandair, Iceland's flag carrier airline, to launch a new low-fares airline. The move was a response by Icelandair to a new rival, Wow Air, which had been founded by a local entrepreneur called Skúli Mogensen. Goode and Maxwell were asked to assess the deal.

"Dec had met the guys from Iceland and they were really good operators," Maxwell recalled. The plan was to connect Europe to North America via Iceland; Irelandia asked to take a minority stake and bring its low fares expertise to the table.

"It just didn't work because of the pricing," Maxwell said. "We were getting fares as low as $320 return (to the United

CHAPTER 26: A NEW AIRLINE FOR LATIN AMERICA?

States) but Aer Lingus at the time was pricing $400 return to the US. We felt why would anyone bother stopping off in Iceland just to save an extra $80?"

In a prescient move, Irelandia advised Icelandair not to do it. By early 2019, Wow Air had filed for bankruptcy because it couldn't make its low-fares model work.

Maxwell and Goode were now a team, reporting into Ryan and trying to source the next deal. In 2014 besides Iceland, they also looked at Oman, Brazil and Pakistan. Both Goode and Maxwell were taken with Pakistan where they looked at investing in AirBlue, an airline founded by entrepreneur Tariq Chaudhary. Airblue was located on the twelfth floor of the Islamabad Stock Exchange Towers, and it wanted to start a low-fares airline linking Pakistan to the Middle East. "John and I both felt the airline was absolutely brilliant," Maxwell said. Pakistan was dominated by the state-owned flagship carrier Pakistan International Airlines, and they felt AirBlue was ready to challenge it. It had ten aircraft and was already profitable, making almost $1 million profit per plane a year. "Ryanair would make $2 million per plane per year. AirBlue had a way to go in some areas, but it was in pretty good shape," Maxwell said.

Chaudhary flew to Dublin to meet Irelandia in its office on Barrow Street. Ryan came into the meeting and said: "Look, I've been thinking about it last night, and it's just not of interest to us." He then excused himself and left. Goode and Maxwell tried to reignite talks, but Chaudhary asked if there was any point. "I don't think there is," Maxwell admitted. "Sorry for making you travel the whole way."

Goode and Maxwell were annoyed as they felt AirBlue was an

183

opportunity. Ryan simply responded: "Look, I'm a reasonably successful guy and we've all been lucky. I don't want to spend my time in Islamabad." Ryan asked Maxwell and Goode to take a macroeconomic look at particular geographies to see where they should go next rather than responding to inquiries. "Looking at airlines at a macro level for us means looking at things like population, an emerging middle class, internet penetration, wealth per capita, GDP growth. It was all data you can find sitting at your desk," Maxwell said. "Then you take it to the next level and find out what the low-cost carrier competition is like and other methods of transportation such as buses, boats and trains."

Irelandia prepared a list of potential countries, and then whittled it down to ten. Four of them were in Latin America. "One market was Peru, one was Argentina, one was Central America as a region and finally there was Brazil," Goode said. It was from this research that Irelandia had a new idea. Why not set up a new low-cost airline serving the entire region?

This could help solve the predicament it was in after the VivaAerobus float failed. A new Latin American airline would mean greater scale and a diversity of revenue streams. It would also be capable of a listing in New York.

Irelandia asked IAMSA for its views. It didn't commit to investing or not. But as it had previously been prepared to back Viva in Colombia, Irelandia felt it was likely to follow its lead. Ryan asked a senior executive in Copa Airlines, Joe Mohan, to lead this new business. Mohan wasn't enthusiastic so Ryan sent Tony Davis to try and convince him over dinner in El Salvador in the summer of 2014. Mohan liked the vision, but he turned it down as

CHAPTER 26: A NEW AIRLINE FOR LATIN AMERICA?

he felt Pedro Helibron, the leader of Copa, might retire soon, opening up a vacancy. Helibron, however, was going nowhere, so Mohan came back to Irelandia. In September 2014, he joined the proposed new airline group to be called Viva Latinamerica. Davis and Mohan were now working on this new business as well as VivaAerobus.

Irelandia set up a meeting with IAMSA for Mohan to outline its plan for the new airline group but this was cancelled. A meeting was rescheduled for early 2015 on the fringes of two large airline leasing conferences that take place in Dublin annually. To Mohan's surprise he discovered that IAMSA wasn't very interested in Viva Latinamerica. It wanted to focus on Mexico, where it felt it still had considerable room to grow if it made the airline less low frills and targeted the middle class.

Ryan realised that Irelandia had taken Roberto Alcántara and IAMSA's support too much for granted. "I was drinking too much of my own bathwater," he said.

Irelandia felt that if it could show IAMSA its vision, it would come on board as a partner later. It set up a Panamanian structure for the new airline and built a small team. In April 2015, Stephen Rapp, an airline consultant, joined as a business development officer along with Ruben Gonzalez, who had worked with Mohan in Copa. The plan now was to start the new airline by taking control of Viva in Colombia by buying out its local partners who owned just over 50 per cent. It would also buy out IAMSA if it wasn't prepared to back the new group. The Irelandia team had remained friendly with William Shaw, and he was now working for them on Viva Latinamerica.

In 2014, VivaAerobus made a loss of $7 million, a loss that was largely attributable to rising fuel prices. It was not a massive number, but it came as growth in the Mexican economy was slowing down. IAMSA became concerned about limiting its exposure to Colombia and other risky markets. Roberto Alcántara had just bought a stake in Spain's Prisa, publisher of its biggest newspaper, *El País*, and Irelandia felt maybe he was distracted.

But as time went on it became evident IAMSA had no interest in getting involved in a new regional airline. Nor was it interested in investing in Panama. This created a problem for Irelandia. It was a 49 per cent minority shareholder in VivaAerobus, but it had no exit route. IAMSA was the obvious buyer, but it didn't need to buy them out. Irelandia knew if it tried to force a sale, the Mexicans could low-ball the price.

Declan Ryan discussed the situation with his team in Irelandia and Paul White, his lawyer in A&L Goodbody. Irelandia had a contractual option that could force IAMSA to buy it out, but it was not easy. "We gamed out a few scenarios," White said. "But there wasn't an easy solution."

Howard Millar wasn't sure what was next. It was twenty-three years after he joined Ryanair, a business that he loved and always hoped to lead. Millar had served as deputy chief executive of the airline for more than a decade. By 2014, Ryanair was generating revenues of €5 billion and €523 million in net profit. Millar was fifty-four and due to sign up to another five-year share option stint with Ryanair. "Michael

CHAPTER 26: A NEW AIRLINE FOR LATIN AMERICA?

[O'Leary] had said to me in 1993 or 1994 'I'll be out of here in two years if things work out.' He said numerous times then after that he was going to retire … but it was always two years away!" Millar said. If he didn't become chief executive of Ryanair before he turned sixty, Millar thought it would never happen. He pressed O'Leary to see what he was thinking. O'Leary had said in 2013 there was "no reason for me to leave" before 2018. Ryanair was implementing its new AGB (Always Getting Better) strategy and it had re-energised the airline and its share price. "We were a warmer, friendlier, cuddlier airline, and Michael got very enthused by the whole thing," Millar said. "We'd just been through a difficult period where Ryanair was being aggressive and nasty – but we did AGB and then we launched a much easier to use website and the whole thing changed."

O'Leary said he had no end date in mind as he was enjoying leading Ryanair and he asked Millar to stick with him. "I said: 'Look, I think I'm going to move on Michael,'" Millar said in response. O'Leary respected his decision but insisted he become a non-executive director of the airline.

"Things are good between us," Millar said. "But it was time to move on. I wanted to do something for myself." Millar announced he was leaving a full-time job with Ryanair in June 2014 and Declan Ryan rang him not long afterwards asking him to meet up for a coffee. "Would you do a bit of advisory work for me in VivaAerobus," Ryan asked. "Yeah, why not?" Millar replied.

VivaAerobus had failed to float earlier that year so Ryan asked him to take a look at what the airline needed to do next now it was staying private. "My role was to look critically at the business and see what could be done to improve things," Millar said. "I worked closely with Alan Bird who was the CFO to help him bring in the Ryanair methodology." He also worked closely with 'JC'.

"Juan Carlos was a relatively young guy, very talented but still finding his feet," Millar said. He flew back and forth to Mexico reviewing its cost base and finances to make sure it was aligned with how Ryanair did things. Millar, as CFO, was in charge of Ryanair's IT division for twenty years. O'Leary wasn't enthusiastic about the internet early on – he referred to techies as "the ponytails". Millar, however, had eventually won over his chief executive and the board, and the internet powered Ryanair to ever greater revenues. One of Millar's big tasks was to oversee an overhaul of the reservation systems used by VivaAerobus and Viva Colombia. He spent close to a year working on this and became a trusted sounding board for Ryan and others in Irelandia. Unusually, Irelandia issued a press release to the Irish media on 2 December 2014 announcing Millar's arrival. "I'd heard Declan wanted to do another Ryanair and he wasn't going to compete with Ryanair in Europe, so it had to be outside of Europe," Millar said. "The circumstances that have enabled Ryanair to be successful, such as European open skies, weren't really available in many other places, so I didn't know if it would work. What I did know was it was going to be a fight whatever he did as we'd seen in Ryanair what it was like taking on state carriers and vested interests."

Eleven years after they'd last worked together, Millar was now part of Ryan's team again. He wasn't working too much during these early years on Irelandia's bigger strategy to set

CHAPTER 26: A NEW AIRLINE FOR LATIN AMERICA?

up a new regional champion, but he was where he was at his strongest – digging into the details, and questioning every line of spending to try and build a better airline.

After so many decades with Ryanair, Howard Millar had no need to take on new adventures in Central and South America, but he grasped it and as the years went on got more involved. "Why did I help Declan when he asked? Why did I then start a new aircraft-leasing company? It gets into you," Millar said. "I won't say it's addictive but there's always something going on in aviation."

"Declan could have walked away into the sunset, taken his money, but what would he have done?" Millar said. "Life would have been dull. Declan likes the challenge, the complexity, the achievement at the end. Of course, money is a motivator but it's not the only one. It is success, the achievement of starting an airline and taking it from here to there. What else was he going to do? Start an IT firm? Play golf five times a week? This is what he knows. This is what he does. This is what we do."

CHAPTER 27: TENSIONS RISING

Viva touched $100 million in sales in 2014 in Colombia and made a $5 million profit. The previous August Irelandia had started to bill Viva for its services for the first time. Posada and Migowski disagreed with this at board level, and argued the airline wasn't strong enough yet. From Irelandia's point of view it felt that it was being forced to actively engage with day-to-day operations in Viva and that its expertise was being taken for granted. The Colombian shareholders grouped together to block any further payments to Irelandia, underlining to the Irish firm that they were not in control. Tensions were now mounting. Viva had five new routes, three of which were overseas. Irelandia was eager to do more. It felt Viva was ready for expansion; its website had taken off and was taking 80 per cent of bookings, cutting out agency fees. Yet the Colombians dragged their feet about expanding.

In February 2015, an engine caught fire in a Viva passenger plane, forcing an emergency landing in Bogotá. "A light of fire was seen and I thought the plane would crash. People were

CHAPTER 27: TENSIONS RISING

stunned, frightened. We asked the hostess what was wrong, but she was more scared," recalled passenger Sebastian Jimenez, to Colombian daily *El Tiempo*. The Viva plane touched back down within seventeen minutes but footage of the flames spread on social networks.

The source of the accident was the failing of a ball bearing within an engine. No blame was apportioned to Viva when the local regulator completed its investigation report, and Viva's team under captain Carlos Flores had responded expertly. But it was a scary moment.

Irelandia always prioritised safety and the incident further soured relations with Posada, even if it was not his fault. Posada now knew about Irelandia's plans to form a larger group, and he feared his shares would be diluted. He didn't want to take any risk in Viva that would contribute to this happening.

Posada wanted to be bought out, and other Colombian shareholders in the airline started to think similarly.

"We had five aircraft at the time, but we needed to get up to ten," Maxwell said. Posada said there was no rush to get there. Viva was profitable and Irelandia was worried its competitors would figure out on which routes it was making money. "We needed to spread out our route network because if you're too focused on just a few profitable routes, then rivals will challenge you on those routes, and suddenly you're in trouble," Maxwell said. "We wanted to invest in more routes. But routes aren't instantly profitable and it can create negative cash flow as they bed in. This could affect the short-term valuation of the airline, so there was tension."

Maxwell added: "There was a stage when we were going to board meetings, and thinking what's the point of this? We were saying we need to add new aircraft, start new routes. We need to do this. And they were like 'No we don't want to do that. It adds risk to the business.'"

IAMSA backed Irelandia, but the Colombians were united. The board was deadlocked.

In March 2015, Tony Davis resigned from Viva, and he stepped down as chief operating officer with Irelandia but remained on its advisory board. Davis wanted to spend more time at home in England. "I'd spent eight years in Asia and was going to South America more frequently than I would have liked," Davis said. "We had a lot of challenges in South America and it was obvious I was going to have to go down there a lot more." Davis had gotten skin cancer, which was treated successfully, but it had caused him to think. "It felt like I was burning myself out," Davis said. "The other thing that happened in 2015 was I turned fifty. I realised I wasn't prepared to be a road warrior anymore." Tensions meanwhile were coming to the boil at the board in Viva.

Bernardo Carrasco, a banker from Grupo Bolivar, decided to put his concerns on record. "The disrespectful and offensive phrases only generate confusion and misunderstanding amongst the operational team of the company," he warned.

"I carefully ask that the differences that may exist between shareholders or members of the board of directors are only discussed between ourselves in order that whatever the eventual ownership structure of the company, whether it remains in the hands of the actual shareholders or those of new owners, that the said company is in the optimum condition and its development is not just sustainable but the success it has been up until now."

CHAPTER 27: TENSIONS RISING

Irelandia now wanted Posada out. Goode and Carrasco clashed at board meetings, and relations got so bad that after a board meeting in August 2015, there wasn't another full one for seven months.

Despite this, Viva opened its first routes from Colombia to Miami in December 2015.

Irelandia wanted more routes to the US, but it was still an achievement given all the regulatory hurdles it had to overcome. Viva's passenger numbers were up 10 per cent, but the Colombian economy was turning. Inflation was at 7 per cent. Fuel prices were rising. The peso was weakening against the dollar. It was not a good time for its boardroom to be at war.

"We had three or four board meetings that were very negative," Maxwell said. It was clear to Irelandia that it needed to buy out its Colombian partners in Viva, and increasingly it wanted to sell out of VivaAerobus too.

After the IPO of VivaAerobus failed in February 2014, Irelandia had pushed ahead with its plan for Vivalatinamerica with the backing of IAMSA. Alcántara had backed Irelandia on an IPO for their Mexican airline despite his reservations, and he did not complain when IAMSA picked up its half of the multi-million-dollar bill for the failed float. IAMSA had invested money in helping Irelandia set up a Viva group structure in Panama. From being very close, the relationship between the Irish and Mexican partners was starting to fray.

Near the end of 2014, Declan Ryan hit the roof when a maintenance issue emerged in VivaAerobus. Questions were being asked about a member of its maintenance team carrying out checklists of work. When Juan Carlos 'JC' Zuazua discovered this he fired the staff member and informed Mexico's aviation authorities about what happened.

Despite Ryan's fondness for 'JC', he felt the airline had to take an even harder line on the issue. Roberto Alcántara considered 'JC' like a son, and while he took the issue seriously, he was more supportive of his talented chief executive. Alan Bird felt the same way about 'JC,' as did the rest of the executive team.

IAMSA may have suspected that Irelandia wanted to replace 'JC' with Joe Mohan. Mohan had been interim chief executive of VivaAerobus before and was now working for the Irish firm in Panama, where he was setting up the new Viva Group structure called Viva Latinamerica. Alcántara was adamant he was backing 'JC', so Ryan was overruled by his Mexican partners from taking more severe action. This was a rare disagreement between the Irish and Mexicans

Irelandia didn't feel, however, that its relationship with either IAMSA or 'JC' had been damaged. Ryan felt he had made his point, and he was prepared to move on.

"One thing I love about Roberto is his loyalty," Ryan said. "JC is like his prodigal son. We'd hold an annual performance review every year over dinner with JC, and I would say to Roberto: 'What would you give JC out of ten?' He would always say 'nine'! JC would always then look across at me and say laughing: 'Don't do it!' as I'd always say 'six'!"

CHAPTER 27: TENSIONS RISING

The partnership was patched up. But then another issue emerged. Bill Franke's Indigo partners approached Irelandia in November 2014 to see if it would be interested in merging VivaAerobus with Volaris where it was a shareholder. This offered a back-door to the stock market as Volaris already had a listing, so Irelandia was interested.

The following month Ryan told Alcántara of the approach, and said he was interested in pursuing the deal. Alcántara said he would take over the conversations with Volaris.

Months went by and from Irelandia's perspective nothing seemed to be happening, adding to its frustrations as it wanted to push ahead with Viva Latinamerica with or without IAMSA.

In the first quarter of 2015 Irelandia was also negotiating a new booking software deal for Viva and VivaAerobus. To get a better deal the two airlines were working together on procurement, with Tony Davis acting as pointman. This was a really important contract as it governed not just bookings, but also ancillary revenues like car hire and hotel bookings. As the process came to a close VivaAerobus insisted it had a separate legal contract with Navitaire. It refused to sign the contract otherwise. Irelandia felt this was a signal from its Mexican partners that they were going to go it alone in the future. Irelandia was now very frustrated.

In May 2015 Irelandia and IAMSA were due to meet in Toulouse at the headquarters of Airbus to receive the first of the $5.2 billion of new aeroplanes they had ordered. A board meeting was also scheduled. It was a big deal for the airline. Alcántara and all his team had worked hard to get to this point, as had Irelandia.

But Irelandia didn't show up. The Mexicans felt insulted by the non-appearance of their Irish partners.

On 4 September 2015 Irelandia engaged Barclays to find a buyer for its stake in VivaAerobus and work with it on preparing a sales teaser. Barclays prepared a list of potential investors, including Volaris, and Irelandia told Alcántara and IAMSA this was the route it was pursuing. It wanted to push on with Viva Latinamerica.

A friendship and business partnership that had brought a new airline to life in Mexico was now close to sundering.

CHAPTER 28: THE NIGHT OF THE LONG (MEXICAN) KNIVES

Brian Mulvihill remembers flying into Mexico City for the first time after being in Colombia to visit Viva. It was mid-October 2015 and the then twenty-eight-year-old was going to meet Ireland's co-investors IAMSA for the first occasion. He'd spent the weekend in New Orleans with some of the Irelandia team attending an American football game, and then watched Ireland lose to Argentina in the Rugby World Cup in an Irish bar. The meeting had been switched from the bus operator's downtown office to a hotel on the outskirts of the city. As the plane landed, Ryan told Alan Bird and Joe Mohan not to go to the meeting. Bird, who was CFO of VivaAerobus, recalls thinking this was unusual. Ryan said it wasn't a meeting about operations or finances so he wasn't needed.

Now the Irelandia team – Ryan, John Goode and Mulvihill – were driving out to the Intercontinental Hotel in San José, a suburb of Mexico City, for VivaAerobus's next board meeting. It was dusk when their car reached the hotel. Juan Carlos 'JC' Zuazua came out to meet them. The chief executive of

VivaAerobus was especially close to Goode. Like him, he was in his thirties. The duo had worked hard together on the airline.

"It was as if he wanted to intercept us to let us know this ain't going to be pretty," Mulvihill recalled. "He didn't say it in so many words, but you could see it in his demeanour."

The four men got into a lift and hit the button for the twelfth floor, where their Mexican partners were waiting for them. When Irelandia sat down at the table, it was clear to them that IAMSA was not going to deliver good news.

Sitting beside Roberto Alcántara was Gian Carlo Nucci. Nucci was a former chief executive of American retail giant Walmart in Chile, who was now Alcántara's senior adviser. Irelandia didn't know him.

Nucci led the meeting. He was blunt. The thirty families behind IAMSA did not want to invest in a new airline group based in Panama called Viva Latinamerica. "We will not go beyond Mexico and Colombia," he said. This was a big change of direction, Irelandia felt. IAMSA had been looking at entering the Colombian bus market, but this too was now off the table.

There was a notable amount of Spanish used in the meeting, which Goode could only pick up parts of, but the Mexicans knew Ryan was unlikely to understand much of it.

Alcántara was not prepared to discuss things further, IAMSA had decided. "They had gone along with our charade of setting up a Panamanian structure," Mulvihill said. "But now they were telling us no way. We are Mexicans. We are not interested in taking big risks outside Mexico."

According to Ryan, "It was dark, a heavy meeting. It was one of the tensest meetings, with the exception of a few with Mick O'Leary, I have ever been at. The mood music was like

CHAPTER 28: THE NIGHT OF THE LONG (MEXICAN) KNIVES

you were going to your funeral party. They made it clear we were in their country."

IAMSA were the kingpins of transport in Mexico. They were proud of their Mexican heritage and didn't want to go outside its borders. Colombia was a relatively tiny investment for them and they had decided they didn't want to go any deeper by setting up new airlines across the region.

Ryan told Alcántara the Viva model could go much further. He argued it could work outside Mexico and Colombia, and that IAMSA could be part of creating a valuable new airline group. Nucci reiterated that IAMSA was out. The tensions of the previous year were now all near the surface.

Eventually, realising there was nothing left to discuss, Irelandia got up and left. The Irish group drove back to their hotel in Mexico City and had a beer at the bar. "It felt like we'd been knived," Ryan recalled. "They had left us in no doubt they were in charge. Don Roberto was sitting directly opposite me but said almost nothing."

They speculated about what had caused the break-down between them and their Mexican partners.

Ultimately, Ryan felt the real reason for the fallout was that IAMSA didn't want to take on the risk of leaving Mexico, but there were certainly other reasons to fall out.

It was also a sign of the strength of VivaAerobus that it was no longer reliant on Irelandia to survive.

Irelandia's expertise was needed to launch the airline and close the multi-billion Airbus deal, but as the business matured the Mexicans now felt more confident that they could go it alone.

Ryan recalled visiting Boeing with IAMSA in the early days of the airline. "I brought them in to see the boss man in

Boeing, who didn't know that much about them," Ryan said. "I said these guys order 1,000 buses a year, and the way to treat them is like they order 1,000 aeroplanes too. Boeing was great with them, very respectful. We had helped IAMSA up the curve [teaching them how to run an airline], but now they were there."

From the Intercontinental Hotel meeting on, the relationship between Irelandia and IAMSA seriously deteriorated, despite so many good years. "The relationship was gone," Mulvihill said. "We felt they were telling us we are taking over VivaAerobus."

Back in Dublin Irelandia had a meeting to decide what to do. The team all believed that it was possible to create a pan-Latin American low-cost carrier.

"Dec has an exit time horizon in most deals," Mulvihill recalled. "He gets itchy feet. The IPO hadn't come off in Mexico, and Colombia was looking like a rock star. We felt we'd proven the concept and it was now time to roll it out across Latin America."

It wasn't an easy thing to do, as both airlines were now worth hundreds of millions of dollars, with a pipeline of planes worth around $10 billion.

Barclays found two potential buyers of Irelandia's shareholding in VivaAerobus. The investment bank found Advent International, a global private equity investor founded by Peter Brooke, and Nexxus, a mid-market investor that specialised in investing in Spain and Mexico.

"They were both going to bid for our stake," Paula Doherty recalled. "We wanted them to bid against each other but the Mexicans didn't want this."

CHAPTER 28: THE NIGHT OF THE LONG (MEXICAN) KNIVES

The private equity firms walked away as they had no wish to become minority investors in a business they couldn't control. Irelandia realised it was stranded.

Mulvihill had only started working with Irelandia's aviation arm a few months earlier, but he knew the strain between Irelandia and IAMSA had caused a seismic rift. Like Maxwell, his background was in KPMG, where he'd advised Irelandia on its tax affairs. After four years he'd left the accountants in 2012 to work in tax and financial planning for GE Capital, working through residual loan books across Europe for the finance giant.

"It was a great experience but it wasn't massively exciting," Mulvihilll said. His interview with Declan Ryan for a job in Irelandia lasted five minutes, after he'd first been put through his paces by CFO Paula Doherty.

Ryan's first question was: "When are you fucking off? Everyone your age is going to Australia."

Mulvihill was playing intercounty Gaelic football for Tipperary, so he told Ryan he wasn't going anywhere. Ryan grew up in Tipperary, so he knew the commitment required to play on its senior team. Mulvihill would get a train from Dublin to Tipperary after work to go to training and back, a round trip of more than five hours. Mulvihill's response was enough for Ryan, who trusted that he had what it took.

Irelandia hired him to work in the investment side of its business. "We were tidying up a few things, selling a few properties in Poland we still had. Winding down Growcorp," Ryan said. Irelandia had a stake in a glass maker called Tipperary Crystal which it bought in 1998, and then sold a majority stake to a former bookie called Declan Fearon.

Mulvihill was tasked with selling its remaining shares. "Tipperary was no longer making glass in Ireland so it was less interesting to Declan," Mulvihill said. "It was a brand, and it needed a new home." Mulvihill also worked on managing Irelandia's investment in a tech venture capital fund called Frontline. When Tony Davis stepped back from Irelandia, John Goode took over. He brought Mulvihill across to be his number two. Mulvihill had enjoyed the investment side, but he was now in the deep end, as Irelandia tried to work out what to do in Mexico and Colombia.

CHAPTER 29: A WILDCAT AND GUATEMALAN CHICKENS

Irelandia began the process to buy out Viva's Colombian shareholders. It needed to reach a price with them first before it could try and find an exit from VivaAerobus, where it now saw its only way of getting a return being to sell its stake. Miguel Cortés, the chair of Grupo Bolivar, and a billionaire, led the negotiations on behalf of the Colombian shareholders. Declan Ryan and Paula Doherty had led the initial negotiations, before passing it to Steven Maxwell to work on the finer detail. It was hard to get all the interested parties to agree to a deal, as there was a stack of private investors, each of whose approval was required, as well as the four original founders and Grupo Bolivar itself. Cortés had helped put the original syndicate together, and he was respected by all sides. Colombia is hierarchical, however, and it is possible Cortés felt it was a snub by Irelandia to appoint Maxwell to complete the negotiation as he was only in his late twenties, despite the flecks of silver in his dark hair.

In any event, Steven Maxwell believed he finally had a deal with Cortés and all the Colombian investors, so John Goode flew to Colombia to close it.

Goode and Maxwell met Cortés in a lawyer's office in Medellín expecting to ink a deal. Instead, Cortés insisted there was still a lot outstanding and wanted to continue negotiations.

Goode asked for a moment to talk to Maxwell in a corridor outside, where he asked him why these elements were not already agreed. "They were John," Maxwell responded.

Goode went back into the room and lost his temper. "Guys this is crazy. We've been trying to get a deal done for months and now we're going backwards. Are you playing a joke on us?" Goode asked as he raised his voice. Cortés stood up. "I don't do shouting," he said, before walking out.

Cortés was one of the most powerful men in Colombia, and the only person capable of getting a deal across the line with the Colombians. He had taken over Grupo Bolivar from his father in 2011, and he had played an important role in the peace process in Colombia, as well as employing 21,000 people.

Now, Irelandia had just fallen out with him, as he felt he had been insulted in front of a room full of lawyers. Goode thought about running after him to apologise but knew it would be seen as weakness. The Colombians went silent.

At the next board meeting of Viva, however, Grupo Bolivar's representative raised the issue. "John, you called Miguel Cortés a joke. This is shameful behaviour," he said.

Goode asked Ryan if he could reply. "You can, but take a breath and be calm, be calm," Ryan advised. "I never called Miguel Cortés a joke," Goode said. "But I felt what was happening was a joke. I should not have raised my voice, and I apologise."

Cortés later accepted the apology. He diplomatically avoided

CHAPTER 29: A WILDCAT AND GUATEMALAN CHICKENS

allocating blame. A deal which had come close to being derailed was now back on.

Irelandia started negotiating on two fronts in Mexico and in Colombia. Irelandia knew it needed a new partner if it was to create a new airline group in the region. It asked Barclays bank to find someone. Two potential parties emerged. The first was the private wealth office of David Bonderman, Wildcat Capital Management. Bonderman liked Ryan from their years in Ryanair and afterwards, but he was no pushover. He offered to buy half of Viva Colombia at cost and said in return he would finance Viva Latinamerica.

Irelandia's aviation advisory board met up in New York in April–May 2016 to discuss what to do. Ryan was living in New York at the time, and he organised a brainstorming session in the Met Museum. Bonderman's reputation could not be dismissed. Irelandia spent a few days trying to figure out what to do. In the end Ryan went around the table and asked Howard Millar, Tony Davis, Paula Doherty, Maxwell and Goode what they should do. Everyone turned down the deal.

"We didn't feel it valued the business appropriately," Maxwell said. "We wanted some uplift in valuation because of all the work we had done, but we weren't getting any."

"I wasn't in favour of it," Millar said. "They're private equity so they want to get in on the ground floor and maximise return. They want the cheapest price they can get." Millar felt, along with his other directors, that the price was too low.

Irelandia had hired Joe Mohan. It had a corporate structure in place in Panama. It felt both airlines were positioned to grow. So, it turned down the American multi-billionaire. "We were just a bit up our arse," Ryan reflects today. At the end of every year Ryan made a point of listing his mistakes, and not taking the Wildcat deal would in time take its place on the list.

"We thought we were worth more than we were. Things were going great so we turned the deal down. It was a tight deal but in hindsight we should have taken it as David Bonderman would have helped us with an IPO," Ryan said. "I should have pushed back on my board stronger but I went with it. I should have gone with my gut more but we thought we could get a better deal and we were doing well at the time."

Millar said it was impossible to tell if Wildcat would have worked out. "You can't drive the car looking out the back window," he said. "Who knows what they would or would not have done if they invested."

Another potential investor then emerged in the form of a billionaire Guatemalan dynasty. The family ran a conglomerate called Corporación Multi Inversiones, which employed 40,000 people. It was a huge player in the chicken industry, processing over four million chickens a week. Cousins Juan Luis Bosch Gutiérrez and Juan José Gutiérrez led the business. They ran a chain of chicken food outlets called Pollo Campero, which began in Guatemala and had over 400 locations in Latin America, the United States, Europe and Asia. Over the decades the family had diversified into other restaurant chains, and founded CMI Capital, which invested in other sectors like property and renewables.

"The operation they ran was incredible," Maxwell said. "The main portion of their wealth was from fried chicken but they had diversified into lots of other areas, like energy.

CHAPTER 29: A WILDCAT AND GUATEMALAN CHICKENS

They were making tonnes of money and were looking for new places to invest, like airlines."

Irelandia went down to have dinner with the cousins in one of their homes, a fourteen-storey property with stunning views of Guatemala City, and a cinema downstairs. "It was impressive like a Bond villain's lair," Maxwell said. The next day they flew by helicopter to their lakeside country home to discuss things more. "They basically owned a good chunk of Guatemala," Maxwell said.

The Gutiérrez brothers took Irelandia by armed guard to a barrio to see one of their chicken shops. "It wasn't that big but it was doing big sales," Ryan recalled. "It was shifting a lot of chicken."

Later, Irelandia was taken to meet the then president of Guatemala, a former comedian and actor called Jimmy Morales. It was that kind of trip, as Irelandia was flown by helicopter from destination to destination. The cousins were likeable, but they had a few demands.

"Number one they wanted us to set up in Guatemala, which we weren't sure about, and then number two they didn't want to exit the company," Maxwell said.

"They wanted to hold onto the investment forever, while we wanted to IPO. It just didn't make sense to us." In a decision Irelandia would later regret, it decided to continue to go it alone for the moment and try to buy out Viva by itself then find fresh investors afterwards if required.

Irelandia's early bids were still being rejected by its Colombian shareholders for Viva Colombia, and months of offers and counter-offers then ensued. Simultaneously, Irelandia was trying to do a deal in Mexico City with its bus king partners.

CHAPTER 30: THE MEXICAN WAVE

P aula Doherty gazed down the long meeting room table in the offices of the Mexico City-based law firm Mijares, Angoitia, Cortés y Fuentes (MACF). There were thirty people around the table; Doherty was the only woman. She was directly facing the suave and formidable corporate lawyer Pablo Mijares Ortega. Mijares was a founding partner of MACF and considered one of the best merger and acquisition lawyers in Mexico. He was on home turf representing the bus giant IAMSA against the Irish airline investment firm Irelandia.

It was about a year since Irelandia had encountered IAMSA in the Intercontinental Hotel in a meeting that became known internally in the Irish firm as the 'night of the long knives'. Irelandia had tried to find a buyer for its stake in VivaAerobus, but nobody was prepared to bite by taking a minority stake in an airline that IAMSA wanted total control of.

This had forced Irelandia back to where the Mexicans knew they would arrive: selling out to IAMSA. Irelandia's advisers', Barclays, valued VivaAerobus at a price in the hundreds of

CHAPTER 30: THE MEXICAN WAVE

millions if it was sold on the open market. But IAMSA didn't want that. It wanted to hold on to the airline so it wasn't prepared to pay as much as Barclays said. IAMSA was prepared to sell its stake in Viva in Colombia to get Irelandia off the pitch in Mexico, so this formed part of negotiations too. "We realised the only way out was for them to buy us out. They wanted us out and we wanted an exit," Doherty said. "But we disagreed on price."

Irelandia had a shareholders agreement with IAMSA governing a change of control in VivaAerobus but it didn't have strict provisions around drag-along rights that would have allowed Irelandia to force IAMSA to join them in selling the airline, if they were not prepared to match the highest bid in the market. This hadn't stopped Irelandia from trying to force a bid process by talking to private equity funds and other potential investors, but IAMSA had shot these attempts down.

Doherty knew Irelandia had made a mistake by not ensuring it had this in place when it signed its agreement with IAMSA in 2005. Back then relations were so friendly Irelandia hadn't considered enough what would happen if it fell out with its partner.

It hadn't also considered the dangers of signing a contract written in Mexican law in Spanish – where IAMSA were the experts – rather than American law and in English, which Irelandia was more familiar with.

"It was a big lesson," Doherty recalled. "Going in you have to have a clear exit strategy and an ability to drag our partner with us if we got an offer to buy the airline.

"There was something soft in our agreement about this but it wasn't enough to enforce. We didn't foresee that they wouldn't have the same vision and they might not want an exit."

Mijares was fully aware of the strong position he was in negotiating on the behalf of his client IAMSA. He was charm personified but Doherty could see he was not going to give an inch. Going into the meeting she knew there were a number of outstanding issues besides the price which could derail any deal.

Irelandia was represented by a Mexican law firm called Garrigues, but Doherty felt they weren't strong enough to match MACF. She had brought John Goode with her to the meeting and also Johnny Hanna, a tough tax partner from KPMG Ireland, as she knew this would be an area Mijares would try to get the upper hand on.

Mijares began by saying IAMSA wanted to be bought out of Viva in Colombia first, before agreeing to sell out of Mexico. This was a clever tactic, as it would force Irelandia to come up with $25 million in cash to buy out its quarter stake in Viva. IAMSA could then use this money to help it fund the takeout of VivaAerobus, while knowing that it was out of Viva.

Goode said Irelandia could explore that, thinking it was better not to get stalled on this issue so early on. Doherty, however, wouldn't budge: she wanted both airline deals to be done simultaneously. As CFO she intimately knew Irelandia's cash position. She knew it was asset rich but not cash flush, so it needed the Mexicans to pay it first.

"We can't do that. It has to be at the same time," Doherty insisted. Only minutes into the meeting, there was already a row.

Doherty wanted IAMSA to buy Irelandia out of VivaAerobus first, and then Irelandia would commit to buy the Mexicans out of Viva in Colombia immediately afterwards. Doherty had advised Ryan only to buy out IAMSA from Viva, but Ryan said no.

CHAPTER 30: THE MEXICAN WAVE

"I suggested we keep the Colombians in Viva and just get the Mexicans out," Doherty said. "We could get somebody else in to take out the Colombians later on. I was thinking like an accountant about cash and risk. But Declan just wanted them all out at that stage. They wouldn't move on anything and he wanted to get going." This added another layer to negotiations as Irelandia was not just trying to do a deal with IAMSA but also the other shareholders in Viva, namely Grupo Bolivar and the founders of Viva and their backers. This was the context Doherty and Goode had to constantly consider as they tried to deal with IAMSA.

The meeting in Mexico City went back and forth as Mijares knew getting Irelandia to take IAMSA out of Viva first would give him an edge, but eventually he relented and agreed to do the deal in the order insisted on by Doherty.

The next issue Mijares raised was that the Mexican Revenue might seek to impose a withholding tax on the deal as Irelandia was a non-resident company. He said IAMSA wanted to hold onto 25 per cent of the sale price in case this occurred. Officials from the tax authority in Mexico at the meeting nodded that this could be an issue. Irelandia had tax advice from KPMG that it couldn't be, and it feared that if it left 25 per cent of the sale price in Mexico, maybe it would never get it all back. "There was massive ructions over this," Doherty said. "There was no way we were leaving millions behind in Mexico."

Hanna of KPMG then intervened, just as Irelandia wanted him to. "Johnny literally attacked the Revenue guy," Doherty recalled. "He was like, 'Do you want me to take you outside to explain this? There is no withholding tax issue.'" The Mexican Revenue official backed down. To ensure the matter wasn't raised again, Hanna suggested a deal structure that was even clearer in terms of taxes. "There was never a risk we would have to pay that tax," Doherty said. "But this new way of doing it ensured we got the deal moving again to the next issue."

Negotiations went on for hours, as both sides drilled into the finer details of the sales. "I was just sitting there thinking I'm the only female in this room of thirty guys, and they're all looking at me ... so don't mess it up," Doherty recalled.

After hours of talks, Doherty went for lunch with her team and then flew home feeling a deal was now close. The price was still being thrashed out, and there would be a row later on around anti-embarrassment clauses to ensure IAMSA didn't flip the airline on at a profit too soon after the deal closes. However, Doherty thought a lot of progress had been made, and she went back to Dublin thinking Irelandia was close to an agreement. But progress was slow, as the agreement was done through Spanish and English, requiring both sides to be sure that they were clear of the meanings of every word governing the deal. For Doherty, a lesson for Irelandia was to ensure future contracts were drafted in New York in English and drafted by a leading law firm. "We had written the agreement using Mexican law, when we should have done it in America," she said.

As the deal went through draft after draft, Doherty noticed that IAMSA's lawyers were inserting unmarked changes to the agreement without flagging them to Irelandia. "I told Pablo you can't do this," Doherty recalled. "He told us it was an oversight, and blamed a junior in his office." Doherty didn't buy this and told him firmly not to allow it to happen again.

"I made them go back to the original draft and start again. We literally had to go through the document with a fine-tooth

CHAPTER 30: THE MEXICAN WAVE

comb," she recalled. "You had to constantly make sure they weren't trying to get one over on you." The deal was now becoming bogged down in detail and acrimony. Doherty felt it would never have been done without the chief executive of VivaAerobus Juan Carlos 'JC' Zuazua. Doherty developed a backchannel to JC where the two could communicate with each other openly about the difficulties each was facing.

"The Mexicans trusted JC, and Declan trusted me, and we trusted each other enough to get there," Doherty said. "I remember being in Scotland at my niece's communion and being on the phone to JC in my room at two in the morning. It was just 24/7. Declan was saying just get it done. He wanted out. He wanted to move on."

As lawyers on both sides took umbrage with each other, Doherty and JC were pragmatic, and kept trying to find solutions.

"It was pulling strings from the top that finally got it over the line," Doherty said. "We wouldn't have gotten there without JC."

Finally, a price was agreed with IAMSA for both VivaAerobus and Viva, but it still needed to get its Colombian shareholders in Viva across the line too. Steven Maxwell and Brian Mulvihill were sent to Medellín to carry out due diligence on Viva, and figure out what price to value the airline at. It was tricky as Juan Emilio Posada took away Maxwell and Mulvihill's access to Viva's numbers. The wily Colombian also insisted that he was in attendance at any meetings with senior staff. But Posada was busy as chief executive, so the Irish duo found it hard to get stuck in as he wasn't always free. "It was really hard to do due diligence," Maxwell recalled. "Thankfully, Mully [Mulvihill] had good relationships with staff members which allowed us to meet them for a beer to back channel, speeding things up.

"Dec and the Colombians had shaken hands on an overall valuation of Viva in early 2015. But then relations deteriorated and we found around $20 million of adjustments downwards." The Colombians would not sell out at this adjusted price and hung on for more. They offered to buy out Irelandia's stake instead, but this wasn't taken that seriously.

Eventually, the Colombians agreed on a price that was a mid-point between the value both sides put on the airline. The Colombians didn't want to give certain warranties to Irelandia, so they accepted the price had to come down. Ryan negotiated the final parts of the deal with Miguel Cortés in the McDonald's restaurant in Medellín Airport. It might not have been the most salubrious of surroundings, but the airport was a fitting place to sign the deal. On 19 July 2016, Irelandia agreed to buy out Grupo Bolivar and the other Colombian shareholders, including the airline's four founders. The money wouldn't arrive, however, until IAMSA bought out VivaAerobus.

In December 2016 in Dublin, Doherty sat in her office on Barrow Street, Dublin 2 waiting for the money to arrive from Mexico, before transferring control of its stake in VivaAerobus to IAMSA.

"We had to make sure everything happened at once as nobody trusted anybody," Doherty recalled. When the time arrived for the cash to hit its bank account nothing happened. "I rang the bank, is it in yet? No," Doherty said. "Then I rang JC saying the money hadn't arrived. JC said: 'Well they said it's left.'"

CHAPTER 30: THE MEXICAN WAVE

Irelandia waited. Then its bank rang: the money was in.

Irelandia's team was too tired to cheer. "It wasn't a massive moment," Doherty said.

"We'd been living in the office ... and now we had the cash." There was a pool of money too which Irelandia gave to its team as a reward for their work or in return for the shares they held in the airline. "We had a whole load of work to do," Doherty said.

On 9 December 2016, the deal was closed. IAMSA sold its 25 per cent stake in Viva to Irelandia. Ryan had put $5 million into Viva originally for his 25 per cent stake, but now he was in much, much deeper.

On the same day IAMSA sold its shares in Viva, it bought Irelandia's 49 per cent stake.

"I don't think we got a fully fair price for VivaAerobus," Doherty reflected. "We got a good return but we felt we might have gotten more if we had sold in a fully competitive process." Irelandia had made a six-and-a-half-times return on its money in Mexico, but it felt underappreciated. The Mexicans for their part felt pushed to do a deal. There was a chill, as the joint venture ended.

"The relationship was damaged. Declan and Roberto held each other in such high regard ... and they still do but they might not rush to do deals together again."

Doherty added, "We had worked all the hours. But we knew we could do it. The high of getting what you set out to do ... there's no better buzz, but we were exhausted".

CHAPTER 31: A CHANGING OF THE DOGS

Brian Mulvihill turned thirty as Irelandia took full control in Colombia and exited Mexico. Irelandia went for a meal and pints in Harlem, New York in October 2016 when it knew most of the deal was done. "We were tired but happy," Mulvihill said. "I'd moved to Colombia with Steven Maxwell to do the due diligence, while John Goode decamped to Mexico to wrap up the loose ends there. We felt ready for what was to come." There was also a changing of the guard in Irelandia as 2016 moved into 2017.

Tony Davis and Paula Doherty had stepped back from executive roles to join Irelandia's advisory board. Doherty was spending time with her young family, while Davis was in Cuba looking at it as a potential new market for Irelandia. Relations between Cuba and the United States were thawing for the first time since its revolution in 1959. American President Barack Obama had visited Cuba in March 2016, where he told staff at the newly opened US Embassy that, "It's a historic opportunity to engage directly with the Cuban people." The potential for a low-fares airline linking Cuba

CHAPTER 31: A CHANGING OF THE DOGS

and the United States was obvious. "American tourists were starting to go back to Cuba, and we had some expertise in South America so it made sense to look," Davis recalled. In January 2017, everything changed when Donald Trump took office as the forty-fifth President of the United States. He took a much harder line, killing any hope of launching a new airline in Cuba. "The political liberalisation we were hoping for didn't happen. Ultimately, domestic US politics made it impossible," Davis said.

Back home in Dublin as 2016 ended, John Goode was head of aviation in Irelandia, and Mulvihill became his number two. Mulvihill had just gotten engaged to Aedín Curtin, and was ready to step up. Steven Maxwell became CFO in January 2017. Maxwell and Mulvihill were twenty-nine and thirty respectively, while Goode was only thirty-five.

When she became chief financial officer Paula Doherty had always said she would put her family first before Irelandia, but this wasn't always possible. Doherty gave birth to her third child, Amelia, in June 2014 but she was back taking meetings with Irelandia after four weeks.

She loved her job but to do it required starting early in the morning in order to rush home at lunchtime to mind her children. "My Mum was handing me a screaming baby to feed as I walked in the door," she recalled. "I was like 'What am I doing? What am I doing?'"

It was full-on juggling everything. "I'd go home and try to do stuff with the kids but I was always back on the laptop in the evening," she recalled. Colombia and Mexico were six hours behind so she would work late into the night. "We were trying to sell one airline, and take control of another at the same time. I would have burnt out if it had gone on forever," she said. It wasn't just doing airline deals. In 2015, Doherty had worked on a string of other exits as Irelandia pruned its investments.

After trying to take greater control of its apart-hotel investment Staycity, Irelandia instead decided to cash out. Doherty ended up negotiating against her old mentor Anthony Carragher as they haggled over the price. "It was a bit weird going up against him," she laughed. Irelandia also sold its stake in an English rugby team called London Irish, and it sold off some of its bioscience interests. After Tony Ryan died, he left the Village at Lyons in Kildare to Declan Ryan. This was a redeveloped village that had been burnt down by English soldiers in 1641 before Tony Ryan had restored it as high-end restaurants, boutiques and guest houses along the banks of the Grand Canal in Kildare. No expense was spared as Ryan installed a 400-year-old fireplace from France, and a model of a plane he owned was hung over a fine wooden bar. Ryan also restored a tiny parish church dedicated to the Blessed Virgin Mary, which was to become his final resting place after he died. Ireland's financial crash had caused Declan Ryan to convert the venue into a popular wedding venue managed by his friend Philip Rock, but it was a low-margin business that required a lot of work. Ryan sold the business in 2015 to businessman Barry O'Callaghan, who owned the Cliff House Hotel in Ardmore, Co Waterford. The Ryans also put Tony Ryan's old home, the Lyons Estate, on the market for a reported €80 million around this time, but instead Shane Ryan decided to take it on. Doherty had worked on all of these deals along with managing Irelandia's

CHAPTER 31: A CHANGING OF THE DOGS

airline interests in Mexico, Colombia, Peru and Panama. She was tired and wanted to devote more time to her family.

"I wanted to have my fourth child and I wasn't going to be at work having it. It was too much. Steven (Maxwell) was coming up the ranks and he was hungry for it," Doherty said. "He was just very young. I had more deal experience but Declan was bringing Steven up the ranks and giving him more experience. It was still a massive ask for him to become CFO at his age. But then Declan gives opportunities like that. Declan gave it to me too, a mum, who was going to have more kids. He knows you'll do it for him." Ryan recalls getting an email at 3am from Doherty and realising she was working too hard. "I knew Paula had to have a break, and understood why," Ryan said.

Did Doherty miss Irelandia? "I definitely miss it to a degree," she said. "It's full-on. You're important in business, and then you're not so much. It was definitely a big change leaving but Declan fulfilled his promises. I have a home in Kildare, horses and a place to bring up my children." Doherty said she had only one regret: "I should have called our home Viva!"

CHAPTER 32: SHAW RETURNS TO VIVA

Unsurprisingly, there was a clearout in Viva when Irelandia took control. Juan Emilio Posada had made several million dollars from the deal and resigned before he was fired.

Joe Mohan had waited patiently in Panama to lead the business, and Irelandia now asked him to move to Medellín. For personal reasons he took a job with American Airlines instead. His departure took Irelandia by surprise so there was now a vacancy at the top of Viva. William Shaw said he should be the boss. Ryan was unsure. He knew Shaw had abilities, but worried that he had no operational experience. Goode flew with Shaw to the Bahamas to meet Ryan and discuss who would lead the airline. He had tipped Ryan off that Shaw was likely to make a pitch to become chief executive. Goode went with an open mind.

Shaw was undoubtedly creative and had played an important role in generating publicity. He argued that with the right team around him, he could lead the business. Ryan wanted him to become interim chief executive, but the Mexican's pride

CHAPTER 32: SHAW RETURNS TO VIVA

would not allow this. He felt he'd be starting on the back foot if he wasn't full chief executive. Ryan agreed to give him a chance, and then asked about who would be in his senior team. Shaw said he wanted to replace Eduardo Fairen Soria as COO, but Ryan refused. He felt this was a crucial role for Viva and it needed stability. The trio started to talk about the finance positions in Viva. Shaw was negative towards Viva's CFO Oscar Herrera Restrepo. Goode asked if Viva's head of treasury, Catalina Jaramillo Cardona, could take on the role. Shaw said he thought she could. "There was a sense that there was a new sheriff in town so he needed to shake things up as Viva was underperforming at the time," Goode recalled. Shaw was made chief executive in July 2016, and he appointed Jaramillo as his new CFO, leading to Herrera resigning.

Viva now had two relatively inexperienced people in charge as chief executive and CFO. "In retrospect letting Oscar go was a mistake, as he could run a finance department properly," Goode said.

Irelandia was focused on closing a big aircraft order, but there were tell-tale signs of the reshuffle. Viva was found to have been under-provisioning, so it had to adjust its accounts. This caused a loss in 2016.

Then, a flight attendant saw smoke in a plane, prompting an emergency evacuation. It was only smoke from overheated brakes, but its rivals pounced on it.

On 28 November 2016, a Bolivian-owned charter airline called LaMia carrying a well-known Brazilian football team to Medellín crashed into the mountains, killing seventy-one people. The team was called Chapecoense and travelling to play perhaps the biggest game in its history in the final of the Copa Sudamericana against Medellín team Atlético Nacional. Leaked audio from an Avianca co-pilot suggested that a Viva flight had prevented the plane landing by going ahead of it due to a fault in its cabin.

Juan Sebastian Upegui, a co-pilot from airline Avianca, who was also waiting to land, said the pilot of LaMia (Miguel Quiroga) told the air traffic control tower: "We request priority to proceed to the runway, we request priority to proceed to the locator. We have fuel problems." In the recording the Avianca pilot said he willed the plane to land safely: "I was saying 'do it, do it – land.'" Upegui had shared his thoughts in a voice message on WhatsApp to friends, which quickly went viral.

The LaMia plane lost contact at about 22.15 hours, and crashed soon afterwards in a mountainous area. In the immediate aftermath of the crash when the audio recording emerged there was anger. Britain's *Daily Telegraph* syndicated a story around the world that claimed that the LaMia plane "crashed after it was denied the opportunity to land because another plane had already started an emergency descent". Other media reports also linked Viva to somehow being to blame for a terrible tragedy that saw just six people survive, in some cases with horrific injuries, of the seventy-seven onboard. The reports, however, were not true.

An official report by the Colombian Civil Aviation Authority, backed by accredited representatives from the United States, Bolivia, and Brazil, outlined what really happened. It said the causal factors of the crash included: "inappropriate planning and execution of the flight, by the operator, because the quantities of fuel required to fly from

CHAPTER 32: SHAW RETURNS TO VIVA

the destination airport to an alternate airport, including reserve fuel, contingency fuel and minimum landing fuel were not considered". It said the sequential flame-out of the plane's four engines was due to it running out of fuel and that there had been "inadequate decision making" by the aircraft operator and a "loss of situational awareness and wrongful decision making by the flight crew", who while aware of the low fuel remaining "did not take the corrective actions required". The official report also found a number of contributing factors to the crash, including the "absence of timely calls for 'priority' or declaring an 'emergency'", which would have alerted others to the fact that the plane was running out of fuel. Viva did have an issue when a light went off in one of its planes' cockpits that its pilot could not explain, causing it to request the right to land. Air traffic control had given Viva priority because the LaMia pilot hadn't told it how perilous a position he was in. Why the LaMia pilot did not alert traffic control sooner is a matter of speculation, as he died in the crash landing. He had failed to put enough fuel in his plane for the journey, and it is possible he didn't want to own up to it for fear of being fined. His co-pilot was inexperienced and didn't overrule him.

A lengthy and moving article by the journalist Sam Borden for ESPN published in 2018 considered all the reasons for the crash as well as the devastating impact it had on the team, their families, and others on the plane and it makes no mention of Viva, as by then it was clear that the Irish-owned airline had nothing to do with the tragedy. It does, however, quote a grieving family member as saying about

223

Quiroga, "The pilot is a murderer." Being linked to the crash did, however, impact Viva, which had prided itself on its commitment to safety.

Shaw had good contacts in the local media, and he managed to contain the story by telling them Viva had nothing to do with it. It was a tragic and unlucky start, as any high-profile crash causes passenger numbers to fall for all airlines nearby as people are scared.

Shaw tried again to break Viva into Peru, but its competitors hit back. Viva gained passengers but made little money there. A crisis was brewing for various reasons both above and below the surface. Irelandia didn't see it, however, as it was busy closing the largest aviation deal in the history of Colombia and working on other big strategic decisions.

CHAPTER 33: 'MAKE THEM FEAR LOSING'

When Viva launched in 2012 in Colombia, its first set of planes were a dozen years old. They were Airbus A320s because there was a glut of them in the market at the time, making them cheaper than the world's other commercial airline maker to Boeing. Airbus A320s from around the turn of the millennium are workhorses, but, from a fuel and maintenance perspective, they cost more money to run than newer planes. Irelandia had seen in Ryanair, Tiger, and VivaAerobus how having newer planes and a lower cost base allowed challenger low-fares airlines to compete hard against incumbents. Allegiant had taken a different approach when Irelandia was an investor as it used older, less expensive aircraft flying less frequently.

In the second half of 2016, as Irelandia took over Viva fully, it felt it was ready to try and do a multi-billion-dollar aeroplane deal. "We passed the billion passengers mark in 2016 on the airlines which we invested in," Ryan said. "These were crazy numbers, but we felt there was untapped potential in the region." Irelandia's minority Colombian investors had held Irelandia back from taking risks but now it was prepared. John Goode, Irelandia's head of aviation, started to run the numbers, and it was quickly obvious new planes would give Viva a serious edge.

Viva typically flew shorter routes but it was flying in mountainous areas and near the Caribbean, so conditions took a toll on its older planes. Newer planes were more robust and fuel efficient.

"With new planes it can be six or seven years before you have to spend significant money fixing engines," Goode said. Overhauling an engine in full cost millions and took up to three months.

"Parts are insanely expensive too," Goode said. "It is like the Gillette razor model – the handle is cheap but they nail you on the blades."

He added: "Then there is the airframe itself – the tube – there are big six-year and twelve-year checks. So again, with new planes you've got this really long time period before you have to do either."

"The move to new aircraft delays and spreads costs out over time. They are also generally more reliable so there are less breakdowns, delayed flights and time that planes are out of action."

There was another important part to the strategy. Buying a large number of new planes was a way of bringing tens of millions of dollars into Viva by doing sale and leaseback deals with lessors. It was also the route for Viva to get the scale required for a listing on the stock market. Ryan told Goode, Mulvihill, Maxwell, and the Irelandia team to test the aeroplane makers and see what deals were available. Ryan

CHAPTER 33: 'MAKE THEM FEAR LOSING'

wanted to do an aeroplane order for lots of reasons, but one was to position Viva for an IPO.

"Declan is always thinking about 'How do we exit?'" Goode said. "We needed to have a business that people would invest in by fixing all the problems in Viva. Airlines tend not to get insane valuations … but if we got the fundamentals right then we would have an IPO story.

"We needed a growth platform and we needed to reduce our costs. One of the ways you can do that is by bringing in newer aircraft at the right price."

With VivaAerobus, Irelandia had managed to buy new aircraft for less than it was able to sell them on in sale-and-leasebacks to aircraft lessors, so it knew it could generate cash from this arbitrage.

It wanted to do the same with Viva. But to get the best price it needed to buy a lot of planes. The challenge for Viva was it wanted to do a multi-billion-dollar deal, but with a relatively tiny balance sheet.

"We could see how we could generate a lot of cash flow by taking in five or six planes a year and then leasing some or all of them out," Goode said. "Instead of Dec always putting his hand in his pocket to fund growth we felt this was another way we could do it."

Irelandia had worked closely with Conor McCarthy on its VivaAerobus deal, but it was now three years later and the market wasn't as soft.

The demand for new planes had intensified as the world put the financial crash behind it so Irelandia wasn't in as strong a position as it had been in Mexico.

The big manufacturers told Irelandia in late 2016 they might

227

not have more new planes available until 2022, and even then, they could expect to pay much higher prices.

Goode kept trying to get a firm offer from the manufacturers to start negotiations.

"The first couple of rounds with Boeing and Airbus went nowhere," he recalled.

By November 2016, Declan Ryan told him enough was enough. "Just kill it," Ryan said. "I don't want you spending more time on this. We'll use older planes for now and try again when the market cools."

Howard Millar, however, took Goode aside in Irelandia's office on Barrow Street. "Airbus has only one strategy," Millar told him. "What's that?" Goode asked. "Beat Boeing," Millar replied. "Once you understand that then you just keep pressing and pressing."

"The fear of Boeing winning an order in South America will put pressure on Airbus to make a counterbid," he added. Boeing's biggest foothold in South America was with Brazilian airline Gol. "Airbus won't want it to win another foothold," Millar predicted.

"John, they are never going to move until they feel like they're going to lose," Millar advised Goode. "You must make them fear losing. Boeing and Airbus are happy if you don't buy from either one, but they don't want to miss out."

Goode listened to Millar and decided to change tack when he next met with Boeing. "Guys, you need to put something in front of me quickly or this is going to be another deal you're going to lose to Airbus," he said bluntly. Boeing asked Goode if it was using external advisers, as it had in Mexico. Airbus had won the contract with VivaAerobus, so

CHAPTER 33: 'MAKE THEM FEAR LOSING'

it wanted to know who it was up against. "We're the only ones running the process," Goode said. Boeing got off the fence and put up a term sheet for fifty planes. Airbus had won a series of big deals in Latin America, so Boeing was eager to build up its position by winning Viva in order to position itself for more deals if it later created a regional airline group. Irelandia now had a card to play.

John Goode took a different approach to Airbus when their sales team flew down from Miami to meet him in Colombia. "I didn't try to convince them to improve their bid. I told them I wanted to be upfront with them: 'We're going with Boeing.'"

Goode added: "It's a pity because I know you have been our provider to-date and you have come on this journey with us. But I get it. You don't have any aircraft available for years, you're sold out, so what can we do? Nobody can make planes appear from nowhere. It is what it is."

Airbus asked Goode to not rush into making any decision. But Goode said he didn't have that luxury.

"Boeing has slots available very soon and I have a two-week window to accept it or they're going to go give the [manufacturing] slots to somebody else. I have to make up my mind," Goode explained. The board of Viva, he said, was prepared to back him going with Boeing. This was credible as Airbus knew that Millar was a director, as was Ryan. Both had cumulatively bought hundreds of planes from Boeing with Ryanair.

Airbus told Irelandia not to rush any decision. A week later, it rang inviting Goode and Ryan to New York. Maybe Irelandia had options.

CHAPTER 34: THE WINGS CLUB

The Wings Club in the MetLife building in New York is steeped in American aviation history. Founded in 1942, it has been led over the decades by Juan Trippe, the founder of Pan American, Herb Kelleher of Southwest Airlines, and Jeana Yeager, who co-piloted the first non-stop, non-refuelled flight around the world.

Ryan, Goode and the Airbus sales team sat down together in a private corner of the club to discuss a deal.

Kiran Rao, deputy to the chief operating officer, led the talks on the Airbus side. He had previously done the Tiger Airlines deals and was friendly with Ryan as a result.

"Airbus said: 'We've heard you loud and clear.' They put an offer in front of us that was night and day better," Goode recalled. Airbus made a detailed presentation outlining what a deal might look like and when Viva could expect its first deliveries.

Ryan and Goode sat stoney-faced as the slides turned. "Conor McCarthy had told me in the VivaAerobus deal to watch our body language," Goode said. "They'll have somebody in the meeting looking at how you react to what they suggest."

Each time Airbus put forward a proposal its teams' chairs swivelled to see how Irelandia was reacting. Ryan and Goode were studiously expressionless.

"It's an improvement, but we are not anywhere close to being there yet," Goode said. Ryan and Goode asked to leave the meeting room to discuss the offer in private. "What do you think?" Ryan asked.

"It is a serious move forward," Goode replied. "We are now in the realm of where we might do a deal – but we can't tell them that."

Ryan and Goode went back to the meeting and tried to appear downbeat. They said they would think about the offer. They were due to fly to Seattle to visit Boeing, but Ryan didn't want to say that to Rao as it might appear disrespectful.

Goode quietly let one of the Airbus team know instead, so they knew they were in a fight.

A few days later Irelandia met Kevin McAllister, the chief executive of Boeing, in its campus near Seattle. "We did a tour of Boeing beforehand," Goode replied. At one stage an engineer who delivered the first Boeing plane to Ryanair, in a deal Ryan had helped broker, came out to greet them.

Ryan and Goode then retired for a private meal with McAllister and some of the Boeing team.

Ryan and McAllister clicked and got on well. "Let's try and do this," McAllister said. "Now that I've met you it's more personal. I want to win this deal." McAllister turned to his sales team and said: "Go and fucking win this deal. We are not going to lose to Airbus again."

Boeing hesitated to make a firm offer while Irelandia was in

CHAPTER 34: THE WINGS CLUB

Seattle, but instead asked for more time. "I don't know what the machinations in Boeing were but I think they wanted to think about it one more time," Goode said.

Boeing did come back with a better offer and one of its ideas was that Viva would use pre-delivery financing from Bank of China Aviation to fund the deal.

Before any plane is delivered it is normal for airlines to put up between $10 million and $15 million towards the price. This was a problem for Viva's relatively small balance sheet, especially as more and more of the fifty aeroplanes rolled off the line.

"We'd only about $10 million in cash on Viva's balance sheet at the time," Goode recalled. "It is absurd to think in some ways you can buy fifty aircraft with so little money but that's how we did it." At the time lessors financing pre-delivery payments to manufacturers was unusual as Boeing and Airbus normally insisted on airlines putting a minimum amount of cash up per aircraft. "Very few airlines with our balance sheet could get the deal we did but we managed it because of Irelandia and Dec Ryan's reputation," according to Goode.

The Bank of China Aviation deal being proffered by Boeing was attractive as it would ensure Irelandia could finance its Viva deal. "How it worked was, say you take delivery of one aircraft there might be a down-payment of $12 million – and you pay some of it on signing of the contract, more on various anniversaries like twenty-four months, eighteen months, twelve months before delivery."

Bank of China Aviation was proposing to make all of these payments in return for being allowed to purchase the aircraft from Viva and then lease it back to the airline for a twelve-year period. In the event Viva defaulted, it would just take back the planes. "They were taking on the risk," Goode said. "But in return they wouldn't have to compete with anyone else on the sale and leaseback side."

Two days after Irelandia's meeting with Kevin McAllister, Lorenzo Garay, a sales director with Boeing, flew to Medellín. He refused to put his offer in an email in advance but instead gave Irelandia a hard copy. "I was like holy shit," Goode said. "It was much better than we were expecting – several million dollars better per aircraft."

Goode called Ryan and told him he was recommending Boeing. "I told Dec the price, the availability of aircraft and it was just wow, we should do this deal," Goode recalled. Irelandia still felt it could squeeze a little more out of Boeing, but it was now almost there.

Goode rang Airbus to tell them. "I don't think there is any way back," he said. Airbus, however, said it wanted a chance to make one more offer.

Boeing then hit a speed bump. It was offering a combination of newer and older model planes. The older planes were called Boeing 737 Next Generations, while the newer ones were called Boeing 737 Maxs. At that stage there were no safety concerns about Boeing's Max but there was a bit of a backlog in terms of delivering them to airlines.

Some of Boeing's bigger and older customers were demanding more next-generation planes, pushing newer

CHAPTER 34: THE WINGS CLUB

airlines like Viva back in the queue. "Somebody senior in Boeing said we will have to give those aircraft to somebody else first," Goode recalled.

This pushed out delivery times, changing the economics of the deal. "The more time that goes by the higher your purchase price," Goode said. He re-ran his model based on later delivery times and now Boeing's offer wasn't as strong. "The delays hurt Boeing," he explained.

A gate opened for Airbus to come back again. "They improved their offer and promised to us aircraft sooner from 2018 on. All of a sudden, they found aircraft to give us," Goode said.

Irelandia now needed to make its mind up, as both Boeing and Airbus pressed for a decision. "We had a final bake-off in Miami," Goode said. Irelandia booked a hotel meeting room in May 2017 to listen to final presentations from the aeroplane makers and then decide.

On the Irelandia side were Ryan and Goode.

Boeing and Airbus both had teams in Miami, and Irelandia tried to wring the best deal from them. In the mix was not just how much Irelandia would pay for the planes but how they would finance them.

"The Bank of China said it would finance twenty aircraft – so it is prepared to put up a billion dollars of financing for a company like Viva which at that stage had about $10 million in cash on its balance sheet and was losing money," Goode explained.

"But that's where the Ryan brand and the Irelandia name really counts because if we weren't who we were, none of these deals would happen.

"If you were Viva – the exact same company but the original founders and not Irelandia – there is no way a deal would happen. Not with Viva in the condition it was."

Irelandia scheduled Boeing and Airbus in back-to-back meetings just five minutes apart.

"You want them to see each other walking in and out to let them know they are in a fight," Goode said.

"I left the Boeing presentation closed on the table when the Airbus guys came in. I took notes in the Airbus meeting using a Boeing pen."

"Boeing came in and they improved a couple of things, but not the price that much."

It did, however, put forward a financing proposal with a big lessor that kept it firmly in the race. It was now the turn of Airbus to make its final presentation led by Kiran Rao.

Ryan listened to its proposal but it wasn't as strong as it could be. Irelandia told Airbus this, and its team asked to be allowed to leave the room. They returned a few minutes later with a revised offer, but it still wasn't good enough. "We're going to go with Boeing, Kiran," Ryan said. Ryan had huge respect for Rao, but he had to level with him. "At this stage I was watching the body language of the Airbus guys and they were eyes wide open as they couldn't believe they were going to lose," Goode said.

Rao remained calm. He asked Ryan to explain why Irelandia wasn't choosing Airbus.

"Okay Dec, can we leave the room for a few minutes and come back to you?" Rao asked after listening.

Rao came back in with an improved offer. Airbus he said would support Irelandia raising financing and make some other concessions.

CHAPTER 34: THE WINGS CLUB

Irelandia didn't want to tie up too much cash in paying for its planes, as it felt it might be needed in Viva. Boeing had been first to suggest that Irelandia might be able to raise finance from lessors and it indicated Irelandia might need to put up over $10 million of its cash to close it. Typically, an airline owner would have to put up many times more than this to close a deal of this scale, but Boeing wanted to win. This was a key reason why it was ahead of Airbus. During one of his exits from the meeting room to discuss the deal, Rao had come close to matching this. He relaxed how much cash Irelandia needed to put up, allowing Airbus to draw level on this crucial point.

Ryan pushed again, asking for some improvements on the deal. He wanted better terms around the first aircraft being delivered, as this would help Viva's cash flow. Airbus came back a third time with an improved offer. Ryan shook hands with Rao. They had a deal.

Goode said the Airbus deal was now much better, but it wasn't a clear winner.

"Strictly on the numbers, Boeing had made a formidable offer," Goode said. "But Dec made the decision that we were too fragile a company to undergo that conversion from Airbus to Boeing."

Irelandia had a multi-billion-dollar relationship with Airbus in Mexico that was working.

Even though Boeing was ahead, Irelandia felt it wasn't enough to risk changing aeroplane makers.

Afterwards, Goode told Ryan he felt they could squeeze Airbus harder and get them to match Boeing. But Ryan said it was over. "John was world-class in those negotiations. I sat back and let him do it but I know when someone is done deal wise," Ryan explained. "We had drained Airbus and got the best deal we were going to get."

Goode agreed: "In hindsight, I don't think there was any more in Airbus. We had stretched them to the pin of their collar on price and they'd given us earlier slots and so on. It was the best we were going to do."

CHAPTER 35: THE PARIS AIR SHOW

Le Bourget Paris Air Show takes place every odd year over a week in June with more than 300,000 people in attendance from the general public to the biggest names in aviation. In 2017, at this prestigious event, Viva signed a memorandum of understanding with Airbus to purchase fifty new A320 aircraft. The planes had a list price of $5.5 billion. The real price being paid for the narrowbody planes was confidential but in the billions. About thirty-five of the planes being bought by Viva were so-called A320neos and were to be kitted out with the new engine option – or next generation of aircraft engines – while the remainder were CEOs or current engine options which were tried and tested. "This order reflects our long-term commitment to our customers lowering fares further due to the benefits of this new fleet," William Shaw proclaimed.

John Leahy of Airbus, known as the trillion-dollar man for selling over 10,000 planes, inked the deal. "Airbus is pleased to play a major role in supporting Viva Air in its exciting journey to develop the low-cost model throughout Latin America," he said.

Just before signing Leahy had picked up a stack of papers in relation to the deal.

"This is the contract?" he asked.

"No, it's just our letter of intent (LOIs)," Goode replied.

Leahy remarked that most letters of intent were two pages. "Ours was over twenty," Goode recalled. "I just wanted to try and agree on everything as once you sign the letter of intent you won't get anything extra."

Goode, at thirty-three years of age, signed the deal for Viva. It was the biggest aircraft deal ever done in Colombia. Ryan didn't go to the signing, preferring to let Shaw take the plaudits and Goode put his name on the contract. "Dec is not a limelight guy," Goode said. In a rare interview afterwards, Goode spoke about how Viva intended to grow, telling the *Sunday Times*: "Latin America is the last great frontier for low-cost airlines."

Afterwards salesmen milled around Goode trying to convince him to buy their equipment – from seating configurations to cockpit equipment – to kit out Viva's planes. "It was like being a popstar," Goode laughed. "You're getting your photo taken and everyone wants to talk to you. That feeling didn't last very long as we still had a lot of work to do."

After the signing there were still another six months of negotiations to close the deal. Viva with funding from Irelandia had put down a $5 million deposit. It was then asked to put up another $7 million towards the planes in late 2017. Steven Maxwell told Ryan not to put up this money, as he felt Irelandia's exposure to Viva was getting too big. It had only just bought out the other shareholders in the airline, and it was continuing to fund its losses too. Ryan said, "Everything

CHAPTER 35: THE PARIS AIR SHOW

you are saying is accurate but we all know the benefits of having new planes to the business so I think we should do it.'

Ryan knew the Airbus deal negotiated by Goode and his team was one of the best done that year in the world, and he felt the demand for new planes was strong in the lessor market. He took the risk, but he was now invested even deeper into Viva. Irelandia did, however, slow the deal a little to give it more time to strike the deal with lessors.

"In truth the contract could have been done a lot faster," Goode said. "But the day we signed the contract we were on the hook for $100 million – so we couldn't sign the contract!"

Irelandia had to pursue multiple tracks to close the deals. One of the big ones was with Airbus to close off every aspect of the deal but it also had to deal with the lessors from which it was raising financing to pay the aircraft maker the required pre-delivery payments (PDP) before it started to receive its planes. Aircraft lessor GECAS initially refused to provide PDP financing. "Okay, well you've no chance then," Goode replied. "If you're not 100 per cent financing then forget about it."

Goode said Irelandia already had offers from other lessors to provide this type of financing. GECAS came back and said it would finance them. "They probably almost broke their own rules to finance us several times over," Goode said. "And that would later come back to bite us in the ass when we tried to re-negotiate with them in the years ahead."

Irelandia struck financing deals with GECAS for ten planes and CALC (China Aircraft Leasing Company) for another five. Finally, Irelandia had all the pieces in place, and Viva had access to a pipeline of fifty planes.

"It was an insane six or seven months closing," Goode said.

"It was probably the steepest learning curve of my life, but we got a pretty good deal away." Irelandia had pulled off a staggering deal that gave Viva a strong financial backbone and advantage over its competitors. But it didn't have long to celebrate.

Closing the deal with Airbus in December 2017 was just the start of dozens of more negotiations with suppliers of everything from trolley providers, to carpet makers to seat manufacturers.

"It is not like buying a car," Brian Mulvihill said. "There are forty or fifty negotiations with different vendors before you have a plane ready to fly."

By far the most important supplier, after the plane itself, was the engine provider.

Irelandia knew that the list price for the 100 engines plus spares needed in a fifty-plane fleet could easily top $3 billion but it hoped to pay less than this because of the scale of its order.

Irelandia was under pressure to decide on its engines as its first plane was due to roll off the assembly line in Toulouse before October 2018.

It needed to select an engine before then or it would not be able to fly the first plane in its new fleet to Colombia.

Viva had two engine makers to choose from: CFM International, which is part-owned by GE, and Pratt & Whitney.

Irelandia had chosen a mix of old and new A320s from Airbus, so it required a mixture of old-generation and new-generation engines for the appropriate planes.

CHAPTER 35: THE PARIS AIR SHOW

The usual thing to do in such a scenario is to try and negotiate at the same time a deal for the old and new engines with each of the two manufacturers, as Irelandia would be able to drive a better bargain by dangling a bigger cheque in front of the two manufacturers.

Irelandia went to talk to the engine makers and both CFM and Pratt & Whitney were prepared to cut a deal on their older engine models. These engines were tried and tested over twenty years and had been used by aeroplanes in all conditions.

It was a different scenario with the newer engines. Pratt & Whitney had a new engine that was seen in the market as being more advanced than CFM International but there were reliability issues.

"There were a lot of teething issues at the time with Pratt & Whitney's brand-new technology," Mulvihill recalled. "We were hearing that other airlines were having to take them off wing after 1,000 cycles to fix them when they were supposed to go to 15,000 cycles without having to be taken off."

CFM International knew about these issues so it felt it was in a strong position. Its sales team came down to Medellín to meet with Goode, Mulvihill and some of Viva's executives.

It was January 2018 and Irelandia urgently needed to make a decision. "We were on the clock with Airbus in France who were putting us under pressure to pick an engine," Mulvihill recalled.

CFM International said it was prepared to do a deal on its older engine types with Irelandia but it wouldn't budge much on price on its newer engine lines.

"They said, 'Well our engine is reliable so we don't have to be creative on the deal,'" Mulvihill recalled. "There was this weird dynamic where one provider was in trouble with its new technology and really scrambling while the other wasn't so it didn't have to play ball."

After listening to them, Goode told the CFM sales team to leave. "We thought you were coming here to do a deal with us but clearly you're not," he told them.

Back in Dublin Irelandia tried to figure out what to do. It decided to split the deal, something that was rare. It also created risks as prices might rise more. "We just thought, why are we killing ourselves to do both deals?" Mulvihill said. "Let's try doing one, and then the other later on."

Irelandia decided to seek the best deal it could from the two engine makers for its older-model planes – and then wait at least another year before trying to negotiate a deal around the new engines.

It hoped that after a year Pratt & Whitney would have fixed its issues so CFM would have to be competitive again.

The first aeroplanes it was due to receive from Airbus were all its older models, so it didn't have to immediately decide on what new engines to buy. Irelandia ended up picking CFM for its 'current engine option' engines, which were for its older model AirbusA320s. The decision to split the deal would prove to be fortuitous.

CHAPTER 36: GOOD KARMA

Declan Ryan was watching the Syrian refugee crisis on the BBC in his apartment in New York. It was a wide-ranging report about the 6.8 million refugees who had fled their country because of war. An image of Alan Kurdi, a two-year-old Syrian boy, who drowned in September 2015, appeared during the report. Kurdi died when a rubber boat taking him to the Greek island of Kos capsized about five minutes after it left Bodrum in Turkey. Ryan was moved by the report and decided to quietly reopen the One Foundation, three years after he had shut it down in 2013.

He wasn't sure what to do at first but started to support UNICEF in its work in Jordan and Lebanon, where millions of refugees were living in tents and sheds in boiling heat. Ryan went to Zaatari refugee camp in Jordan, where 80,000 people lived, with his niece Danielle Ryan. "The main street is called the Champs-Élysées as it is where all the shops are," he recalled. "There was humour and hospitality like I never had experienced. I was amazed by the people and how resilient they were."

Ryan decided to try and do something. His foundation paid for a spotter plane to help boats rescue refugees from drowning in the Mediterranean. Ryan could see how hard the refugees wanted to work, so he funded a start-up event with UNICEF in Zaatari. Back in Ireland, One tried to push Ireland away from its direct provision model for refugees that restricted their ability to work, towards a more inclusive model. Ryan had built up good political contacts and knew how the civil service worked, from when One was at its peak, so he tapped again into these networks. The focus of One became helping refugees wherever they were.

From 2015, millions of refugees had fled Venezuela into neighbouring Colombia. "Venezuela and Colombia are like good first cousins," Ryan said. "In the office in Medellín when something bad happens in Venezuela I can see our team get low." Ryan decided to set up the Viva Foundation to support refugees and other good causes locally. His plan was to allocate a percentage of the airline's profits towards the foundation but until that happened he picked up the entire bill. "Someone called me an activist the other day," Ryan said. "That isn't a million miles away from where I want to go. I don't want to be a Geldof but I do care deeply about this stuff."

From 2016 on, Ryan went back and forth to refugee camps trying to figure out ways to help. He was in a refugee camp in Lebanon when he got a call in February 2019 from Irelandia's aviation team asking him to go to Boston to meet Chaker Chahrour, the powerful vice-president of GE Aviation. John Goode and Brian Mulvihill were at that stage near to closing the second part of Viva's aviation engine deal for its newer-model planes.

CHAPTER 36: GOOD KARMA

"We went back to the market for our new engines after about fourteen months," Mulvihill recalled. "Pratt & Whitney had got their act together and the market was starting to trust them again. The split turned out to be an inspired move as now CFM was starting to lose deals, so they had to be competitive."

Irelandia had run a second bake-off for its new engines, and CFM again emerged the winner. "CFM had lost a few campaigns to Pratt & Whitney so the market dynamic swung in our favour," Mulvihill said. Director Howard Millar backed their decision to go with this engine maker. "Howard said: 'Even if Pratt are ahead, we are taking delivery of these engines in 2020, 2021 and 2022 so there will still be a risk it hasn't resolved all its issues – whereas we know CFM will work straight out of the box,' Mulvihill recalled.

By splitting its engine deal in two and deferring buying its neo engines until 2019, Irelandia had saved Viva tens of millions of dollars. After months of negotiations, it was time for Ryan to close the deal.

"When we felt they were at their best and final offer and there was no further push then we sent Dec in," Mulvihill said.

"We always hold him back in reserve for the final push with whoever the CEO is as he is so experienced."

Ryan got on a plane from New York to see if he could squeeze out a few final concessions.

After five minutes of talking to Chahrour, Ryan knew he wasn't going to budge. Instead, their conversation switched to football, before Chahrour asked him where Ryan had come from. Ryan had flown in from New York, but he'd been recently in Jordan and mentioned it.

Chahrour asked him what had brought him there, and Ryan said to visit a refugee camp. Chahrour said he had grown up in a refugee camp after his family was forced to flee conflict in their home in Lebanon. He shared some of his story of how he made it to the United States, studied engineering in the University of Illinois, and worked his way up to doing multi-billion-dollar engine deals.

Ryan was fascinated and sent him an email the following day telling Chahrour to write his story down, as it might inspire others. Chahrour replied saying how he'd enjoyed the meeting, and then unprompted said he couldn't reduce the price anymore for CFM's engines, but he might be able to do something with the first engine delivery which was due in April 2020. He said he could frontload various discounts that Viva was due on to this first engine. Irelandia knew it could do a sale and leaseback deal on the engine which would bring more cash into Viva. On 1 April 2019, Viva announced a fifty engine deal. The list price for the engines – both for the ceo and neo – was $3.2 billion, with the actual price being less than this because of the scale of the order. "It's an historic day for Viva Air Group," Felix Antelo, the chief executive of Viva said. "We believe the engine will prove to be a very valuable asset in terms of the full efficiency and industry leading daily utilisation it will be to the new A320neo fleet."

The terms of the deal struck between Irelandia and GE Aviation was not disclosed, but within it was the Chahrour engine deal. It would later turn out to be a vital lifeline for Viva at its darkest moment. "I didn't know it then but it was karma," Ryan said. "The kindness of a former refugee, and a man who helped without being asked."

CHAPTER 36: GOOD KARMA

When the Airbus deal closed, but before the engine deals were all completed, Irelandia had refocused on Viva, and quickly realised its financial reporting had lapsed. Irelandia now couldn't tell where it was making money and where it was losing it. "When I think back to that meeting in the Bahamas and some of the decisions we made I can feel the hairs on the back of my neck," Goode recalled. Irelandia had approved Shaw as chief executive despite his inexperience and they backed him when he shook up its finance team, replacing an experienced CFO with its head of treasury who wasn't ready for the role.

"It took a lot to recover from that," Goode said. Closing the deal with Airbus and all the other parties had been time-consuming, and while hugely important it was also distracting from day-to-day operations.

Viva was burning cash, and Irelandia was losing faith in the charismatic Shaw. "We took our eye off the ball and that took a long time to fix," Goode said. "We were heading into a dangerous place."

In his 2017 private memoir *Almost Famous*, Declan Ryan reflects on the importance of cash to anyone running an airline. "It sounds boring, but so much of success in business is about the management of cash. I pore over the weekly reports from the airlines, but the No. 1 thing I'm looking at is the cash balances – I always know how many days of cash we have. That's what I learnt at Ryanair. Michael [O'Leary] was obsessed with it too. At one stage, he was personally signing every cheque. Think about cash balances and you think about cost disciplines. Contrary to what people sometimes say, you actually should sweat the small stuff, because the cash balance never lies."

As Ryan's attention turned back to the operations of Viva after closing the Airbus deal, he realised when it came to cash, worse than being lied to, nobody knew what was going on.

CHAPTER 37: BACK AS TOP DOG

On 24 October, 2018, a bright-pink new Viva aeroplane was revealed in Medellín. It had been freshly flown across the Atlantic from Airbus's home in Toulouse in the south of France.

The pink was part of a campaign by Viva to promote breast cancer awareness, an idea William Shaw had come up with to honour his mother Charmian, who had died from the disease.

Goode asked Airbus to make its first plane pink and to cover the cost of doing so.

Shaw was not there to receive it, as he had left six months earlier. During the twelve months Shaw was in charge, factors outside his control had hurt Viva. Growth in the Colombian economy had slowed. VAT had been increased from 16 per cent to 19 per cent, and a temporary surcharge was imposed on flights to Medellín to fund a road tunnel. Irelandia had been flat-out on the Airbus deal, so they weren't there to hand-hold as much as they had been at other times. Shaw had also made mistakes. For example, four out of Viva's eleven planes were grounded on one particular Friday due to technical issues, causing dozens of flight cancellations. Viva still had old planes in its fleet, and Irelandia felt Shaw was too inexperienced operationally to manage them. Nobody denied he knew how to sell seats, but what was the point if there were no planes. Every quarter Shaw was in charge, Ryan was being forced to put in more money. "There was a moment in the summer of 2017 when I thought the whole thing was going to go," Ryan said. Ryan had fondly given Shaw the nickname "Will Ferrell" as he reminded him physically of the star of *Anchorman* and *Elf*. But now that Shaw was responsible for the daily operations of Viva he wasn't laughing. Things came to a head. In late 2017, Ryan flew to Colombia to find a company in disarray. Growth was stagnating, financial reporting was poor, and planes were breaking down. Viva had put in an industry veteran called Eduardo Fairen Soria as chief operations officer in 2014 to be in charge of operations and maintenance. He was stretched as Shaw didn't have the skills to help him.

Ryan asked Shaw for a plan to turn around Viva and return it to profitability and growth. 'William, what would you do differently, what would you change?" he asked. Shaw replied that he would fire Eduardo Fairen Soria as his head of operations. Ryan was furious that Shaw wasn't taking any responsibility.

At a Viva board meeting in Miami before Christmas 2017, Ryan told Shaw he needed to leave. Shaw disagreed and warned that another change in leadership would be risky. "Dec was like enough's enough," Goode recalled. "He was right, without a doubt."

Ryan told Shaw to stay on but in a different role. The Mexican felt slighted and resigned. He remained a non-executive director

CHAPTER 37: BACK AS TOP DOG

for a period, but soon left entirely. Shaw had lived with John Goode, Steven Maxwell and Brian Mulvihill at various points in Medellín. All four had bonded over hard work and late nights, but nobody objected. He had run out of chances.

"A regret of mine was I didn't call him when I left," Goode reflected. "At that point I really struggled to separate the person from the business. It was a mistake on my part not to call, and it destroyed our relationship.

"In learning that lesson, I lost a good friendship. Willam has a big heart. He's not cut out for an airline CEO, but he's a very decent human being."

As William Shaw left, Viva appointed another board member: Rupert Stebbings, a managing director in Bancocolombia. The Englishman had worked in New York for Deutsche Bank before moving to Colombia in 2006. He was Britain's honorary consul to Medellín, and friends with the president of Bancocolombia, Carlos Raul Yepes, who was also on the board of Viva.

Stebbings met Ryan for breakfast in the Intercontinental Hotel in Medellín for the first time. "I've got no idea what Declan Ryan looks like as he's not on any social networks," Stebbings recalled. He remembers a smartly dressed Irishman coming towards him, but it wasn't Ryan.

"It was Steve (Maxwell). And then kind of ten metres behind him was a guy in shorts, and an outfit that might have cost ten dollars," Stebbings said.

Stebbings and Ryan spoke for two hours. Both shared a love of books and Colombia. Stebbings was fluent in Spanish, and well-connected. A few hours after their coffee, Ryan rang him and asked him to be non-executive director of Viva.

"Dec was looking for a bridge between the different factions on his board," Stebbings said. Conscious of his reputation, Stebbings discreetly checked things out. "How did they not fall into corruption? They didn't, despite all my digging away. I didn't come across any bungs or handouts," he said.

"Colombia is very dangerous, but not to everyone. If you run a small local business company here, you could be stuck paying bribes to everyone, but foreign companies in general get left alone in my experience."

Stebbings became a go-between between Irelandia and the other members of Viva's board during the difficult times ahead. Shaw had played this role, but Stebbings was tougher. He was more financially astute and clued into the banking scene in Colombia. He helped in other ways with his understanding of local business culture, and he knew who was who in the region. His wife, Tatiana Vasquez, was a former journalist who had also worked as a communications adviser in politics in Colombia. Stebbings found the Irelandia team different from other businesses he had worked with in Colombia. It was less hierarchical and tried not to take itself too seriously. Stebbings recalls seeing Ryan and one of the Irelandia team turning up at a staff party dressed as female Avianca air flight attendants. "Everyone knew Irelandia was Irish but until they got to know them they had no idea what that meant," he said. "They took the business seriously but we had a lot of fun too."

Declan Ryan was now back where he started with Ryanair. He owned a loss-making airline in need of a leader. Ryan

CHAPTER 37: BACK AS TOP DOG

asked John Goode to be chief executive, but he turned it down as he felt he didn't have the experience and he was not fluent in Spanish. Ryan decided to move to Medellín for six months as chief executive until he could find a replacement. Goode volunteered to come with him as deputy. The two moved into apartments beside each other, and got stuck in. "Viva was crying out for leadership and the only person who could really give that was the person writing the cheques," Ryan said. "I was shocked at the chaos I found. Suppliers were sending us default notices. It was ironic, because many of them were aircraft lessors from Ireland – and I had to say to them, 'guys you know you're going to get paid'.

"Frankly I only got away with it some days because of the Irelandia reputation. But these were dark times."

Ryan started to rebuild Viva's culture and reinvigorate its spirit. "There was an immediate response," Goode recalled.

"Just seeing Dec on the ground, and how much he cared about the business, people started to believe in it again. Everyone knew Viva was losing money, but Dec's arrival showed we were committed."

According to Mulvihill: "Dec was in his office every day, music blasting out of it. He took his dog in and would get up and ask how everyone was doing. In Colombia it can be hierarchical, so they hadn't seen this before. Dec built back up the culture."

Ryan wore shorts, and his dog Waffles became Viva's mascot. He went for beers with his team, and he brought Gary Keegan, an Irish high-performance sports coach, to help revive morale. Keegan was best known for his work with Irish boxers where he led a team that won Olympic,

World and European medals working with champions like Katie Taylor and Michael Conlon.

"He was a huge hit because he is an outsider and also Latinos love boxing," Ryan said. "He taught the team about David versus Goliath and how the principles of boxing apply in life."

Maxwell added: "He was getting people to take pride in Viva. One of the videos he showed was of Paddy Barnes (an Irish Olympic-bronze-medal-winning boxer) sparring with a heavyweight boxer. He was massive but Paddy (a flyweight) took the fight to him. Gary really helped people to take pride in Viva, especially its uniform and what wearing it meant."

Ryan worked long days as he tried to turn it around. He had the biography of Tony Ryan translated into Spanish, so the Viva team could understand Irelandia's history. He flew the author of this book, Richard Aldous, down to Colombia to do a workshop on Tony Ryan and Ryanair. "That's what we're doing for Colombia," Ryan said after Aldous was finished. "It's going to work." As Ryan looked around the room, he felt his team was starting to believe it. He was too. "I had almost forgotten I had the skill set, knowledge and drive. It was like the possibility of failure had jump started the engine again," Ryan said.

Ryan tried to lighten the mood and encouraged staff to share any problems. "Viva needed more of the fun that Ryanair had in the early days," Ryan said. "That brilliant sense that we were blazing a trail by challenging the big boys and vested interests. We were anti-establishment, for the people, democratising. That was the mission and if the staff didn't believe it, who would?"

He became friends with Monica Gil Coca, the head of flight

CHAPTER 37: BACK AS TOP DOG

attendants in Viva. Gil Coca cared about Viva as he did, and, like him, she was a keen cyclist.

The two talked about what was happening to Colombia, where many people were living in poverty, especially among the 1.5 million refugees who had fled violence and political instability in nearby Venezuela. Ryan decided to set up the Viva Foundation to help, modelling it on the One Foundation. Ryan started to explore Colombia more – sometimes with Gil Coca as his guide. It was a country with mountains, the Amazon, two different oceans, but Ryan had been too busy to really see it. "The people are proud but warm and funny, especially in Medellín," Ryan said. "It's Munster, but with better weather."

As Ryan fell more in love with Colombia, his heart also turned towards Gil Coca.

Goode meanwhile concentrated on building up Viva's financial reporting and structures again. "We needed good financial reports so we could make decisions," Goode said. "The monthly production of detailed financial reports had just collapsed."

Viva had a good chief information officer, but he was in a silo. "He was taking on too much," Goode said. "And becoming a crutch that everyone else was leaning on. What we really had to do in Viva was to get people to take responsibility and to work together. We knew we couldn't change everything, but we could change attitudes."

Viva rose to it. Its staff already turned up at 6.30 in the morning, but now they had leadership.

Goode realised Viva had made some cost cuts that did not make sense. "We had a great fuel analyst for example," he said. "But she had a computer that kept crashing because nobody had bought her a new laptop. She was responsible for analysing a fuel bill of between $30 million and $40 million and couldn't do it because she needed a $2,000 laptop. It was penny wise, pound foolish." A new laptop later, and she was saving Viva $700,000 a year.

Irelandia could now see which routes were working. "Before, the operations and commercial side of Viva weren't talking enough," he said. "So, commercial were selling flights, and then operations were cancelling them as we couldn't deliver. Communications internally were failing, and everyone was blaming each other."

Viva was now receiving new Airbus aeroplanes regularly, so Ryan had to figure out how many planes to deploy on Viva's routes or try to lease out to other airlines. He looked for new routes both domestically and internationally for Viva to fly to.

Stebbings was a wingman for Ryan as he pushed for better deals for Viva. He recalls accompanying Ryan to a regional airport near Santa Marta, a coastal city in northern Colombia, to negotiate a landing deal. Ryan listened to a PowerPoint presentation from its management justifying why they were not going to reduce their charges for Viva. Ryan gave it twenty minutes, then stood up before they had finished. "Clearly there's an issue here. Thanks for coming. We'll see you around," Ryan said.

He then walked out. Stebbings, who was used to long meetings in Colombia, scrambled to catch up. Santa Marta had a population of 500,000 and was a busy port city that

CHAPTER 37: BACK AS TOP DOG

was also a gateway for visitors to trekking in the Colombian jungle and its famous Lost City of Teyuna.

It was not an unimportant city for Viva, but Ryan was not in the mood for nonsense. At dinner that night with Stebbings, Ryan excused himself to take a call. It was the airport officials ringing. "It was like a girlfriend who had been dumped," Stebbings said. "The next day we had exactly the kind of deal we wanted. You can't do what Dec did when you're inexperienced. He knows how to negotiate."

But it was still very tight. Viva was still losing money every month, so it needed to generate cash from doing deals with lessors. At Christmas 2018, Ryan told Mulvihill there was overcapacity and he needed to place three aeroplanes elsewhere quickly. "I had a month to do it," Mulvihill recalled. "I pounded the pavements of Europe."

Eventually, he found a Lithuanian holiday operator prepared to take the planes. "We have countercyclical summers in Colombia," he explained. "Our high season is from October to January, which is Europe's low season. An aircraft is the world's most expensive paper weight on the ground, so we got the planes to Lithuania and made some cash."

Viva was turning around, but Ryan was still being forced to lend millions of dollars more to the airline. As chief financial officer, Maxwell started to become worried that Irelandia was becoming too exposed to just one investment. If Viva went down, it would be on the hook. Irelandia believed in Colombia and Viva, but it knew it needed a new partner, and fast.

CHAPTER 38: DON'T CRY FOR ME ARGENTINA

Viva had raised $30 million from friends and family of Irelandia in 2018 and 2019. The money came in two tranches – an initial $20 million and then another $10 million. Irelandia was making money from its aircraft deal by leasing its planes to air lessors, but it knew it needed more funds. The $30 million was intended as a cushion while Viva tried to find a new partner. Declan Ryan had a big exposure to Viva, and Steven Maxwell was worried this was too much. "Too much of Dec's personal net worth was in one place," he said. Ryan asked his brother Shane Ryan, niece Danielle Ryan and nephew Cillian Ryan if they would like to invest. All agreed, quickly.

"The nickname for me in the family is the 'elder lemon' as I'm now the oldest," Ryan said. "None of my family had any problem helping – it was lovely. It made me go into fifth gear. It was no longer just my money if I got it wrong."

Could Ryan have kept funding Viva alone? "People forget how much I put into One Foundation," Ryan said. "I put in over $100 million. I've no regrets and I wouldn't change a

CHAPTER 38: DON'T CRY FOR ME ARGENTINA

thing. I wasn't going to put it all into Viva, I couldn't."

Maxwell had read the journalist Matt Cooper's 2016 book called *The Maximalist* on the rise and fall of Tony O'Reilly. Once Ireland's richest man, O'Reilly had gone bankrupt after he put too much money into too few places: a glass maker and a newspaper group. "The O'Reilly story really stuck with me," Maxwell said. "Going broke was the one thing I never wanted to happen to Dec."

Keith Ryan was the head of the Dublin office of Julius Baer, a Swiss bank which advised high-net-worth individuals. Irelandia knew Ryan, so it asked him if he could introduce them discreetly to potential investors. They met a few Irish clients of the bank after Ryan introduced them. "It was structured as a secondary sale from Dec, as the aim was to de-risk him," Maxwell said.

"But we also thought there was a huge amount of opportunity. Dec is not going to sell a pup to anyone, especially his brothers and his brother's family."

"At the time we didn't need the funds but it was prudent to raise them. The plan was only to put the money into Viva if it was needed. But then it did in typical fashion."

As this money started to come in, Viva hired Felix Antelo as its new chief executive in April 2018. A tall Argentinian, Antelo was calm under pressure. He'd spent thirteen years with LATAM, leading its Peru operations. His background wasn't low fares, but he was a corporate leader. Antelo wanted to go back to Argentina, but Irelandia convinced him to buy into its vision for Viva. As when it lured Tony Davis to join Tiger, Antelo was excited about leading an airline to the stock market. He built his own team with his first hire, a new head of communications, Catalina Rendón Jaramillo, who had previously worked in the fashion industry. Rendón recalls her instructions as: "We are low-cost but not cheap. You don't have to pay for smiles."

Antelo's arrival allowed Declan Ryan to step back and concentrate on finding Viva a new co-investor. He hired Bank of America to help. It suggested he talk to JetSmart, which was backed by Bill Franke's Indigo Partners. "Colombia, Peru, and Chile kind of made sense," Maxwell said. Franke, as always, was tough. Viva and JetSmart couldn't agree on a new capital and ownership structure if the airlines merged.

The talks ended, but they had taken up time. Meanwhile, Viva's rival Avianca had slashed its fares to bring in cash.

"Avianca during a period of economic stagnation in Colombia was chasing cash by cutting fares," Maxwell said. Viva could not compete, and Ryan was again losing lots of money. Viva made money in the first six months of 2018, and then went to a $20 million loss in the second half. Finding a new partner was now vital if Viva was to survive.

CHAPTER 39: A LION LOOKING AT A ZEBRA

Declan Ryan asked John Goode to come to New York to meet potential investors towards the end of 2018. It was one of two trips that were among the darkest times for Irelandia. Viva was losing millions a month, and they knew its value was falling daily. There were a dozen meetings lined up, but the most in-depth were with a fund called Cyrus Capital Partners. Founded by Steve Freidheim, the investment advisers managed about $3.5 billion from its base in a thirty-six-storey skyscraper called Park Avenue Tower. Freidheim's father Cyrus was vice-chairman of consultancy firm Booz, Allen & Hamilton. He had worked in the distressed debt arm of Och-Ziff, before he renamed the business after his father in 1999 and took it fully independent in 2005.

Freidheim had backed Richard Branson when he launched Virgin America in 2005 and made a fortune when the airline was sold for $2.6 billion to Alaska Air in 2015. Cyrus had early on put a term sheet on the table, valuing Viva at more than Irelandia had put in. "It wasn't a down round," Goode said. "But it was close to our cost of capital after years in the business."

Maxwell recommended the deal as it would recapitalise Viva and repay a significant portion of Ryan's loans to the airline. Cyrus asked to meet Felix Antelo and was impressed enough to begin due diligence. "We let them start before we were ready," Goode said. "So we sent them financial information, and they saw a mistake. Then we sent them more information, and another mistake. It started chipping away at our credibility. The golden rule, which we learned painfully, is that time kills deals."

The errors were not that serious but caused delays. Viva's losses kept growing, and Cyrus started to harden its approach. "It started getting very private equity like," Goode said. "They added in more terms in order to protect themselves and gain more control."

Cyrus asked to visit Colombia, where they met Ryan and other Viva executives. After Ryan left, an airport tour was arranged. "Let's skip the airport tour," Freidheim told Goode. Catching him alone, the Cyrus team grilled him. Cyrus wanted exclusivity and a $5 million break clause.

Goode said Cyrus should pay Viva a $5 million break clause and said Ryan would have to be consulted. An Argentinian nicknamed by Irelandia as the 'black monk' became visibly irritated: "Are you allowed to decide anything, or do you always have to check with Dec?"

Goode paused and looked hard at him, and the 'black monk' backed off. The meeting was an ambush, which Cyrus claimed later was because they were frustrated they weren't getting enough information. Goode kept his cool despite the provocation. He knew Irelandia couldn't walk; Cyrus was the only party really interested.

CHAPTER 39: A LION LOOKING AT A ZEBRA

"It was constant questions and death by a thousand cuts," Goode said. "I remember thinking coming up to Christmas, this is fucked. It is not going to happen, and we are fucked too."

Irelandia had projected to Cyrus that Viva would make money in the last quarter of 2018, but with Avianca still slashing its prices, it was losing money. "Avianca were charging $30 a fare and less, the same as our average fare," Maxwell said. Antelo had to match them, causing Viva to lose more money. Just before Christmas, Goode told Ryan: "Dec I can't recommend that you put any more money into this because I don't know if it'll ever be the last cheque."

The Irelandia team took a few days to recuperate in Ireland over Christmas. "We'd put so much into it. I knew Viva could be turned around but we needed a sizeable chunk of capital to get there but I didn't think we would make it," Goode remembered thinking.

Over New Year, his mindset changed. "I thought if we're fucked, we're fucked. But we can't go down without a fight," he said. "Whatever happens I'm not going to have any regrets that we did not do everything possible to save Viva. We're going out on our shields."

Goode went back to Colombia in a last push to save Viva, while Ryan went back to New York to try and find more money. In late January, he rang Goode. He had a bite. Goode came to New York for a few days but ended up staying six weeks. The investor was called Cartesian Capital Group. It was an early investor in Brazilian airline Gol, backing the business not long after it was founded in 2001. It had made a lot of money from the deal. Like Irelandia, it had passed on AirAsia. More recently it backed Flybondi, a low-cost airline in Argentina backed by among others Michael Cawley, a former chief operations officer in Ryanair. Ryan didn't ask Cawley for the introduction but instead relied on Tom Mullins in Raymond James. "Myself and Michael Cawley would be like two Jack Russells in a room," Ryan said. "I preferred to contact them independently."

Ryan and Goode booked into the Andaz, a five-star hotel on Fifth Avenue near Bryant Park, just a short walk from Cartesian's office in a skyscraper at 505 Fifth Avenue. Ryan wanted to make a good impression so didn't mind the cost as they didn't intend to stay long. He had met Cartesian once already, as had Steven Maxwell and Tony Davis. All three liked Peter Yu, the founder of Cartesian. Yu was a former chief executive of AIG Capital Partners, and in the 1990s he had served as an economic policy adviser to President Bill Clinton. To allow Goode to come to New York, Maxwell went to Colombia. His orders were to turn off the cash taps until a deal was reached with a new investor. "There was no money leaving the company without my say-so," Maxwell said. "It was squeaky bum time. We didn't want to use Dec's cash again. We needed to make Viva work." Irelandia still hadn't given up on Cyrus either as it had done a lot of due diligence, but the deal was drifting. Before meeting Cartesian, Ryan and Goode went to meet Steve Freidheim from Cyrus again. Freidheim was still not certain, and then one of his team piped up: "What other assets do you have?" Ryan said he had a house in the Bahamas. Would he sell it? Cyrus said it wanted security on Ryan's personal assets before it would fund Viva.

Ryan said he might give them more security, but it still wasn't enough as Cyrus kept coming up with more questions.

CHAPTER 39: A LION LOOKING AT A ZEBRA

A frustrated Ryan told Goode privately: "We need to fucking know if there is any deal they would do." Ryan played his last card. He said Viva needed a bridging loan at once, and if he didn't get it the airline would go bankrupt. "Steve, is there a deal you would do?" Ryan asked.

Freidheim walked across his expansive office to pour himself a glass of wine. "We drink wine on Fridays," he explained. "It is a way of staying balanced and stopping people getting burnt out. It looks like Dec you're in a tight spot." Ryan replied: "Steve, if there's an offer, make an offer."

Freidheim said: "Are you sure? I don't want to offend anybody." Ryan said none would be taken. Freidheim said that Cyrus had a separate division that dealt in distressed assets, who he could bring in. From private equity, Viva was being passed to the undertaking arm of the business. A few days later, Ryan got a call. Cyrus was prepared to put up to $70 million into Viva, but Irelandia had to cram down its creditors, and give them shares in the airline if needed. Ryan's loans were to be converted into shares too, and he would become a minority shareholder. All the cash he had put into the business was gone, and he would no longer be in control.

"They wanted Viva to go into Chapter 11, except outside of court," Goode said. Ryan sent Goode to meet with Cyrus to find out more. "They were professional, but it was like a lion looking at a zebra with sympathy before he eats it," Goode said.

By now they'd been weeks in New York and moved to an Airbnb downtown to save money. Goode had insisted upon it. "I will never forget coming downstairs into the Andaz Hotel for breakfast and asking for eggs," Goode recalled, adding that the only thing the hotel had was scrambled eggs and lobster. "The bill was $59. I felt guilty eating it, as Viva was going bust and all our people could lose their jobs."

Ryan and Goode tried to find other deals through endless conference calls sitting at the kitchen table in their apartment. At one point the washing machine went off, and Goode got up to empty it. The camera on his computer was off, so the potential investor could not see him but Ryan could. "Dec just stared at me open-mouthed as if to say what am I doing?" Goode recalled. "From then I used the laundromat down the street." Irelandia felt if Cyrus was the only deal, then they'd have to do it. "It was better than total failure," Goode said.

Irelandia also looked at going into Chapter 11 and met with a boutique investment bank that specialises in bust businesses. "My head was spinning after that," Goode said. "It was like climbing a steep mountain and you get to the top of it and realise there is another mountain five times taller."

After that meeting, Ryan said to Goode: "What's wrong, your energy's changed?"

"It was that last meeting," Goode replied.

"Don't let that happen, don't dip your head," Ryan said. "We have to keep going."

CHAPTER 40: THE CARTESIAN EQUATION

Cartesian hadn't gone away. Yu had told them: "You know Dec, I might invest in another airline in Latin America. I wouldn't rule it out." But then Irelandia didn't hear from him for a while.

"At this stage I took everything with a pinch of salt," Goode said. "Everyone we met in New York loved our story at first, but then they looked at the numbers and started worrying.

"We had really emphasised to Cartesian the value of the aircraft order we had and the potential profits we could make from it." Irelandia had received its first few planes from Airbus and could show it could raise money from air lessors by giving them these planes. Yu invited Irelandia for breakfast one morning. He put a term sheet on the table. "Here is what I am thinking," Yu said. "I will invest our money into the entity where the aircraft profits are and not the airline itself." This would reduce its exposure to the airline, while giving it first call on any money raised from lessors. Irelandia knew its Airbus deal was world-class. "It was one of the best-priced deals in the world,"

Maxwell said. "So, Cartesian thought of an innovative way to invest in Viva and get an exposure to that deal." The term sheet said Cartesian would put $50 million into the procurement company within the Viva Group that held its aircraft leases.

"I'll take a shareholding in that," Yu said. "You need the capital quickly and I think that is a good business. There's less due diligence too than looking at the entire group."

Cartesian retained an option to become a shareholder in the main airline within two years. The size of the share it would receive if exercised would depend on how Viva was performing. The big risk for Cartesian was that if Viva failed entirely it could lose all its money.

"That was the key thing Cartesian needed to take a view on," Goode said. "Was Viva going to survive?"

Irelandia felt it could earn $150 million from its procurement company managing fifty aeroplanes.

To protect itself, Cartesian said it wanted 1.75 times its money before Irelandia was allowed to make a cent.

"It was a conservative bet if you assumed the airline didn't go broke," Goode said. "We now had a good management team and $50 million so it looked like a sound decision."

Cartesian's due diligence went smoothly. Irelandia had structured and built the model behind it, so they could answer all the questions. Back in Medellín, Viva's team had no money to pay its staff. The Friday before payday, they looked at Viva's bank account hoping the money would arrive. They refreshed the screen: $50,000,000.

"It was like the clouds parted and the sun came out," Goode recalled. "We had the capital and relative to what

CHAPTER 40: THE CARTESIAN EQUATION

the Cyrus team was proposing it was a fucking great deal."

On 11 May 2019, Viva Air announced the $50 million investment by Cartesian. "We are delighted to have found a partner with the level of experience and calibre of Cartesian Capital Group, a globally known engaged investor, who not only adds capital, but also brings knowledge and experience and it is a huge vote of confidence in our company and business," Goode said.

"With a valuable orderbook of A320s and world-class management team, Viva Air will continue Irelandia's demonstrated track record of democratising air travel around the world. We are privileged to be their partner," Yu added. Viva had another chance.

The den of thieves

As they negotiated between Cyrus and Cartesian, Declan Ryan had sent an email to his team in Irelandia. Its subject line was: "Den of Thieves: Wall Street". He said getting a deal had been a "rollercoaster" and "on many occasions we had to position ourselves as cool, calm and confident, while inside we were the opposite.

"Ironically my lowest point was at a very friendly meeting when a 20-something fund manager from LA said he loved the Viva Air business but was restricted because his Fund's bite size (investment threshold) was a minimum $200m!" Ryan confided.

"I told him he could buy several airlines for that. As they say in Tipperary he had 'Notions'!" Steven Maxwell and Howard Millar, he said, had been "sanity checks come cheerleaders" as he and Goode tried to get a deal.

"One of the thieves, in the den called Wall Street, smelt blood," Ryan said. "They are brilliant bottom fishers ... The NYC hedge funds are ruthless – they use words like partnership and I'm investing in you Declan, because I believe in you. But at that moment you can hear the drop of your jocks to the floor.

"The other issue is that low-cost carriers in Latin America are not a popular investment product. For example, take Doug from Omaha who makes vast investment decisions for his clients but probably doesn't hold a passport and thinks emerging markets are everything south of the Mississippi.

"Re The Deal for Viva Air," Ryan added. "It's looking good and though it's not finalised the future is looking remarkably better. To the team at Irelandia, our lawyer Paul White, our investment bankers (that's a fee sensitive comment), Felix [Antelo] plus Rapper [Stephen Rapp, an aviation consultant] in Medellín and anybody else I've missed - A massive, mil gracias."

CHAPTER 41: WHO YOU GONNA CALL?

Declan Ryan knew Ruairi Blaney from when he was a child. His father Patrick had worked with Tony Ryan in GPA. Blaney was a school friend of Ryan's son Conor, and after studying economics and politics in UCD, he wanted to get into aviation leasing. Blaney met Maurice Mason at a dinner in his parents' home and heard him talking about Irelandia. This sparked an interest.

In 2011, he wrote to Declan Ryan and asked him for a job and got an internship. He then went to England to work for his uncle Hugh Blaney, who had a fund that invested in urban regeneration and renewable energy. After three years there, Blaney's mother Camilla had Alzheimer's, and he wanted to move back to Ireland to be close to her. On a trip home for Conor Ryan's birthday, he ended up talking to Declan Ryan, who told him to talk to John Goode.

Goode met him in October 2015 and asked him if he had a passport. He did. Goode put him on the next flight to Panama to help set up Viva Latinamerica.

Blaney ended up sharing an apartment for a few days with Steven Maxwell and Brian Mulvihill, cementing their friendship. "Dec definitely didn't need me when he hired me," Blaney recalled. "But he knew it was an avenue for me to get the next job."

After nine months with Irelandia, Blaney got a job as a credit risk analyst with Orix Aviation. He learned about balance sheets, reporting and putting together deals, but it wasn't as exciting as Irelandia. In December 2017, he was invited to Irelandia's Christmas party in its office on Barrow Street. "I was taken aside by each of the lads at different times and they were asking me what I was up to and telling me about the aircraft order they were working on," Blaney said. "I remember leaving the party and thinking that was random."

On New Year's Eve 2017, Declan Ryan sent Blaney a text message: "I'm going to Colombia on Tuesday as CEO of Viva. Do you want to come with me?" Blaney asked his father, and he told him to go for it. On 2 January 2018 he handed in his notice to David Power, then group chief executive of Orix. Power was encouraging: "Just go. Whatever happens, we'll figure it out." By the end of the week Blaney was living in Colombia. He didn't speak Spanish and knew nobody. It was a steep learning curve. He ended up sleeping in the office trying to figure out how to deal with all the complex paperwork required to receive a new plane. Blaney spoke to his father about Irelandia and Viva when he came home months later. "I would tell him about some of the stuff and he said people look at the GPA story and they just think about the start and the end,"

CHAPTER 41: WHO YOU GONNA CALL?

Blaney said. "He said the best part was the middle, the journey. Irelandia is like that." The journey for Blaney and Irelandia in Colombia, would turn out to be much harder than either could have imagined.

———◆◆◆———

CHAPTER 42: PANDEMIC

Thousands of decisions have to be taken when an airline is being grounded, and that's what Declan Ryan, John Goode, and Ruairi Blaney found themselves doing when they arrived in Medellín in March 2020 as the pandemic ground the skies to a halt. Ryan and Felix Antelo had called their staff together. "We're shutting down. We have to. This is happening worldwide," Ryan told them. It would be the last time they would see most of the staff in person for many months.

Viva put its staff on holiday leave, hoping that Covid-19 would not last. However, it soon became apparent they would need to cut pay. Antelo took a 70 per cent cut, and it cascaded down. Three weeks went by. The Irish men did not know when they could leave.

A group of Peruvians were trapped in Miami and Viva was asked to bring them home, picking them up on 14 April. The Irish trio decided to hitch a ride to Miami. They got a special letter from the Irish Embassy permitting them to leave. The letter arrived with just hours to spare. Medellín airport was

CHAPTER 42: PANDEMIC

dark and cavernous when they got there. "We were escorted by police to the plane. It was very surreal," Blaney said. They were the only passengers on their flight. "The load factor on this flight is awful!" Blaney joked. Behind his facemask Ryan couldn't help but smile: "Shut up."

At Miami airport, officials greeted them in surgical clothing, gloves and masks.

Their temperature was taken, and they were hustled through empty corridors to their next flight.

Ryan had chartered a plane, as no commercial flights to Ireland were flying.

"As we flew back it felt like all of the world was shutting down," Blaney said. Irelandia didn't know if Viva would survive long enough to open again.

Back in Ireland, it regrouped.

An executive committee was formed to cut cash burn, comprising Declan Ryan, Felix Antelo, John Goode, Steven Maxwell and Jason Bewley. Ryan had seen the Gulf War and the terrorist attacks on the Twin Towers. But he had seen nothing like this. Airlines have three main costs: aircraft leasing costs, salaries and fuel.

Fuel was easiest; as Viva wasn't flying, it wasn't using any.

Wages could be cut, but Viva knew this would hurt their staff. Some would go hungry. If it didn't support its pilots and cabin crew at all, there was no guarantee they would return.

"It was a time of definite, quick and hefty decisions," Antelo said. Viva cut wages by 30 per cent, and in time it had to put people on silo.

"There was no state support in Colombia," Maxwell said. "No social security, nothing. It was terrible."

Viva decided to pool any income it made among pilots and cabin crew, so at least all got something. "I think we were the only airline in the world to do that," Maxwell said. Tackling aircraft leasing costs was another matter.

It had to pay rents to its lessors whether its planes were in the air or not.

Within a week, Viva was in contact with its lessors trying to cut a deal. "We really pulled back the sheets and showed them everything," Bewley said. "We were upfront saying: 'We've a good story. Don't give up on us. We can get through this but I can't pay you right now.'"

As nobody knew how long the pandemic would last, there was a mutual self interest in airlines working with their lessors. When Viva asked for six months relief, the lessors said they'd think about it.

Viva had twenty-three planes in its fleet made up of fifteen new Airbus planes, and seven older planes which were due to be given back to their lessors at the end of 2021 when they would be replaced by new models.

Viva sent back two of its older planes to GECAS by flying them to Phoenix, Arizona. In June, GECAS agreed to a short-term deal, giving Viva some breathing room. China Aircraft Leasing Group (CALC) agreed to the same deal that GECAS did.

Three of Viva's older planes were leased from DAE (Dubai Aerospace Enterprise), and one apiece from Air Lease Corporation (ALC) and Arena. It sent three of the DAE planes back in mid-April, and convinced ALC to do a deal too. It didn't have a deal with Arena yet.

The board of Viva now realised that the pandemic was

CHAPTER 42: PANDEMIC

going to last longer than three months, and the airline was forced to tell CALC it couldn't sign a three-month deal as it wasn't long enough.

CALC agreed instead to extend its repayment profile, so it was less of a cash drain.

Talks with Arena were harder as its plane required a so-called Airframe Check-6Y, a major airframe structural check that takes place every six years in planes.

This check cost $1 million, and Arena said it wouldn't pay this unless Viva had paid its rent up-to-date. "They didn't have another customer for the plane so they'd no incentive to resolve things," Blaney said.

In the third month of lockdown Viva almost caused a diplomatic incident. About 100 Colombian doctors had been trapped in Cuba since 25 March, where they had been receiving training.

Gustavo Petro – a left-wing political leader, former member of a guerrilla group, and a future president of Colombia – was also on the communist island at the time.

On 19 May, Colombia and Cuba had agreed mutual repatriation flights, with Panamanian airline Wingo set to carry out the flights. Wingo pulled out due to concerns about Covid-19 safety, so Viva stepped in. Blaney contacted Viva's insurance company, an American firm called Gallagher, to inform them. Gallagher warned Viva if there was an incident it could not pay out anything to the Cuban government because of economic sanctions.

"It got a little lost in translation and our commercial team took that as a no," Blaney said. The Cuban Embassy in Bogotá kicked up and Petro tweeted to his 4.5 million followers that Viva "has defaulted and suspended Monday's flight". Viva clarified things quickly but not before the tweet went viral. "It was a storm in a teapot caused by translation," Blaney said.

Ryan was now writing multi-million cheques every month as Viva remained largely grounded. It was then he reached out to Chaker Chahrour asking him if he would honour the deal he offered before the world changed. Chahrour said he would, and he moved Viva's engine deliveries forward to May from October. "We managed to get a very large discount on an additional spare engine, the benefit of which we realised in the middle of no flying in pandemic 2020, when the multimillion financial gain from the discount was much needed and welcomed!" Mulvihill recalled. It was enough to buy Viva another month.

In October 2020, Viva struck another deal with CALC where it paid a small fee and gave up its deposit in return for being allowed to break its lease.

As Viva tried to send planes back or get rent cuts, it was due to receive eight new planes from Airbus in June 2020. Airbus agreed to give it only four, and push delivery back to the end of 2020.

It also agreed to extend delivery of all fifty planes out until 2025.

Viva was making progress, but it still hadn't cut a deal with GECAS.

Even parking planes created its own difficulties. Most of Viva's planes were in Medellín but it had a few in Bogotá and some in Barranquilla, a coastal area where there was the risk of erosion.

Viva couldn't afford to deactivate its fleet, so it reached

CHAPTER 42: PANDEMIC

an agreement with its insurers to fly each plane at least once a month. By now, Viva was picking up small gigs such as flying cargo, transporting medical supplies and repatriating people. At other times it had to just fly its planes around in circles.

Viva did about 150 humanitarian trips, going as far north as Chicago. It took whatever it could trying to earn income and ensure its planes and team didn't lose their ability to fly. Despite all its efforts, Viva was still burning millions of dollars a month just standing still.

———•◦•———

Viva had one lucky break at the start of the worst crisis in global aviation. While John Goode focused on closing the final parts of its engine deal, he asked Brian Mulvihill to find a leasing company prepared to buy the first Neo engine which was due to be delivered by CFM in June 2020. ELFC, an engine financing and leasing company, owned by Tokyo-stock-exchange-listed Mitsubishi HC Capital, agreed to take the engine in early 2020. ELFC was in forty countries but it had been headquartered in Shannon since 1989 to be close to GPA historically and then to avail of tax breaks brought into the region by the Irish government because of Tony Ryan's success. Viva's revenues fell to almost zero from the end of March 2020 but ELFC had signed all the paperwork and committed to honouring its deal. ELFC paid market price for the engine and then agreed to lease it back to Viva over 12 years. Irelandia's deal with Chaker Chahrour , who grew up in a refugee camp to become an aviation engine executive, meant however that Irelandia had to pay much less upfront for the first engine. Just when Viva needed it most the deal he did came good for Viva, giving it a vital cashflow lifeline. Karma, unexpected and unlooked for, had arrived.

CHAPTER 43: PROJECT AIR – RESTRUCTURING TEAM

Declan Ryan was, however, still convinced Viva was on its way to being finished. Month followed month and Colombia remained in lockdown, longer than almost anywhere else in the world. Ryan was continuing to support Viva but he was now getting worried, and he told his grown-up children in the autumn of 2020 to expect the worst. "I told the kids Viva was gone," he said. "The kids weren't worried. They said: 'Well one out of six ain't bad' in reference to the other airlines. I said: 'You're meant to fail at the beginning not at the end!'" Ryan had a $120 million personal exposure to Viva which he felt could go to zero. It was a big portion of his wealth. He knew the $30 million raised from his friends and family would be lost too. Ryan had broken up Irelandia to avoid this very situation. Cartesian was also facing losing $50 million. Ryan felt he could put no more money in, and Cartesian wasn't prepared to either.

Declan Ryan's biggest worry was the 1,000 people who depended on Viva for a living. He had been moved by their resilience and commitment to the airline, and felt he was letting them down. He had put $1 million of his own money into the Viva Foundation to try and help them and others in Colombia impacted by the pandemic. He had no more to give. Monica Gil Coca was running the foundation, and she supported him during these hard times.

If Viva went bankrupt, Howard Millar knew the conclusions that would be drawn. "I was personally concerned for Declan. I have known him for a long time, and I knew how much he'd put into Viva," he said. "I was there in the summer of 1992 when GPA blew up. I saw how it impacted him, his Dad Tony, and all the Ryan family. Airlines have this horrendous ability to suck up all the money you have and more. I knew people would say if Viva failed: 'Ah yeah, it's happened again. The Ryans flew too close to the sun.'"

Ryan knew too the headlines would inevitably be linked to his father Tony Ryan's past. It would be frontpage news back home. Ryan didn't think about that: "Failure is individual, not shared."

Irelandia trusted KPMG. Maxwell, Mulvihill and Doherty had all trained there. It was its auditors and tax advisers. Secretly, Irelandia asked Kieran Wallace, the head of KPMG's insolvency team, to create a plan to place Viva into Chapter 11, a US form of bankruptcy.

Wallace had liquidated Anglo Irish Bank, the biggest bankruptcy in Irish history. He had taken control of the Quinn Group, when its founder, Seán Quinn, went broke. Wallace put together a tiny team that included Andrew O'Leary, a specialist in working capital and insolvency, Theresa King, a director of KPMG, Patrick Murphy, a consultant, and Kieran O'Brien, lead advisory partner in the aviation finance arm of

CHAPTER 43: PROJECT AIR – RESTRUCTURING TEAM

KPMG. All were sworn to secrecy, and even within the firm their work was need-to-know. They code-named their work 'Project Air'.

Wallace was a deliberate choice. "We wanted him as the harbinger of doom. If anyone Googled him, they would know we weren't messing around," Maxwell said. Irelandia needed to show its creditors it wasn't bluffing. It was prepared to file for bankruptcy. Video calls went back and forth, but everyone kept their cameras turned off. Irelandia levelled with KPMG: it was near the end of its cash.

KPMG tried to figure out how much Viva owed, and then worked out when its money would run out. Viva owed its suppliers $100 million. It had a little over twenty planes in its fleet, so it was facing a bill of between $6 million and $8 million in rent a month to lessors. Viva still had some Cartesian money, but most of it had been exhausted.

Irelandia also had debts related to its new plane orders. In March 2020, Brian Mulvihill had arranged new financing deals for fifteen planes with an international lessor, but it had pulled out due to Covid-19. Viva only had its aircraft financed until the end of 2021. Unless it started flying again after that point, its planes might be taken off it. Viva's pressing concern was its lessors, who could pull the plug at any moment.

KPMG drew up a plan where Viva would go bankrupt in both Colombia and the United States. It said the only way this could be avoided was if Viva could squeeze its creditors outside the courtroom – and raise a lot of capital.

Another reason to go bankrupt was that all of Viva's rivals had already done so. Howard Millar remembers the Viva board frequently discussing Chapter 11. "It was very close.

Right to the precipice," he said. One by one its rivals went over.

Avianca went first, followed by LATAM. Avianca was already on edge even before the pandemic, in part because of its price war with Viva. In August 2019, a video had gone viral of its chairman Roberto Kriete saying the airline was "bankrupt". Avianca tried to explain this away by saying his message had been lost in translation, but it hadn't fully been.

At the same time that Viva looked at bankruptcy, Irelandia appointed investment bank Raymond James to find fresh capital. Finding capital for a small airline in an emerging market was a big ask, so the odds favoured Chapter 11.

Airlines were now failing globally, but the worst impacted ones were in emerging markets where their governments were not prepared – or resourced – to bail them out.

Peter Cerda, vice-president for the Americas at the International Air Transport Association, told the *Financial Times* just 1 per cent of the $130 billion in government bailouts worldwide was given to Latin American carriers "and of that 1 per cent, only two countries stepped up – Brazil and Colombia."

Declan Ryan's big hope was that Viva might access some of this support. On 29 August 2020, Colombia announced a $370 million plan to bail out Viva's biggest rival, Avianca, with a soft loan.

Avianca was four months into its bankruptcy, and such a loan would be enough to resuscitate it. Viva was getting nothing.

Only two months earlier, the president of Colombia, Iván Duque, said Avianca was not getting any special treatment. He told the *Financial Times* that Colombia would help the sector as whole: "We're not ruling out any plan that is

CHAPTER 43: PROJECT AIR – RESTRUCTURING TEAM

sensible and involves a sustainable restructuring."

Now Colombia was giving everything to one airline. It was an iconic Colombian brand, but it was also a private business headquartered in Panama.

Iván Duque's sister, Maria Paula, was chief customer experience officer in Avianca. Any suggestion that her position had anything to do with her employer's bailout was dismissed. Viva had asked for a $50 million government loan, but now Declan Ryan felt compelled to write formally to President Duque. On 6 September 2020 he told him: "We make an urgent call for an equitable support package for the airline industry, to survive the worst crisis in the history of world aviation."

Viva, he said, had invested $200 million in Colombia so far, and would put another $650 million into its new fleet. He outlined that the airline was ultimately going to invest $1.75 billion in Colombia, if it survived.

"Following communications with you, Mr President, and other senior government officials relating to the support of the airline sector, we felt content and assured in the promise that all airlines would be treated equally on support packages given," Ryan said.

"It is with great disappointment that we observed Avianca receiving preferential treatment in not only the proportional quantum of a $370 million loan but also the structure whereby the loan is being issued directly from a government-controlled fund," Ryan said.

"We note that this has all been agreed while Avianca remains in a foreign bankruptcy process and where they have publicly announced that they intend to slash their active fleet size by more than seventy-three planes (50 per cent of the fleet) for 2021, this will undoubtedly have severe repercussions on connectivity and employees." Viva, he said, was committed to twenty-five planes by the end of 2021.

"While we recognise that Avianca was historically a larger airline, we believe that no other airline has been offered the same pro-rata quantum or structure of financial support as Avianca," Ryan said. "Favouring support to one airline would have a catastrophic impact on the competitiveness of the industry as well as having negative economic ramifications all whilst going against previous government communications on equality."

Ryan finished his letter by asking Colombia to give a $100 million loan to Viva on the same terms as Avianca. President Duque did not respond. Some further back channelling came to nothing. After Ryan realised Avianca was getting nearly all the state support he went public, telling Jude Webber in the *Financial Times*: "It makes Colombia look like a banana republic."

Under Colombian law any citizen is allowed to challenge public decisions, and one of them filed a lawsuit trying to block the Avianca loan. This was enough to stall it, and in the end Avianca never drew down the loan. The offer of a loan served its purpose, as it told the market that Colombia was not going to let Avianca fail. Viva was by itself.

CHAPTER 44: AT WAR WITH GECAS

Viva and Irelandia now realised they were alone. In September 2020, KPMG completed its Project Air report. It set out in stark terms what would happen to Viva and all its creditors if it went bankrupt. KPMG had studied what was happening to Avianca and LATAM during their bankruptcies and extrapolated this across to Viva.

Irelandia could see how Avianca was progressing in Chapter 11, and how it was striking incredible deals with its creditors. Even if it survived until the pandemic ended, it knew if it couldn't get similar deals that it would be finished anyway as it couldn't compete. Back home in Dublin, Paul White in A&L Goodbody recommended Viva bring in Skadden, a hard-nosed American law firm that specialises in restructurings. Skadden had worked with KPMG and A&L Goodbody before in dealing with some of Anglo Irish Bank's US liabilities, so the firm came highly recommended. Two of Viva's lessors, DAE and Carlyle, had decided to sue Viva in New York to try and force it to pay up. Skadden's first task was to head them off. But its bigger task, working alongside Irelandia and KPMG, was to do a deal with Viva's biggest creditor, GECAS. If Viva couldn't do a deal with it, then an out-of-court restructuring would fall apart. There was a negative history between Irelandia and GECAS already that made a deal unlikely. GECAS's origins were in GPA, so in theory the Ryan name should have meant something. It did perhaps in the early days, when Viva signed its big aircraft order with Airbus in 2017, and GECAS had agreed to finance ten planes. But after Declan Ryan took over Viva in 2018 as chief executive, he has asked for GECAS to relax its payment terms to free up cash flow so he could fix the airline. GECAS's credit committee had only recently approved Viva as low credit risk, and now Ryan was making them look foolish by asking to be given a break.

"It blew up the relationship," Blaney said. "And it didn't really recover after that." As Viva struggled to bring in the Cartesian investment it had always paid GECAS. However, some payments were late. "We had payment issues with them," Blaney said. "In April 2019, I'd told them we might not be able to pay them at all until the Cartesian deal closed the following month." Ryan had heard rumours that GECAS had considered pulling the plug on Viva and pursuing him personally, rather than wait for Cartesian. It was unclear if this was true or false, but for Blaney trying to negotiate with them it was like coming in "mid-divorce". "Nobody liked anyone anymore, but we're trying to keep the show on the road," he said. Irelandia still had a good relationship with GECAS's commercial team, but its credit team took a harder line.

Now with Covid-19, Viva was back knocking. GECAS gave it three months relief, but when the airline asked for longer it

CHAPTER 44: AT WAR WITH GECAS

dug its heels in. "They refused to do anything," Blaney said. "I think it was because of earlier issues and who Dec is. They thought if they pushed hard enough, he'd put more money in.

"We tried a couple of times to reset the relationship, but we never got anywhere. Credit's view was that we kept coming back looking for more and they were not giving it to us this time."

Irelandia could see how its people in Viva were hurting. Blaney recalls telling thirty people in Viva's engineering team they had to go on unpaid leave, and then hopping on a call with an airline lessor. "He is sitting in a penthouse and telling me he can't do anything for us," Blaney recalled. "It was hard not to take it personally."

Despite the pressures, Irelandia was making progress cutting deals with its various lessors. Antelo and the Irelandia team got on with Priscilla Branco, a regional manager with GECAS. She previously worked with Azul Airlines, a Brazilian airline founded by David Neeleman, the founder of JetBlue Airlines, so she understood the low-fares entrepreneurial approach taken by Irelandia.

"We had a deal in principle in October 2020 that looked pretty good," Blaney said. Irelandia didn't get as much as it wanted, but it wasn't far off. Branco, however, went on maternity leave before the deal was signed. A Dubai-based South African called Jonty Nel took over. He took a harder line, and the deal fell apart. Irelandia decided to let it rest and try to cut deals with all its other lessors first.

It started with Aviation Capital Group, a California-based but Japanese-owned lessor co-led by Jorge Castillo, a Chilean who gave Viva its first plane. It took five phone calls to reach an agreement on restructuring its leases with Viva. It gave Viva twelve months relief on its aircraft, with the money to then start being repaid after that. "In terms of support it was pretty chunky, like $16–17 million in 2020 and 2021," Blaney said. By November 2021, Irelandia had another deal with CALC. There were a few rows to get a deal done, but again CALC was pragmatic and did a deal after a handful of calls. Arena Aviation Capital also agreed a deal by the end of that month.

Viva had a components deal with Air France to supply its older fleet. But as Viva had moved these planes on, the arrangement was no longer required. Viva had stopped paying Air France in April 2020, and now it reached a deal to buy out its contract for a few million. In return Air France didn't charge them an early termination fee.

It also had to recut part of its deal with Airbus. It had a service agreement based on flight hours, but now its planes were barely flying. Airbus agreed to a new deal.

In Colombia, Antelo, Bewley and treasury manager Juanita Forero were cutting costs on everything from fuel suppliers to on-board-drinks providers.

In mid-October, Declan Ryan and Blaney flew to Colombia to help on the ground. Ryan's presence was also about showing his team in Viva he remained committed. Irelandia reached out again to GECAS, and it said it was still digesting Viva's previous proposals. Two calls were arranged between KPMG and GECAS, but again they were inconclusive.

In late November 2020, GECAS came back with an offer. It wanted Viva to lease five more planes from it in 2022, in return for a small reduction in rents and an extension of lease terms. It also wanted Irelandia to increase Ryan's personal

CHAPTER 44: AT WAR WITH GECAS

exposure if the airline failed, and it wanted Viva to raise $50 million in new capital. "We just couldn't sign up to it," Blaney said. "We couldn't guarantee that new equity was going to come in." Another row ensued, so Irelandia asked KPMG to step in again and try and resolve things.

In December, KPMG made a presentation showing GECAS a way it could break – even if it gave Viva more time. GECAS came back with a slightly improved offer, but Irelandia still couldn't accept it. Goode and his team were working around the clock now trying to reach a deal – but to no avail.

On December 23, GECAS wrote a letter threatening to ground its part of Viva's fleet if it did not sign up to its deal. GECAS leased ten planes to Viva, so effectively it was threatening to put the airline out of business. KPMG wrote back asking for more time, as Irelandia would need board approval to agree a deal. It was too close to Christmas to get that, it said.

Ruairi Blaney drove home to Tipperary on Christmas day to cook dinner for his family. "I was shattered," he said. On the 28th, he drove back to Dublin to prepare a fresh proposal for GECAS, but this was rejected too. GECAS was now preparing to issue grounding notices on Viva. This would be game over for the airline as other lessors would follow suit, taking all of its planes away. A late call was arranged on Friday 22 January between Dubai-based Jonty Nel, an executive vice-president in Viva, and Paul Wilson, who was leading its restructuring team in Latin America. John Goode and Howard Millar were on the call for Irelandia. Wilson laid out the facts bluntly. Viva had run up arrears of $55 million, so GECAS was pulling the plug. "The call started off very aggressively," Millar recalled. "Their initial position was we are going to ground you. We are tired of excuses as we've heard them all before. We knew we were down to the wire." Millar knew Nel so there was a rapport there. They had done a deal together in the 1990s and bumped into each other maybe a dozen times over the years. It was a long call, but gradually Irelandia convinced GECAS to pull back. Nel told Millar if he was engaged in the process and prepared to put his reputation behind it, then GECAS would try one last time to do a deal that would prevent them issuing a grounding notice. "It was the precipice, definitely the precipice," Millar recalled. "But somehow we came back from it."

Goode and his team still had weeks of negotiations ahead to defer and rescheduling Viva's debts with GECAS, but Viva was no longer facing extinction.

The discussion changed to if Irelandia was open to consensually giving it back some of its planes. "They said we'll take five planes back. One night it was just decided that was going to be the way out," Blaney said.

On 19 March 2021, a provisional deal was signed, and a full agreement was in place by 30 April 2021. Paul Wilson wrote to Goode and Millar that day thanking them both for their efforts and Millar for his "timely intervention". He said GECAS looked forward to remaining a key lessor to Viva in the years ahead. Unknown to Irelandia, GECAS had a home for these planes with its rival Avianca, which was preparing for life after bankruptcy and looking for new

CHAPTER 44: AT WAR WITH GECAS

planes to boost its relatively old fleet.

At the same time, Goode cut a deal with Carlyle and DAE, who were suing Viva in New York. Viva would give back some planes, and in DAE's case lease terms were extended on one plane. Finally, in secrecy and outside the courts, Irelandia had restructured Viva's entire balance sheet. It was ready to go again if it could raise enough money to do so.

On 14 December 2020, the United States had vaccinated its first person after enduring a death toll that topped 300,000 people. The United States announced plans to vaccinate 100 million people by April 2021, and soon it was making vaccines available to anyone who turned up at a medical centre or pharmacist. Colombians who could afford it flocked to the United States, and Viva's planes were full to capacity bringing them there. Viva was now in a much stronger position. In total it had written off $120 million it owed to its suppliers, halved its rents to lessors, and now its sales were rocketing.

In the wings was its co-investor Cartesian, which had feared it was going to lose all of its $50 million investment. Under the terms of its agreement with Irelandia, Cartesian, had an option to take a share in Viva. Talks began about Cartesian becoming a shareholder in Viva, a deal that would free up more cash for the airline. On 23 June 2021, Cartesian agreed to take a 30 per cent stake in Viva, but held back on announcing this until after the summer. Viva had 15 per cent of the Colombian market before Covid-19 but now its market share shot up to 24 per cent. Viva's flights were landing at a 95 per cent on time rate, and Antelo was running a tight ship.

In September 2021, Cartesian's stake in Viva became public knowledge. "Even in the midst of an unprecedented crisis, Viva has shown great resilience," Peter Yu, the chief executive of Cartesian, told *Finance Colombia*. "Felix [Antelo] and the entire team have consistently demonstrated the agility, creativity and tenacity that make Viva a world-class airline. We look forward to the continued growth and success of Grupo Viva."

Antelo added: "Viva found opportunities in challenging and crisis times, adapting to new ways of managing this complex business. Today we can proudly say that, with the commitment of our employees, the evolution of our strategies, and the support of our suppliers and lessors, we have consolidated our position as the leading low-cost airline to/from and within Colombia and Peru." Goode said the arrival of Cartesian on Viva's capital table steadied nerves. "Other investors could have been spooked if Cartesian did not want to be involved in the equity play at the Group level," he said.

In total Viva had reduced or deferred bills of $224 million from negotiating with multiple airline lessors, Airbus, hundreds of suppliers, staff and so on. It had also managed to generate $83 million in cash that came into the business. Much of this was from ticket sales but it also got a $25 million loan from banks that was guaranteed by the Colombian government; and it raised $30 million from the sale and leaseback of its fleet of airlines, and finally it had been able to free up cash to put into the airline by convening Cartesian to become 30 per cent shareholders. "We were one of the only airlines globally to generate a cash buffer while all our planes were sitting on the ground," Maxwell said in an email to his colleagues in Irelandia. It was an immense amount of work by Irelandia, Viva and their advisers.

CHAPTER 44: AT WAR WITH GECAS

All in, about a quarter billion of debt and deals had been restructured. With the restructuring finally done, Irelandia and its advisers in KPMG finally met up in person for a trip to Powerscourt Distillery in Co. Wicklow. After an arduous year they sipped whiskey, as the Irelandia team toasted the restructuring experts. Thankfully it hadn't needed them to take Viva into bankruptcy.

CHAPTER 45: EL DOG

The Kriete family led El Salvador's flagship carrier TACA through a civil war that lasted from 1979 to 1992 between a military junta-led government and left-wing groups. It is one of the wealthiest families in the Central American country. Its leader Roberto Kriete has been steeled by fire. The *Financial Times* called Kriete a "straight shooter with a Midas touch and a social conscience".

Cordial and friendly, it is possible to underestimate Kriete, but he is formidable.

Kriete, like Declan Ryan, had grown up in the aviation industry. His grandfather first invested in TACA, and Kriete trained as a pilot and had a penchant for flying two-seater aerobatic planes. He'd been involved in TACA since 1980 and built TACA from $35 million to $1 billion in revenues.

In 2009, TACA merged with Avianca, which was controlled by a Bolivian entrepreneur called Germán Efromovich. Efromovich grew up poor from a family of Polish Jewish immigrants who fled to Bolivia after escaping World War II. He told *Forbes* his first house was a twenty-four-foot

CHAPTER 45: EL DOG

container where his bed was a trunk with a piece of foam for a mattress and that he set up his first company at sixteen to sell quail eggs.

He made money in the oil business then he got his start in aviation by taking an aeroplane rather than money to pay off a debt. In 2004, he bought Avianca for $64 million when it was almost broke.

Avianca was the second oldest airline in the world, tracing its roots back to 1919.

It was a trophy asset with a storied history stretching back to when German immigrants and some Colombian businessmen founded the airline in Barranquilla, a port on the North Caribbean coast.

Avianca had a history of merging with other Colombian and regional airlines, but its merger with Kriete's TACA was its most ambitious ever deal.

Kriete could see the benefits of greater scale and bought into the vision of combining the two airlines.

Efromovich enjoyed the trappings of being a billionaire, and he built up an array of other business interests. He liked giving media interviews and became the face of Avianca after the merger closed in 2010, creating the fourth biggest airline in Latin America with revenues of $3 billion carrying seventeen million passengers.

After the merger, Kriete told *FlightGlobal* he was a "supporter of consolidation" and that there were "tons of synergies". Declan Ryan first met Kriete in 2016 in El Salvador in the old TACA headquarters in its capital. He had flown in to meet him to see if he was interested in buying his stake in VivaAerobus.

Besides his stake in Avianca, Kriete also owned the MRO Holding company, an aircraft maintenance business in El Salvador that employed 3,000 people. He was also a quarter shareholder in Volaris, a rival of VivaAerobus, so it made sense to see if he was interested in buying out Irelandia in VivaAerobus.

"I have never been to a scarier country than El Salvador and I have been to a lot of scary places," Ryan recalled. Brian Mulvihill was on the trip with Ryan. "There were lads with pump-action shotguns guarding the corner shops," he recalls.

In 2016, El Salvador's murder rate was three times higher than that of Colombia. Gangs controlled parts of its big cities. Kriete's office was impressive but fortified.

"It was almost like something out of Batman; it was so secure," Ryan said. "Kriete had his own separate place to park his car, and separate lift to his separate office."

By the time Ryan sat down with him, relations between Kriete and Efromovich were terrible.

Ryan and Kriete talked for hours, delicately testing each other. "There wasn't a direct ask or a direct question," Mulvihill said. "We were just sussing him out to see if he was interested in our stake in VivaAerobus, giving us another option other than IAMSA."

"He made a comment, asking us if we would fancy buying out Efromovich, and doing Colombia together?" Nothing came of the 2016 meeting, but Irelandia now knew Kriete.

In the years afterward, Roberto Kriete's relationship with Germán Efromovich continued to worsen.

Efromovich controlled 78 per cent of Avianca, while Kriete had 22 per cent.

CHAPTER 45: EL DOG

Kriete had certain veto powers to protect his minority interests, but he soon realised Efromovich was in charge, and didn't want to listen to him. Kriete spent years being suppressed by Efromovich at boardroom level. He watched as the Bolivian ran the airline in a way he strongly disagreed with.

Kriete believed Efromovich was using Avianca to prop up his other business interests. As it turned out, Efromovich had borrowed hundreds of millions from a bank to invest in a Brazilian shipyard secured on a company called Synergy Aerospace Corp, that held his shares in Avianca.

Efromovich's loan went into default, and his US bank put it on the market. The buyer in 2015 was Paul Singer's Elliot Management. Elliot is teak-tough, famously pursuing Argentina for years in relation to its sovereign debt. Singer told Efromovich to put Avianca up for sale in 2016 and pay it off.

A trio of big airlines were interested: Delta, United Airlines and Panama's Copa Airlines.

Delta and Copa put a $2 billion price tag on Avianca, but they wanted Efromovich to exit the business. United took a different approach by offering Efromovich a loan of about $450 million. This was enough to get rid of Elliott, and it offered Efromovich a chance to hold onto Avianca, with strict conditions. The airline put a "box" around him, where it could foreclose if Avianca failed to reach agreed targets. When Kriete heard about this, his firm, Kingsland, filed a lawsuit in New York in March 2017. He said Efromovich had "secretly negotiated" the deal for his "own benefit at the expense of Avianca and all of its other shareholders". Kingsland said

Efromovich had "forced" Avianca to do the deal because "Efromovich's other companies are bleeding financially". The *Financial Times* described the war between Kriete and Efromovich as like a "John Grisham novel". Efromovich however denied everything. He told reporters: "We are not in the Al Capone days ... I [even] begged Roberto to take court action. But what's our job? To be the most important airline from the Rio Grande to the penguins of Patagonia. And we'll get there."

Efromovich ordered Avianca's lawyers to countersue Kriete, accusing him of "disloyalty" and a "smear campaign". Kriete was enraged at this attack against his reputation, but Efromovich forced through the United deal.

Efromovich soon hit trouble. In order not to default on his deal with United, Avianca slashed its fares to bring in more cash. Viva, its competitor, came under pressure. But inevitably Efromovich couldn't hit his numbers, allowing United to call in his loan and take control. But there was a problem.

Under the terms of its contract with its pilots in the United States, United could not control another airline without their approval. Along with antitrust, it could take United months or even years to gain control. Instead, United Airlines decided to give its voting rights in Avianca to Kriete. In the long-term it still wanted Avianca, but this was a good stop-gap measure.

Kriete agreed to take the rights, but he was frustrated too and unsure how well he would be able to work with United. He had put an option in his contract whereby he could sell the US airline his 30 per cent stake in Avianca for the highest share price in a sixty-day period at any point in the next two years.

CHAPTER 45: EL DOG

Kriete was now chair of the board of Avianca, and he had most of its voting rights.

He fired Efromovich immediately. "Kriete kicked Efromovich out of Avianca, getting his revenge," Declan Ryan said. "It was like *War and Peace* or Cain and Abel."

Kriete then brought in a new chief executive, a Dutch native called Anko van der Werff, who had been chief commercial officer with Grupo AeroMexico. He brought in an ex-Credit Suisse banker called Adrian Neuhauser as CFO.

Avianca's new management regime cut costs and refinanced debt, putting the airline in a better position. It tried to do an out-of-court restructuring. But then March 2020 arrived, bringing with it Covid-19, so Avianca decided to instead file for formal bankruptcy protection by going into Chapter 11. Prior to that happening, Kriete exercised his option. United now had to pay him a substantial sum, and it had no choice but to pay him. To get through Chapter 11, Avianca needed debtor-in-possession (DIP) financing to pay its bills pending the completion of its restructuring. Kriete put the money he had just made back into the airline, increasing his stake. Elliott Management reinvested in Avianca via DIP financing alongside Kriete. The American investor knew Avianca intimately and could see a turn.

Elliott, portfolio manager Johannes Weber, who previously worked with Carl Icahn and firms like Goldman Sachs and Anchorage, led the investment.

Kriete was on his way to becoming the biggest shareholder in Avianca, with Elliott riding shotgun. By patience and boldness, Kriete had emerged on top.

CHAPTER 46: GURDIAN OF AVIANCA

Steven Maxwell was at a friend's wedding in the Irish countryside, when his phone buzzed. It was Declan Ryan: "I've just got a call from one of Roberto Kriete's guys – a guy called José Gurdian. He wants to talk."

It was 18 March 2020, and Maxwell was just back in Ireland after Viva's board meeting in Lima where Howard Millar had warned about Covid-19. It was still unclear what was going to happen, and public events like weddings were still taking place in Ireland.

Gurdian was the cofounder of a private equity fund called Caoba, which worked with various wealthy families in South America and managed Kriete's stakes in Avianca, Volaris and MRO Holdings, and his aircraft maintenance business.

Gurdian wanted to feel Ryan out to see if he was interested in talking about the future of Viva.

Gurdian is a big-picture dealmaker who thinks many steps ahead. Previously a partner with accountancy firm EY, Gurdian had run the finance side of TACA for Kriete. Ryan was cautious. He felt Avianca was in an even more

CHAPTER 46: GURDIAN OF AVIANCA

precarious position than Viva. He pressed Gurdian on whether Avianca was going into Chapter 11, but he was non-committal.

Nothing firm came out of the call, but a first contact had been made.

By May 2020, Avianca had filed for Chapter 11, and Ryan felt that was the end of Caoba's interest. But as Colombia began to ease out of lockdown, Gurdian invited him to Miami. On 9 October 2020, Ryan met him in a law firm's office. Roberto Kriete and his son also attended. Ryan had KPMG's Project Air report on his laptop, and he knew it valued Viva at potentially zero in a worst case scenario. "I would have sold Viva to them for very little that day," Ryan recalled. "We had been closed for six months. I couldn't put more money in. We had 1,000 staff who I felt terribly responsible for. I would go through a wall for them and was prepared to do any deal to save them."

Caoba began by saying it wanted to either buy or invest in Viva. It was thinking ahead, working way past Avianca's bankruptcy and towards the creation of a new regional airline champion. "They were all airline people," Ryan felt. "Respected, experienced. Roberto knows the region inside and out. Maybe something was possible." After the meeting, Ryan went for lunch with Gurdian and the Krietes. "I now knew Viva was worth more than when I went into the meeting," he said. He came back after lunch to his hotel, and to Monica. "Why are you smiling?" she said. "We might not be going bust," he replied. "Someone might buy Viva."

Caoba had indicated a price for Viva of $125 million, but as the deal became more granular there was a misunderstanding. Ryan had loaned $40 million to Viva, and he presumed these loans would be repaid. Caoba felt its price was $125 million tops, not including any loans. A way around this was to peg the price to be paid to Viva to that of Avianca. In that way, Viva's value could rise in value to pay Ryan's loans off, assuming the market recovered. The other big draw was the promise of a 10 per cent stake in a new holding company set up to house Avianca, Viva, and whatever other airlines might also be acquired. Kriete said the plan was to go to the stock market eventually, so these shares could be very valuable.

In November 2020, Caoba changed position. It was now prepared to back pay $30 million of Ryan's loans and do an all-shares offer that valued Viva at $175 million. Cartesian would do well in this deal, and it gave Ryan the chance to recoup his losses. Ryan liked the shares in Avianca idea, as it echoed his own plan for Viva Latinamerica, and had the potential to reach the stock market.

Irelandia was getting on with Caoba, but nothing could be taken for granted. As Irelandia and Caoba negotiated, the market was recovering. Irelandia could see a new wave of mergers and acquisitions starting in the region. The Irelandia team started to regain their confidence. They knew they had done a world-class deal with Airbus, and Viva had the youngest fleet in the region. The average age of an Avianca plane was eleven years, so it needed access to Viva's Airbus deal to grow. Avianca could try and do its own deal with Airbus, but the next available manufacturing slots would leave it years behind.

Viva had a good management team, and a lean business.

CHAPTER 46: GURDIAN OF AVIANCA

Ryan could see the transformative effect Viva could have on Avianca. Over beers one of the Caoba team said doing a deal with Viva could be worth $1 billion to it in the long-term. "I knew then there was a deal to be done," Ryan said.

CHAPTER 47: THE BAD BOY OF BRAZILIAN FINANCE

Irelandia was impressed by Caoba and its vision. "José really knows the details – he knows about engines, how airlines work, everything," Maxwell said. "He's a deal guy who will make you laugh, but he's also no-nonsense. He will tell you directly if something will work so he's very reasonable to deal with. He's not nitty gritty, or obsessed with valuations, but he is huge on the opportunity and the vision."

Maxwell added: "José is really smart. But he's a typical aviation person too, as he is a little out there. To give you an idea, I got on a call with him and Cartesian at one stage and he had an actual gun on the call. He was like: 'Oh sorry guys, I was just out shooting rabbits.'"

But at the same time Irelandia had been jilted before and knew nothing could be taken for granted.

It needed competitive tension. In January 2021, Irelandia appointed Tom Mullins from investment bank Raymond James. Maxwell, meanwhile, resigned from the board of Viva to lead a "clean team".

The plan was to find out if there were any other potential

CHAPTER 47: THE BAD BOY OF BRAZILIAN FINANCE

new investors or buyers out there.

Brian Mulvihill, Michael Lynch and Alan Bird all joined the clean team too. Lynch ran Irelandia's non-airline arm, but he slotted in. Bird was a former CFO of VivaAerobus and an adviser to Viva, so he had an in-depth understanding of the airline. Ryan didn't put John Goode on the clean team, because he was too important to the operations of Viva.

Ryan felt confident Mullins and his team would find the best deal. "People in our industry like Tom," he said. "They know when he says something he is not bullshitting."

Private equity was looking to invest in airlines but there were also trade buyers too. Irelandia had already spoken to JetSmart about a merger pre-Covid-19, and now they spoke again.

"The guys in Indigo are amazing but they are tough," Ryan said. "They were a logical M&A opportunity as they were in Chile and Argentina, while we could bring them into Colombia. But we just couldn't do a deal with Bill Franke." Spirit, a Florida-based low-fares airline, was another logical partner.

Mullins was friendly with Spirit and pushed hard for a marriage. Spirit hired Barclays to do due diligence on Viva. "They liked our network. They were already flying into Colombia, but we could really move them forward," Maxwell said. "Spirit was the best fit strategically in our view, but its management team wasn't behind it." A deal to buy Viva went to Spirit's board, but its executive didn't push it.

Irelandia wanted a cash deal, but Spirit had received $334 million in payroll support from the Treasury Department in the United States during the pandemic. It was worried about the optics of buying an airline in Colombia. Irelandia said it would be prepared to take stock instead, but Spirit felt its shares were undervalued so it didn't want to give them.

An offer never materialised. As it would turn out, Spirit's management was working on a bigger deal – in February 2022, Spirit announced plans for a $6.6 billion merger with Frontier Airlines, a carrier led by Viva's old chief executive Barry Biffle.

There was also private equity interest in Viva, which Irelandia took seriously.

The first was Castlelake, a fund founded by Rory O'Neill in 2005, and backed by TPG. Castlelake was interested but then it rang Irelandia to say it couldn't do more due diligence due to a conflict of interest. It couldn't say what this was. But it later turned out to be helping to refinance Avianca out of Chapter 11.

The other interested private equity firm was Brazil's Opportunity Capital. It had invested in Brazilian airline Volaris as part of a $165 million fundraise in the last few months of 2020. Mulvihill knew Opportunity from when Irelandia was looking at Brazil. "Opportunity had raised money, so they contacted us asking to invest," Maxwell said. This happened first in May 2020, but now, it had returned. "Opportunity had a bunch of special ops money to invest in the region and it felt Viva was an interesting prospect," Ryan said. "They liked it, and its story."

Founded in 1994 by three bankers, Opportunity had $10 billion in assets under management. One of its co-founders was Daniel Dantas, a former fund manager with Citigroup. He was heavily involved in the privatisation of Brazil's telecoms sector in the late 1990s and had a controversial history.

Bloomberg even called him "the bad boy of Brazilian

CHAPTER 47: THE BAD BOY OF BRAZILIAN FINANCE

finance". Opportunity offered $70 million in cash, and then increased it to $75 million, in return for between 25 per cent and 30 per cent.

Maxwell analysed the two private equity bids.

Both were subject to due diligence. Castlelake couldn't do more of this, so it might not materialise. "Neither offer was a shit-hot deal that you'd jump over the table for," Maxwell said.

Some of the Irelandia team liked the private equity route.

They felt Viva would get stronger as markets recovered, but Maxwell, however, was against P.E.

"My personal view was we've taken on $50 million before from Cartesian and it was gone in two years. What was the benefit of going again?" he asked. As April ended, Opportunity was the best offer.

But Dantas's past in business now became an issue. He was sentenced to ten years in prison in 2008 and fined $5 million after a São Paulo court convicted him of paying a $1 million bribe to a police officer in return for him dropping all investigations into Dantas and his associates on a business deal.

Later Dantas was cleared, but Cartesian didn't like it, as it would have to explain what happened to its investors.

On 5 May 2021, Opportunity sent a letter explaining what happened. "Following an eight-year legal battle, all proceedings against Opportunity's founding partner and executives have been formally and definitely dismissed," it said. "In 2011, the Brazilian High Court of Justice declared null and void the conviction of Mr. Daniel Dantas of Opportunity and all related proceedings, including the ones with allegations of corruption and crimes against the Brazilian national financial system."

Irelandia accepted this explanation, but Cartesian remained concerned. It didn't block the deal, but it indicated it might prefer another one.

Opportunity valued 100 per cent of Viva at $175 million. Irelandia needed $90 million to get its money back, as well as repay the friends and family consortium. On top of this was Ryan's $42 million in loans, and then there was the Cartesian $50 million. At this price Irelandia lost $10 million. "It wasn't the end of the world," Maxwell said. "Given what we'd gone through."

But Maxwell knew neither Opportunity nor Cartesian would be happy with that. Cartesian had a liquidity preference clause that said if Viva was sold they would get 1.75 times their $50 million investment. This equated to $87.5 million. Opportunity, once it found out about this clause, would ask for it too. At a $70 million investment, this equated to $122.5 million. What did this mean for Irelandia? It meant if it sold Viva in the future, it would only make any money if it was sold at a price above $210 million.

Irelandia realised this was a very risky deal to do. Worse still, there was every likelihood Viva might need more money again. If that happened Irelandia's position could be diluted to almost nothing. Maxwell argued against going the private equity route. "We will be having the same conversation in five years about needing more capital," he told his colleagues. "This business is always just around the corner from making lots of money."

It wasn't all bad news. Viva's performance was improving. Avianca was also getting its act together. Its chief executive,

CHAPTER 47: THE BAD BOY OF BRAZILIAN FINANCE

Adrian Neuhauser, who joined in April 2021, was expertly cutting deals in the Chapter 11 process. He was an M&A banker, so Irelandia knew it was credible for him to buy other airlines to form a group.

Irelandia wanted to go back to Avianca, but not without a second bidder. Ryan greenlighted a rebranding of Viva in May 2021 which changed the livery of the airline to bright yellow with Vs in the logo, now a distinctive boomerang shape to signify its rebound. Viva also relaunched its website, and dropped the word Air, a word Spanish speakers found hard to pronounce, from its branding, making it just Viva.

That same month, Irelandia approached American Airlines, after ignoring it before because it was competing with it in Colombia.

"We looked at everyone else first. When we finally talked to American Airlines, they were interested," Maxwell said.

Viva could feed American Airlines with tens of millions of passengers from Colombia and Peru. American had a codeshare deal with LATAM in the past that had shown this model could work. This fell through in 2019 when Delta bought into LATAM and pushed it out.

"American wanted to do something in the region after their LATAM divorce," Maxwell said. Declan Ryan was friendly with AA executive vice-president Steve Johnson, who was an ex-general counsel at GPA. Johnson had also worked with Indigo Partners, including on Tiger. "I've known Steve for a hundred years," Ryan said. Doug Parker, the chief executive and chair of AA, was less sure. "Steve couldn't get Parker to agree to buy us at first," Ryan said. But as American Airlines entered talks to invest in JetSmart in Chile from Indigo, adding

Viva made a lot of sense. "American were actively looking for partnerships," Mulvihill said. "And had already done something with Gol in Brazil."

Headquartered in a metroplex in Dallas-Fort Worth, the code-name for the American Airlines/JetSmart deal became "The Dallas Buyers Club" in Irelandia. Avianca was nicknamed "Little Red Riding Hood", after the distinctive red peaked caps worn by its air hostesses. There was a double reason, as Irelandia hoped it wasn't a wolf.

By July 2021, AA announced it had bought a minority stake in JetSmart, with Vasu Raja, its chief revenue officer, saying: "This would enable JetSmart and American to grow aggressively and profitably across Latin America as demand recovers, while preserving the best aspects of each carrier's business model." AA had never bought into a low-fares carrier before.

"Things were getting serious," Ryan said. "It was a bit like the Four Seasons [a five-star hotel] buying Ibis [a two-star]. Steve [Johnson] had a great comment about: 'There are so many low-cost people in the market we just have to do deals with them.'"

Mulvihill thought investing in JetSmart meant AA had to buy Viva. "It was a game changer," he said. "JetSmart and Viva had the two youngest fleets in the region and the best on time product. We could do the last leg of a connecting flight that was originally sold in New York."

By July 2021, there was a term sheet for an all-cash purchase of Viva from Dallas. "American Airlines had made an offer. They'd improved it twice. It looked like it was going to happen," Mulvihill said.

Irelandia knew that Indigo would be tough negotiators in due

CHAPTER 47: THE BAD BOY OF BRAZILIAN FINANCE

diligence. "We call it the corkscrew," Maxwell laughed. "It will fight over every cent." Maxwell knew that when Irelandia had spoken to Indigo about investing in Viva in 2019 just before Cartesian, Franke offered $60 million at first. But he'd reduced his price to $45 million later on.

This made Irelandia wary of American Airlines. Irelandia board adviser Howard Millar remembers telling Ryan he was concerned too. "Bill Franke is constantly reworking the offer. I know how he operates," he said. Millar respected Franke, but he also knew how tough he was.

Ryan knew this too from experience, but he felt at that stage American Airlines was the best deal.

He asked John Goode and Steven Maxwell to meet him in his home near the Grand Canal in Dublin to discuss things. "I think that's the deal," Ryan told them. "I want to take the Dallas Buyers Club deal. That's done, it's in my head, we're done."

Caoba stayed in touch, but it was busy with Avianca, and may have thought it was the only game in town. Maxwell rang Gurdian to tell him Irelandia had found a different buyer.

Gurdian asked what he needed to do to win, and Maxwell gave an indication. He then rang Mullins, who told him Irelandia wasn't bluffing.

Three days later, Gurdian made a new bid. It was cash, shares, and a seat for Declan Ryan on the board of the merged airlines. "It was 95 per cent of what we had asked for," Maxwell said.

Caoba said it would pay enough to pay off Cartesian. Next, Ryan would be allowed to repay his personal loans from money generated by Viva. And finally, Irelandia and its friends/family investor group would have 10 per cent of the merged airlines.

"The offer was much more than where they started from back in Miami," Maxwell said. The ultimate value of the deal was all about the shares. Ten per cent of Avianca merged with Viva was worth a lot of money, but it could easily be worth more in a few years.

"I was of the view that the enlarged group could IPO at $3 billion," Maxwell said. "Upside scenario, it might reach $4 billion. But you need to stick around, and nothing is certain."

Antitrust was a real risk too. Irelandia went back to the American Airlines-led deal, but it was at its limit. "The Dallas offer was all cash, but Little Red Riding Hood trumped it," Ryan said.

Mulvihill said: "Caoba could see American were writing cheques in the region and they were prepared to do deals with low-cost carriers. It could see if it had to respond or get overtaken." Irelandia was in a better position as Viva was surging back with 28 per cent of the Colombian market. It was profitable again, so options were opening up. Going with Caoba offered the potential to be part of something that would transform flying in Latin America. Ryan, Goode and Maxwell tried to look at the deal from every angle. Maxwell was the first to favour it, as he'd been impressed by how Caoba stayed focused on the big picture rather than sweating the detail too much. Goode could see the strategic advantages. Ryan asked Millar what he thought. "You have to look at Avianca as having IPO potential. This is an opportunity," Millar advised. "We don't know when it will happen. It could be years away, but they will eventually IPO and you're getting a big stake early on." Ryan was by then thinking the same way. It was vision versus cashing out, and Irelandia chose vision.

CHAPTER 47: THE BAD BOY OF BRAZILIAN FINANCE

Now that Irelandia almost had a deal, it needed to talk to Cartesian Capital and convince it to do something to ensure the deal occurred.

Irelandia had kept Cartesian Capital updated as it tried to find a new investor and contemplated filing for bankruptcy. From telling Cartesian to expect to lose everything in the summer of 2020, now as things moved into the second half of 2021, its conversations were more positive. Cartesian was now a shareholder in Viva, with 30 per cent of the airline, so any deal needed its imprimatur.

In October 2021, Irelandia signed an exclusivity agreement with Caoba. Paul White in A&L Goodbody suggested that Irelandia use Steve Hollander, a partner in New York law firm Watson Farley & Williams, to close the deal. Hollander was Cartesian's lawyer too, so it was a way of ensuring they felt comfortable with the deal. Ryan wanted to get Cartesian off the capital table post-merger. "Dec didn't want Cartesian as a back-seat driver," White said.

Cartesian had liked AA's all-cash offer, but there was now more to think about. This was cash and shares, and Cartesian tried to get paid in cash today, and then have the option of sharing in any upside if the value of the shares rose. Irelandia didn't like this, as it felt Cartesian was having its cake and eating it. There was a stand-off and then in February 2022, Declan Ryan flew to New York to try and close a deal over breakfast with John Goode and the boss of Cartesian, Peter Yu. There was a lot of respect between both sides, but now things were tense. Yu admired how Viva had been managed during Covid-19, but as always, he wanted the best deal he could get for his investors. He wanted his money today, and a big share in any future upside.

Goode had become close to Yu and his team during the crisis, but he wasn't budging. Ryan told Yu that Cartesian could have lost everything, and he reminded him of all the other private equity firms who had been wiped out investing in emerging-market airlines.

Ryan and Goode were adamant Cartesian had to take the deal being offered. It represented a return of 1.75 times its capital in less than three years for an investment in an emerging market during a pandemic. Gradually, Irelandia wore Cartesian down.

The New York investors were tough, but they appreciated Viva had been among their best-managed investments of their portfolio of twenty active positions. Gradually Irelandia won them over, and eventually a deal was done that gave it a significant upside. It also got a tiny 0.2 per cent stake in the combined Avianca and Viva.

"Cartesian had their return and were now playing with house money by holding onto some small shares," Mulvihill said. At a time when investors in airlines lost tens of billions of dollars Cartesian had held its nerve and pulled off a good return. Its trust in Irelandia and Viva had paid off. Irelandia could now focus on what it thought was the last lap of closing the deal.

On 1 December 2021, Allegiant announced plans for a fully integrated commercial alliance agreement linking it to VivaAerobus. Allegiant said it planned to invest $50 million in the airline, and its chairman and chief executive Maury

CHAPTER 47: THE BAD BOY OF BRAZILIAN FINANCE

Gallagher was going on its board. The US-Mexico market was the largest international travel market at the time, and among the first to rebound post the pandemic. "This groundbreaking alliance should reduce fares, stimulate traffic, and ultimately link many new transborder cities with non-stop service. In short, it will bring meaningful ultra-low-cost carrier competition to the US-Mexico market for the first time in history," Gallagher said. More than 250 routes had been identified as part of the alliance. "Allegiant is a little bit like Ireland's Kerry Group," Ryan said. "Nobody understands how successful and good they are until you get up close."

Ryan said Viva had twice tried to form an alliance with Allegiant during the pandemic, but Mexico was the more obvious next step for the Las Vegas airline. "It was too far of a stretch geographically," Ryan said. "Mexico made sense." Ryan sent Gallagher and Juan Carlos Zuazua, the chief executive officer of Viva Aerobus, a note of congratulation. "It was like two of my kids setting up a business together," Ryan said. "I was happy for them both and know they will do great things together." As Ryan wrote to his old friends, he was becoming ever more confident. He felt it was only a matter of time before Viva merged with Avianca. But another black swan was coming: war.

CHAPTER 48: A MERGER AND A MARRIAGE

On 24 February 2022, Russia invaded Ukraine, a gross violation of international law that has caused massive damage to the country and the loss of many lives. One of the consequences of the invasion, however, was surging fuel prices. Viva had pre-sold tickets based on lower fuel prices, so suddenly, like many other airlines, it was losing money. Viva had sales of $250 million in 2021 and was trading strongly, but now 2022 looked uncertain. Irelandia might have closed the deal before the invasion, but on 11 December 2021, Avianca had emerged from Chapter 11. The Avianca team was exhausted and asked for negotiations to pause over Christmas. Irelandia didn't mind, as it was doing so well. January and February started brightly. Some in Irelandia wondered whether it would be better even at this late stage to go it alone, but Ryan was sure about the direction he wanted to take. "I reminded them that only eighteen months earlier I was going in naked to meet Kriete and that he had delivered," Ryan said.

Ryan felt Viva was a long way from an IPO in Colombia, which was perceived as a "very exotic place to invest". A Viva

CHAPTER 48: A MERGER AND A MARRIAGE

merger with Avianca and other airlines would be big enough to attract big investors and support a New York listing. Building a new aviation champion had worked for Willie Walsh in Europe. The Irishman had merged British Airways with Iberia in 2011 and then acquired BMI (2011), Vueling (2012) and Aer Lingus (2015). A South American IAG was an exciting prospect. Irelandia asked Caoba/Avianca if it was concerned about Ukraine. "This is a bit like Afghanistan," one senior airline executive said. "We didn't see the Irish very worried about Afghanistan when it was invaded." Irelandia feared the war would be an excuse for its deal to be recut, but that didn't happen. The repayment term for Ryan's personal loans was extended by twelve months but that was it.

However, Irelandia and Viva were now close to burn-out.

Susana Mantilla, the chief legal officer of Viva, nicknamed Irelandia "the vampires" because they never slept. Ryan was impressed by Mantilla and her tiny team's work ethic too. He was worried about Steven Maxwell, who had taken only one day off, for his daughter's christening, in the previous year. "Steven is one of my team and a pal, but I could see how hard he was working. We were fucked without him. He was the one person most across everything," Ryan said.

But Maxwell had real grit. Giving up wasn't an option.

The merger of Avianca with Viva was announced at one minute past midnight on the Avianca website on Friday 29 April 2022. Rumblings of the deal had broken about nine days earlier in local newspaper *La República*. But it hadn't been picked up outside the industry. It did, however, give the impression Avianca might be buying Viva rather than merging with it. Irelandia and Viva were determined this wasn't how the transaction, so long in the pipeline, should come out. Avianca's Adrian Neuhauser had the idea to include a diagram showing the corporate structure of the deal. This made it clear it was a merger and that the airlines would be independent and would actually be competitors and under different brands. The headline of the release read: "Avianca and Viva shareholders join economic ownership in a new holding company".

Roberto Kriete explained the logic of the deal in the statement: "This new and strong group of airlines would benefit customers by having a more efficient cost structure that would allow them to offer even lower prices, as well as a route network that would promote direct connectivity between destinations, a strong loyalty programme and a service friendly and efficient according to the needs of today's traveller."

"In addition, it would give Colombia and Latin America a new and stronger competitor that is sustainable over time, encouraging both players to remain relevant in the Latin American market."

Kriete was to become chairman of the board of directors of the new holding company for the merged airlines, with Ryan becoming a director. In the same statement, Ryan said: "This is an important day for Viva as it is the perfect setting to continue with our growth and expansion strategy, maintaining the flag of air inclusion and strengthening our company.

"In addition, if in the future the authorities approve the management of both groups in the same holding company, it will encourage the air transport market to continue growing,

CHAPTER 48: A MERGER AND A MARRIAGE

promoting low rates for users and a good service with the best punctuality, giving everyone the opportunity to fly to many destinations around the world.

"Likewise, it will be a source of generations of quality employment, giving more and better job opportunities to current and future collaborators, as well as continuing to positively impact the connectivity of Colombia, the region and the economic development of the country."

There was a delay due to legal issues with the announcement, which created a problem for Ryan as he was supposed to be in Cartagena, on the Caribbean coast of Colombia. Ryan was to be a witness to the wedding of his partner Monica Gil Coca's sister Diane. "Diane is my sister, and she's been with her partner for twenty-three years who is like a brother," Ryan said. "I had to be there no matter what business was going on."

On his last day in Viva, Ryan said goodbye to Felix Antelo and his senior team before he left. There was a strong bond between Ryan and Viva's senior management. They all knew how close Viva had been to going under. Antelo and Ryan knew once the deal went through they would have to keep a distance from each other until any antitrust investigations were over. Ryan gave the Argentinian a personalised licence plate with the letters "DFIU" as he left, standing for "Don't Fuck It Up". Antelo laughed and said he would try not to. Ryan caught a late flight to Cartagena, to join Gil Coca and her family. She loved Viva as much as Ryan did, but this was her sister's wedding. She wanted him in the church nearby and texted him telling him to take a break. "You have to sign the registry, or they're not married," she texted. Ryan replied:

"Can somebody substitute for me?"

Ryan was trapped in a hotel room in a former nunnery as the ceremony went ahead. At last, all the documents were signed, but he still had to brief the broader Viva team.

On a video call, Felix Antelo said Viva's spirit would thrive as part of the bigger group, and that it secured Viva's future. Ryan said less due to regulatory concerns, but he also assured Viva that jobs were safe.

Next, there was a two-hour call with Viva's pilots, who needed to be reassured their status wasn't going to change. At this stage Ryan was very late for the wedding. "You can imagine the brownie points I lost that night," Ryan said. Unknown to Ryan, Gil Coca had dyed her hair red for the wedding, the colour of Avianca. "It was a bit like someone from Ryanair dying their hair green for Aer Lingus," Ryan laughed. "The wedding ran over the whole weekend, so at least I could make things up to her."

There is a toughness to Declan Ryan. He is warm but can switch to reveal a steel. He relates to other people, and is kind. He is not someone who is content for long. Ryan was born with a cleft palate that is noticeable even after being operated on many decades ago. "It's a huge part of me. It made me who I am. I had so many scraps as a kid – countless," Ryan admitted when asked about it. "The slagging at school was relentless but it taught me so much."

The nickname some of the kids in school gave him

CHAPTER 48: A MERGER AND A MARRIAGE

was Caliban, a character in Shakespeare's The Tempest *who was half-man, half-monster. It was a cruel thing to say about a child whose speech was impacted by it, causing other kids to do impressions of him. It can't have been easy in a boarding school facing this daily. It is part of why he doesn't give up easily.*

CHAPTER 49: A BATON PASSES

Not everyone was happy with the merger of Avianca and Viva. William Shaw, one of the four original founders, tweeted a meme image of *Star Wars* with the caption: "You have become what you swore to destroy." Shaw was now running a new rival airline called Ultra Air in Colombia, with a few aeroplanes.

He called for his followers to send him more memes, but not many arrived. Ryan wasn't bothered. It was good to have start-ups like Ultra Air in the industry.

A post by another founder of Viva did catch Ryan's attention. In a LinkedIn post Fred Jacobsen said he did not think the merger would serve the Colombian market well. "We are going back to the pre-2012 conditions with airlines unwilling to compete on price to the detriment of millions of Colombians that need to travel by air," he wrote.

"As founders, we dreamed of Viva to be the rebel airline that would allow millions of Colombians to travel by air when no-one believed it was possible. The regulators should not approve this merger."

CHAPTER 49: A BATON PASSES

Ryan admired Jacobsen, who he knew played an important role in the Viva story.

The comment stung a little, and the two men would meet the following month at Viva's tenth-anniversary party on 20 May. "Fred had come out and said we'd sold ourselves out," Ryan recalled. "I love Fred, so I had to say something to him." The conversation went as follows:

Ryan: "Fred, you know that comment you made about us selling to the red devils."

Jacobsen: "Yeah."

Ryan: "You owned Tampa Cargo. Who did you sell to?"

Jacobsen: "Avianca."

Ryan: "People in glass houses Fred."

Jacobsen burst out laughing. He had gone through a lot with Ryan, and his response had been in the moment. He shared a beer with Ryan, and the two men recalled the many twists it had taken to get to ten years.

Ryan had been told not to go to the Viva party. Susana Mantilla, the chief legal officer of Viva, rang to say their Bogotá lawyers had concerns it might give the wrong impression.

"Susie, let's say you and I were married, and we got divorced, but our ten-year-old kid was having a birthday party – am I allowed to go?" Ryan asked. "Of course, you are, Dec," she said. "That's how I feel about Viva," Ryan said.

Ryan was careful, however, not to say too much at the party. He avoided speaking of the future or the intricacies of the recent deal. Only Monica Gil Coca and Ruairi Blaney went with him. No other member of the Aer Dogs attended.

Blaney had resigned from Viva on 28 April. "For me the party felt like it was goodbye," Blaney reflected. "I will always go back to Colombia but my time at Viva is done. To get such a positive outcome was almost unthinkable two years ago but now it is done it is a relief."

Blaney was usually the last at any party, but this time he left early. He thought about Christmas 2021 and flying with his father Patrick and his siblings to the home of Airbus in Toulouse, to collect Viva's twenty-fifth plane from the French aircraft maker. When they got near the nose of the plane, there was a cloth covering its name. Underneath, to his family's surprise, was their mother's name, Camilla Blaney, emblazoned on the side of the plane. Camilla Blaney couldn't be with her family in France due to early-onset Alzheimer's, but her son showed her a picture of the plane afterwards with her family in front of it.

"My Mum would have loved the whole Viva story as she was always up for the underdog," Blaney said. Even if Viva was now in his past, there would be part of his family in its skies for many years to come.

A few days after the party Jacobsen posted again on LinkedIn, but now he acknowledged all that had been achieved: "In 2008, four dreamers joined forces to build a new airline alternative in Colombia. At the time, less than 6 per cent of the population travelled by air. Domestic airfares were prohibitive, and as a result, more than 160 million people used the bus."

No serious investor was prepared to back them, until Irelandia. "We put our credibility on the line and worked relentlessly to make our dream come true," Jacobsen wrote. "During the public hearing that gave us the green light to start the certification process, I remember listening to our competition's lawyers laughing and betting how long we would remain in business."

CHAPTER 49: A BATON PASSES

"Later, the Chairman of the Board of Avianca [Germán Efromovich] was outspoken and did not save any effort to let the public know that our project would fail, that we were reckless rebels. In a way, I didn't blame them. Before us, there had been four start-up airlines in Colombia that never materialised – Universal, Cosmos, Estelar, and Aeroasis. And we were going to compete with three of the most solid airlines in Latin America and deal with a regulatory environment working against us. The odds were clearly in their favour. So, they initially ignored us; then they laughed at us and fought us hard, and ten years later, I can say we won. We became the rebel airline that brought affordable air travel to Colombia."

"The VivaColombia story is now a relay. As we passed the baton to others some years ago, I am delighted that those who took it continued to run forward with passion and conviction to achieve bigger and better dreams. Declan's commitment to Viva and Colombia has been extraordinary," he said.

"I hope each member of this team will never forget that the reason for being this airline is to make travel affordable and fun for the many while keeping the people, every stakeholder, at the core of the strategy."

CHAPTER 50: VIVA COLOMBIA, VIVA IRELANDIA

On Friday 6 May 2022, the entire Irelandia team met to celebrate the deal closing in a hotel in Miami overlooking 600 feet of beachfront. The city was buzzing as it hosted the Miami Grand Prix Formula One race. At 4pm Irelandia met up in the Indigo meeting room to debrief. Declan Ryan, John Goode and Steven Maxwell talked about how the deal had played out. "My father said if you want to sell a cow in the mart in Nenagh, you just need two bidders and thankfully we had that," Ryan said. Irelandia had operated in cells during the deal so not everybody knew everything. Ellen James, Ryan's PA, Aoife Gallen, head of finance, Michael Lynch, partner, and Louise Coen, finance manager, all listened. Each had played a part in keeping Irelandia going while its aviation team fought to find a deal to save Viva.

All the Irelandia team agreed that a big lesson was to keep an open mind. "There were so many bumps and near derailments," Ruari Blaney recalled. "As long as you focus on getting it done you will find a way of getting there." Colombian investment manager Natalia Laverde, who was based in

CHAPTER 50: VIVA COLOMBIA, VIVA IRELANDIA

Medellín during the deal, said her lesson was: "Everyone had each other's backs, and did better together."

For John Goode the lesson was to always look at the big picture. "Caoba didn't sweat the small stuff," he said. "They always saw the bigger opportunity."

Steven Maxwell said the ability of the team to rely on each other had been crucial. "I wasn't too involved in restructuring leases at Viva, but I knew I could trust everyone else. It took teamwork."

On Saturday night, Irelandia had dinner in a Greek restaurant with the senior management team in Viva. They took a private room at the back and arrived to find basketball great LeBron James glowering at them. "LeBron James is a God over in Miami," Ryan said. "We'd taken the room that he wanted, the restaurant told us. So he was stuck outside sitting scrunched up at a little table."

It was good for Viva and Irelandia to meet again. They could not talk to each other about the ongoing merger for regulatory reasons, so stuck only to talking about the past.

Susana Mantilla, the chief legal officer of Viva, silenced the room with her heartfelt words. "Susie left Avianca to join us," Ryan recalled. "For her it was really bittersweet, the sale to Avianca. She did the whole deal with just a team of four people. She never once lost her calm."

Mantilla finished by giving Ryan a gift on behalf of Viva's 60-strong executive team. It was a forest in the Amazon with a tree named after each member of Irelandia, including one named after Tony Ryan.

Felix Antelo said a few words, but it was tough to follow Mantilla, who had brought the room close to tears. Antelo spoke about missing his family at home in Argentina, and how grateful he was to Viva and Irelandia for their loyalty. Antelo recalled a car journey two-and-a-half years earlier with Brian Mulvihill as Viva was losing money. "We will look back and laugh at this day in a couple of years," Mulvihill said. "That comment stuck with me," Antelo said. "I am happy to be sitting in a restaurant today celebrating a positive outcome but there were bleak times." Antelo said he was buying a new home in Medellín, and he saw his future in Viva and the larger group.

Then it was Ryan's turn to speak. He spoke only briefly. "I'm honoured to be in this room. This room is a group of great aviators, we have loads of experts, knowledge and experience," he said. "You guys are Aer Dogs – military-like and efficient. Being here with you is both an honour and a pleasure."

Ryan spoke about how it had hit him when Viva had to provide food parcels to some of its staff when they were hungry. "That's when I realised how hard it was for the troops and how serious things had become," he said. He said Viva had come close to failing many times. "That day of 9th October 2020 in Miami in Roberto Kriete's office, I would have accepted nearly anything for the company and now here we are celebrating," he added. "As they say in Dublin – enough said."

The final speaker of the night was Richard Aldous, the biographer of Tony Ryan. Aldous had visited Colombia in 2018 and he had been following the Viva story.

"Three things seem important to me," Aldous said. "First, that spirit of 'you'll never beat the Irish.' No matter what

CHAPTER 50: VIVA COLOMBIA, VIVA IRELANDIA

happens, whatever the challenge is, there's that fighting spirit."

Aldous told a story about how, in the 1970s, Cathal Ryan had won a relay swimming race as a boy while outnumbered and how proud Tony Ryan had been of his son for winning as the underdog.

Aldous then spoke of the hard times when GPA went bust. "GPA would have knocked most people down for good, but Ryanair emerges from the rubble," he said.

"Now Dec and Irelandia have done it again with Viva during a global crisis. So the story seems to me to be a quintessentially Irish one about a never-say-die mindset.

"Second, it is a cliche, because it's true, that Ireland is a land of saints and scholars but that rarely gets applied to Irish business, but it's as relevant here as anywhere. It's that same imaginative, disruptive capacity to envision an entirely new world. They did it with GPA, did it again with Ryanair, and then Irelandia spun it out around the world.

"Third, it's democratising. That's particularly been the case with Viva – opening up markets in an environment much more challenging than the EU and United States were from the 1980s onwards," Aldous said.

"But it's been true of all the projects. In Ireland families would even have to choose who could fly home for funerals because flights were so prohibitively expensive – Ryanair changed that by opening up flying to everyone.

"What would Tony Ryan have thought of the deal? I asked Declan Ryan earlier and he said there would have been an interrogation, was there more money to be squeezed out of the deal? And not much in the way of praise.

"But once the whisky and cigars came out, which is the stage of the night where we are now, Tony would have caught Dec's eye and he'd have given him the nod. Job well done."

Aldous said he wished Tony Ryan could have been there to give the speech instead of him.

"But we are here instead, and I would like to say how proud Tony would have been, how Dec had forged his own path and succeeded in times that none of us could have foreseen."

Then a toast: "Viva Colombia, Viva Irelandia."

CHAPTER 51: SUNSET IN MIAMI

On the last day of their weekend in Miami, Declan Ryan took a yacht around the bay with his Irelandia team and their partners. The skyline was beautiful, and he watched as his young team messed around and enjoyed themselves. For the aviation team – John Goode, Brian Mulvihill and Ruairi Blaney – it would be the last time they worked together. Mulvihill and Blaney were setting up a new aircraft leasing company called TippAero. Ryan was funding their overheads to get going but it would need to raise hundreds of millions from others. They had a trip to the Middle East and North America lined up.

Goode was planning to visit Venezuela to meet his girlfriend Liz's family for the first time a few days later. Venezuela's economy had been devastated by an authoritarian government, sanctions and hyperinflation. More than six million people had fled a country racked by violence. Goode was planning to propose to Liz at Angel Falls, the world's tallest uninterrupted waterfall.

Goode also met Roberto Alcántara around this time. He had

learned so much from the Mexican and was sorry how things had ended in VivaAerobus. Alcántara would have none of it and embraced him. "John, we did one of the best deals I ever did together," he said. VivaAerobus was again looking at the stock markets he said and it was worth more than ever. "What I want to say to you is, bring me more deals like that John."

As he sat legs dangling on the edge of the yacht, Goode didn't know what was next for him as he looked out on the bay. He was hoping Liz would say yes to his proposal and knew it would change his life for the better (she did say yes).

Goode had been through so much with this small group; he knew whatever happened they would remain friends. He wanted to work with Ryan again but wasn't sure how or if it would happen.

Steven Maxwell planned to stay with Ryan but perhaps focus more on his other investments, like drones and bus software. He had a second child on the way so was hoping to travel less for a while.

After elation, Ryan now felt sadness. "I am looking out at the Miami skyline, and it is near sunset. A few tears ran down my face and then I realised it was quite a few tears! Why not?" he reflected.

"We had rescued Viva from the jaws of bankruptcy and then sold it for a good price. I desperately wanted at that moment to shoot the breeze with Tony and my big brother Cathal."

He could imagine them teasing him for being too old to be an Aer Dog. Ryan was grateful to his team for sticking with him. "The Aer Dogs gave me so much. They left nothing on the pitch, perhaps they gave too much of themselves … But beyond proud are the only words that I can muster up, just

CHAPTER 51: SUNSET IN MIAMI

beyond proud." John Goode saw the tears in Ryan's eyes and came over to him. "Well done head," Ryan said. They hugged.

CHAPTER 52: 20/20 HINDSIGHT

Dec Ryan, 1 February 2024.

What's the difference between success and failure in business? It's perseverance and luck. It's about wanting it and being prepared to put everything on the line and leave nothing on the pitch. In the forty years I've been in the aviation business I've seen how narrow that gap is between a business thriving and going down.

Time and again people – good and bad – have made the difference between us making it and failure. If there's one lesson in this book or in life: that's it.

We've been lucky that, more often than not, the airlines we invested in have worked out. Why? Because we had great people around us.

Not everything worked out to plan, and for every investment we made, we passed on others.

The reason Irelandia asked Tom to write this book is so that people can see that we wouldn't have achieved anything

CHAPTER 52: 20/20 HINDSIGHT

without others. The book is called *Aer Dogs* because it took a team to get there.

When the Ryan family founded Ryanair everyone expected us to fail. Aer Lingus thought we were a joke, and early on the state tried everything not to help us. But Tony wanted to win. He needed to win. And eventually he convinced me, Michael O'Leary and others not to give up on Ryanair when logic said shut it down.

I stepped down from the board of Ryanair more than twenty years ago now, but it was – and still is – my first love in aviation. When Ryanair became the most valuable airline in the world in 2023, I couldn't have been prouder. We'd done it, passing out Delta Airlines, and even our original inspiration, Southwest.

I wish Tony and Cathal had been alive to see this moment. They were the only people in the world who ever believed it could happen. They had the vision.

But nothing in this book could have happened without Tony's doggedness, and refusal to give up.

I have seen that same spirit in my team in Irelandia over the last twenty years since we started trying to bring Ryanair's low-fares DNA to the world.

Irelandia believes low-fares travel between countries is a positive force in the world. Yes, we're going to have to do it differently in the future. We need new low-carbon technologies. But making travel too expensive for anyone but the rich is a big mistake. Wars and conflicts are born out of bad leaders who take advantage of distrust, and people not knowing each other. The world needs to be connected more, not less.

Bringing Tiger from an idea on a page to the stock market helped open up travel in Asia. Allegiant Air is an enduring success in the United States.

Just look at what we did by co-founding VivaAerobus. Yes, we had our differences towards the end with our partners in the airline IAMSA, but together we helped democratise flying in Mexico.

In 2023 over 25 million people flew with them, and they are connecting Mexico to its diaspora and allowing ordinary people to get around one of the best countries on earth.

Tony always loved Mexico, so I'm glad he was there to see it getting off the ground. In a country noted for how often airlines fail, VivaAerobus has really established itself. We were unlucky not to get it to the stock market during our time as investors, but everyone in Irelandia feels certain this will happen in time.

But what about Viva Colombia? This is the airline that captured Irelandia's heart over the last decade. We'd worked so hard at building its brand, and creating a real challenger airline. It disrupted travel in Colombia by making it accessible for the first time to millions.

For a long time during the pandemic we thought Viva was going bankrupt like so many other airlines around the world. But the Aer Dogs in Irelandia and in Viva kept it alive.

Selling the airline in April 2022 was the right decision. The prospect of Viva becoming part of a larger new airline group in Latin America was a real result. We felt the culture

CHAPTER 52: 20/20 HINDSIGHT

and Ryanair's DNA inside Viva would help it become an important part of the bigger group.

We didn't know that Colombia's Civil Aviation Authority Aerocivil had other ideas. The long delay in clearing the merger of Viva with Avianca killed it. The lessors seized the planes. The airline ran out of cash. Game over.

The world changed too. Oil prices rocketed as Russia's illegal invasion of Ukraine turned into a long war. To make matters worse, the Colombian peso devalued.

When the merger of Avianca and Viva was finally cleared, it was with a tonne of restrictions, all of which would have to be further negotiated.

It was this combination of delay and economic change that led to Avianca deciding not to merge with Viva.

Could things have gone differently if Irelandia had sold Viva to someone else?

It is impossible to know. The other potential buyers might not have closed the deal either, so we traded.

We now are a significant minority shareholder in a resurgent Avianca, which post Chapter 11 is one of the best-performing airlines in the world. Steven Maxwell now sits on its board, representing our interests.

Avianca is profitable and investing in Colombia and the region. In September 2023 it announced plans to invest $473 million in adding 16 more aircraft, as well as hiring 1,200 more people.

In January 2024, global aviation data firm Cirium named Avianca the most punctual airline in the world. *Bloomberg* has reported that Abar, the parent company of Avianca, is planning to IPO in either London or New York for billions of dollars.

So the future looks bright for Avianca. We know we are helping it learn the lessons of Ryanair in being efficient with capital and relentless on costs. We know someday it will reach the stock market.

And we're spreading the Irelandia gospel in other ways too. Some of the Aer Dogs who worked so closely with me in recent years have now moved on to new ventures – John Goode, Brian Mulvihill and Ruairi Blaney. But they'll always be Aer Dogs. Like those before them they remain friends, and we will always have each other's backs.

Steven Maxwell and Michael Lynch are now running Irelandia, with myself as executive chair.

We're working on getting a new electric airline off the ground, which is as big a challenge as any Irelandia has ever undertaken. That'll be the seventh airline Irelandia will be involved with. Another project started in Ireland.

But this is all some way to go. Nothing is ever certain in aviation. That's why it's an amazing industry to work in. I have gotten so much from it. You're constantly challenged and work with the most amazing people who share a common love of planes. And it's never boring.

I'm very proud to see how many of these people around the world are Irish. I know that Tony had something to do with starting it all off. The Aer Dogs have continued that can-do spirit. And now that Ireland is the global leader for airline entrepreneurs and we have the biggest airline in the world, who knows what we can achieve next. This story is just beginning.